ESCAPING THE POTTER'S HOUSE

AN ANTHOLOGY OF MEMOIRS BY FORMER MEMBERS

JOEL CROSBY

CONTENTS

For more information about this book or to contact the author, visit www.JoelCrosby.com

Escaping the Potter's House/ **Joel E. Crosby.** – 1st Ed.

Paperback ISBN: 9789083192123

Hardback ISBN: 9789083192130

To the current members of The Fellowship: May this book open your eyes to the corruption and hierarchy of your pastors.

To the former members of The Fellowship: May this book serve as a voice to those who have been shunned.

To everyone: read your Bible in context.

INTRODUCTION

The network of churches falling under Christian Fellowship Ministries goes by different names: Potter's House, The Door, Victory Chapel, Lighthouse, or other variations or translations. A city name may be attached to the building.

In 1970, Wayman Mitchell, a licensed (not ordained) Foursquare minister, requested and was appointed as pastor of the Foursquare church in Prescott, Arizona. This was during the heyday of the Jesus Movement, and Mitchell began discipling hippy converts, teaching them to actively pursue opportunities to win other new converts. Many effective methods at the time included rock music and skits in public, as well as meeting weekly in a rented building.

Gradually, the idea developed to disciple these new converts or give them on-the-job training and apprentice them as pastors. This method of apprenticeship and church planting (starting new churches in other cities, states, and countries) seemed successful.

In the early years, this network was known as The Arizona Fellowship, then after crossing state lines, simply as The Fellowship. The idea was that they were a like-minded fellowship of churches cooperating to evangelize the world. At the time, this seemed to be a worthy cause a Jesus Freak could stand behind.

Somewhat concurrently, a friend of Wayman's from Bible school had also garnered a following of churches when he was tragically killed in an accident with his family. Wayman quickly moved in and approached these churches, which were under the name Christian Fellowship Churches, ostensibly about rejoining Foursquare. Agreeing to this, everything was signed over to Wayman, who then merged them with his own churches and began withdrawing from Foursquare. In current Fellowship terminology, Wayman rebelled against Foursquare.

But in 1990, a group of churches that had followed Wayman in leaving Foursquare, or had been established afterward, withdrew from The Fellowship. Wayman viewed this as a betrayal, an act of rebellion, but it was the first of a series of defections that made Wayman more possessive and controlling.

In the aftermath, the changes taking place in The Fellowship accelerated. Wayman became distrustful and controlling while excessively fawning over his accomplishments became standard posturing among those lower in The Fellowship hierarchy.

Standards of behavior were established, and members acquired a status based on their level of vetting and the duration of their loyalty to the organization. Pastors were expected to sign documents relinquishing all claims and rights to church property, equipment, and even members. Members participating in services in a visible way, i.e. on the platform, were required to sign documents of conduct that, among other things, forbade ownership of something as mundane as a television.

And, as with all things corrupt, stories arose of abuse. These stories were consistently denied or blamed on the victim. The records go back thirty years. There were also consistent reports of systematic interference in family relationships when one member was not supportive. Online groups for ex-members share frequent complaints concerning the extortionary method of fund raising that took place in nearly every church service and certainly played a major role in financing the semi-annual conferences every six months. These conference churches supported twenty-five or more baby churches.

Along the way, new doctrines were adopted to justify everything unbiblical that was developing in The Fellowship. A major factor in what went awry in The Fellowship was the incorporation of all ministries into the role of pastor. Actually, the role of pastor as it is portrayed in The Fellowship is false, but it involves every authoritative function described in the Bible, including kingship, all rolled into pastor. This sets the stage for abuse.

This book tells the story of a number of ex-member's experiences in their own words. The participants include a cross-section of members of different support groups of ex-members of this organization from several countries with a wide range of impact. Some used ghostwriters while others wrote their own experiences. That was harder than it sounds.

If you weren't sick of perverted religion already, read on.

—Dennis Crosby

PREFACE

Sometimes we don't want to minister to all the people on a personal level. We want to be a big-shot. We want to stand and give declarations to the people. We want to manipulate them to do our will, and we want to give commands and orders.
—Ron Simpkins, *We Can Take the Land*

There's a lot I can say about why I started writing this book; I could start by describing how and why new members join this church, how a good first impression gradually transforms into a life that revolves around the church. I could make my case by explaining how that afore-mentioned first impression is akin to love bombing and that all members are manipulated in one way or another from the moment they step foot in The Door. I could argue that the abundance of church activities one is expected to attend consequently isolates them from friends or family due to a lack of spare time. Maybe I could walk readers through a breakdown of the B.I.T.E. Model of Authoritarian Control by Steven Hassan and explain which points are applicable to the Potter's House and why.[1] Or perhaps I can start where all rebels start—by disputing tithing, how it's an Old Testament law established to provide for the Levites and is not required under the New Covenant.

Maybe, instead of debating over doctrines, I can make my case through something I didn't even want to discuss with my parents before I left the church: the personal experiences of former members. But I've already added those to the main contents of this book. And these experiences weren't my initial motivation for writing this book (they simply serve to make my case). Neither was the fact that many who shared their story in this book—and far more who haven't—were shunned, ostracized, and kicked out of the church where God himself had supposedly placed them. At least, according to their interpretation of 1 Corinthians 12:18. Here I go, finally resorting to debating over doctrine after all.

Should I step on dangerous ground by arguing the Holy Spirit hasn't been involved in the church as he was in the eighties? Back then, the song services reached a point where the congregation spontaneously erupted in tongues and praise; when you prayed in tongues in the prayer meetings, no one noticed, because everyone was. But now, tongues is scheduled as part of the service at the end of the last song prior to the offering. It lasts no more than two minutes, if that long. And prayer meetings are usually quiet unless there is a visiting pastor. No, I can hear your argument already: But that's not the case in my church! And that's what makes it so difficult; depending on who your pastor is and who his pastor is, the collective experiences of Fellowship members will differ greatly.

I've spent a long time thinking about this preface: what to write and what not to. Finally, I thought I had it: I would make my case how The Fellowship always states they are a book of Acts church, but they are really more like the church of Corinth. Rather than being led by the Holy Ghost, they are led by their flesh and by sinful men. But then it struck me! That's why I started writing this book. Not because I disagree with their manipulative practices, because of the collective negative experiences of former members, a lack of the Holy Spirit, or even that they ended like the church of Corinth. I wrote this book because—and I do not say this lightly—The Fellowship follows *man* and not God.

What I mean to say is this: The way The Fellowship operates and the amount of power a pastor has is unbiblical and reeks of cultism (which they were aware of). Steve Cooper, the author of Go Ye: The Arizona Story, said this: "Why shouldn't a pastor take disciples under his wing and raise them to his level of ministry? Immediately, many are turned off. The idea smacks of cultism. Pastors will become spiritual dictators."[2]

Let me explain, generally, churches refer to the five-fold ministry as the basis for leadership functions in the church. These are based on the well-known passage in Ephesians 4:11. However, The Fellowship sees all the ministries as subordinated to the pastors, except for apostles, which are seldom mentioned. This is even more bizarre when you take the list given in 1 Corinthians 12:28, which doesn't even include pastors.

Titles and positions are a common focus in churches. What the Bible describes are functions—and in the case of functions: you either do or you don't. However, The Fellowship makes pastors central to everything, and nothing is allowed to function without the pastor's consent.

There are many sermons about the authority of the pastors. Nearly all are based on Old Testament passages about the authority of kings, which explains a lot about how The Fellowship (dis)functions. And it's based on taking Bible texts out of context.

Certain functions mentioned in the Bible are explained as actually referring to pastors anyway, such as Acts 20:17 and 1 Timothy 3:2. Of course, the Greek uses different terms in these passages, not pastor. But in The Fellowship, the pastor holds these functions automatically.

The text in 1 Timothy 5:19 is even used to justify ignoring complaints against pastors, although the text clearly says *elder*. This is because elders don't exist in The Fellowship, so they substitute pastor whenever the Bible mentions elders. But the context of 1 Timothy, in particular verses 1 and 2, proves this word does not mean *pastors*. And besides, since The Fellowship teaches that women can't be pastors, they would never give that meaning to the second verse.

As a result, pastors are the only acknowledged authority in The Fellowship and they are given the same degree of authority as an Old Testament king with Wayman Mitchell at the top. In fact, the bylaws that came out in 2004 even state that the pastors of local churches only *hold* the church for The Fellowship. They have no claim to anything in the church and function on the basis of derived authority. (For more information on this, see Appendices I, III, and V.)

In the early days, sermons were commonly about restoring the dignity of the local church. Only gradually did the messages morph into being pastor-centered. In time, the only pastor that mattered was Mitchell, and the local church lost all its dignity to the organization.

Taking all of this into account, it's not just a couple of pastors with bad intentions—or even those with good intentions who fell victim to their own sinful lifestyles. It's the overall organization of The Fellowship, it's the source, Wayman Mitchell—who, from the start, was preaching a doctrine that would only have one possible outcome: a religious organization where leadership has ultimate control over members' lives. In short, it's a cult.

Here are Wayman Mitchell's own words on the matter. "This world will never be our friend. We will never be accepted. The moment you're accepted by this world, you are no longer a citizen of heaven— you're a defector. You are a betrayer. When this generation or society accepts your life-style, testimony, or religion, you're a traitor, a lost colony. You are no longer a colony of heaven."[3]

As the church grew, Wayman was no longer interested in saving souls for God's kingdom; he was only focused on numbers and would be a nightmare to anyone who stood in his way. If any member posed a threat to church growth, he had them removed from The Fellowship— no matter who their pastor was and what city or country they were in. Pastors are to be shepherds. What shepherd would cut a sheep off from his flock?

Churches that split from The Fellowship were met with a lawsuit over church real estate, spending millions of money donated to the Prescott church by their members and the pastors of other Fellowship churches.

One such example is what happened to the church in Fiji. All of this was done just to "make a point", as Wayman stated.

Leadership constantly preached about a common enemy, sometimes known as *the world* or *worldly*—terms that can be filled with whatever content they choose at any time. This was also linked to betrayal, treachery, or treason. It's no surprise that members of this church often become distrustful of anything their pastor didn't approve of: chiropractors, abstract art, television, social media, rebellion against the church, homosexuality, martial arts, alcohol, earrings on men, and fat people (gluttony).

Anyone who left the church was labeled a rebel. As pastor Darren Munzone from the Potter's House in Hurstville, Australia, puts it: "A refusal to do the will of God is called what? Rebellion. Let me take that one step further. A refusal to do what your pastor asks you to do is called what? Rebellion. Some people say: 'I don't have to do what you say.' And no you don't. But if you don't, you're rebellious."[4] This is even more ridiculous when you take into account that Wayman Mitchell first rebelled against the leadership of the organization of the International Church of the Foursquare Gospel (ICFG) when he split from them. Wayman was guilty of rebellion himself—the very thing he called witchcraft.

I lost track of the times members of The Fellowship have tried defending their church against me by stating the Potter's House (or their pastor) had saved them from a sinful lifestyle or even death. They said that their pastor was a brilliant man of God and they were thankful to know him. But it wasn't the church and neither was it their pastor that saved them—they're crediting their pastor and their church for what Jesus has done. "Therefore let no man glory in men. For all things are yours" (1 Corinthians 3:21).

I attended a conference when a prophecy was released, declaring that Wayman Mitchell would not pass away but would bear witness to the second coming of Jesus Christ. However, in September 2021, the news of his passing shook The Fellowship. The Potter's House in Prescott created a tribute with Wayman's former desk and a plaque bearing the church's logo, along with the inscription: "The majority of sermons that have touched and blessed your life were written by Pastor Mitchell on this desk."[5] Additionally, another pastor commissioned a piece of art depicting him and Wayman Mitchell seated at a table, reminiscent of Leonardo da Vinci's renowned painting, "The Last Supper" and also called "The Last Supper."[6] Is this not idolatry? Is the Potter's House the Catholic Church with Wayman Mitchell as their Pope?

In a trailer video that circulated on the internet announcing an upcoming documentary were several extracts of sermons by other Potter's House pastors. One of these extracts said: "There's only one apostle, one man that came with the instruction package. Could you imagine where we would be without our apostle? Could you imagine where we would be in our ministry without the ministry and the teaching of Pastor Wayman Mitchell?"[7]

Wayman Mitchell had always insisted The Fellowship had a unique calling from God just to preach and not do anything else other Christian churches might do, such as organizing charities and community events. This also included Mitchell's private interpretation of what discipleship is, seeing the will of God fulfilled in another human being —which takes the form of heavy shepherding. Allegedly, during one of his sermons, he claimed he got this idea from the shepherding movement (which was exposed as a cult); thus Wayman reproduced the errors men have created in the past.

Problems arise in the discipleship process because it isolates an individual from other Christian sources; it keeps them from learning outside knowledge. And students don't challenge teachers. Everyone is taught to unquestionably believe what they are told.

The Potter's House sees discipleship as a success; the disciple becomes a pastor and continues The Fellowship pattern, creating a circular system that reproduces itself in the victims. Mitchell said that disciples were called Christians in the book of Acts, that God intended all Christians to become disciples. The word disciple and Christian were used interchangeably.

According to their own online sources, The Fellowship now consists of over three thousand churches in more than 125 countries. Each of these churches has their own pastor who is seen by The Fellowship as an entrepreneur. They plant a church and work a full-time job while they evangelize on the side to recruit new members until they have enough members that support their church financially to allow the pastor to become a full-time minister. All church property, however, is owned by The Fellowship—even if it was bought with the local pastor's own money.

Though there are so many different churches with different pastors, the atmosphere in the churches doesn't vary much. They uphold a certain standard. That standard drips down from Prescott to all the other (baby) churches through activities and International Bible Conferences.

As I stated earlier, depending on who your pastor is, your experiences will differ greatly. This is why I've used this preface to show that the source of The Fellowship—the founder, Wayman Mitchell and his doctrines—is the main factor as to why there are problems in this church and, most importantly, why this church is a cult. It is also why I've chosen to add ten stories by former members from all over the world: to illustrate The Fellowship is an abusive church system with victims across different countries, continents, and cultures.

I believe many good people are in The Fellowship who simply don't know any better. Once you discover there is a problem in the church that you don't address, you're essentially perpetuating the problem. When you neglect to take action on a problem that doesn't align with God's will, this gives the devil free rein. It allows false preachers to infect Jesus' flock with false teachings, to abuse people for their own personal gain, and to do as they please without being held accountable.

The Bible never asked us to remain silent against false preachers. Nor does the Bible ask us to pray for them. Rather, it admonishes us to rebuke them sharply (Titus 1:13), stop their mouths (Titus 1:11), expose them (Ephesians 5:11; 3 John 1:10), refuse them and not welcome them into our house (2 John 1:9), reject them (Titus 3:10), hand them over to

Satan (1 Timothy 1:20), and to turn away from them (Romans 16:17; 1 Timothy 6:5).

This book has attempted to do just some of those things: bring the truth to this cult and expose what was done in darkness to the light. May we all draw nearer to that light as we continue to walk closer to Jesus each and every day.

---

1. "BITE Model of Authoritarian Control^{TM}," Freedom of Mind Resource Center, accessed March 3, 2024, https://freedomofmind.com/cult-mind-control/bite-model/.
2. Steve Cooper, *Go Ye: The Arizona Story*, (Flagstaff, Arizona: Potters Press, 1982), 2, https://a.co/d/9N7jdOh.
3. Wayman O. Mitchell, *Blueprint From Heaven: The Divine Blueprint for Disciples*, (Prescott, Arizona: Potters Press, 1986), 31.
4. The Potter's House Cult, "The Potters House is a Cult Defending Historical Christianity (DOCUMENTARY TRAILER)," YouTube video, 2:50, September 21, 2022, https://www.youtube.com/watch?v=VtZqi9kBcVc.
5. Joel Crosby, accessed March 6, 2024, https://www.joelcrosby.com/wp-content/uploads/2024/03/425364382_3238942469735631_8719962136007882317_n.jpg.
6. Joel Crosby, accessed March 3, 2024, https://www.joelcrosby.com/wp-content/uploads/2024/03/709dce68-40d0-40d8-b950-de2ca5309a2a.jpeg.
7. The Potter's House Cult, "The Potters House is a Cult Defending Historical Christianity (DOCUMENTARY TRAILER)," YouTube video, 2:50, September 21, 2022, https://www.youtube.com/watch?v=VtZqi9kBcVc.

CHAPTER 1

THIS IS WORSE THAN WHAT PEOPLE SAY ABOUT US

DENNIS

"Their throat is an open sepulchre; with their tongues they have used deceit;
the poison of asps is under their lips:
Whose mouth is full of cursing and bitterness:
Their feet are swift to shed blood:
Destruction and misery are in their ways:
And the way of peace have they not known:
There is no fear of God before their eyes."
—Romans 3:13–18

I was born into a Christian family. Most of my family had roots in the Ozarks, but the Dust Bowl era had scattered many across the country. We moved often and usually connected with relatives in the area. My grandfather, three of his brothers, and my dad had all been Pentecostal preachers. My mom's side was mostly Baptist, but my larger family included Nazarenes and Presbyterians.

When I was young, we read three chapters from the Old Testament and two from the New Testament every evening, going around the table, taking turns reading a verse. My younger brothers had to sit there and listen until they learned to read, and then they started taking turns too, while I learned patience, sort of. We only read from the King James Version and went through the Bible in a year. Doctrine was often debated in our home.

I memorized Bible verses and always won contests about Bible knowledge. I was unusual and so was my memory. I could pay attention in class and get good grades. I was mostly bored. Besides the Ozarks, we made our home in Arizona and the West Coast states at different times while I was growing up. The Sonora Desert, Klamath Basin, Willamette Valley, northeast Oregon, and eastern Washington have very different geologies, climate, flora and wildlife. I was always the new guy because we moved every two or three years.

All five of us were born in different states. I went to the same junior high school all three years—that was a record. Different schools, different accents, different curricula, always public school based on my address. Different churches too. When we lived near my grandpa, we mostly went to his church, but we also attended Assembly of God churches until we started going to Open Bible in Klamath Falls. That's where my dad decided to switch churches and go to Bible school. We moved to Eugene, Oregon, where Open Bible had a Bible school.

As I grew older, I'd become more skeptical about the Bible and more interested in science. But when I learned in seventh grade biology that no one had ever observed spontaneous generation, I lost faith in science too.

I discovered languages. My first-grade teacher was Mexican, and I was fascinated by the idea of speaking another language. Unfortunately, the US wasn't a great place to study languages back then—especially before high school. So I taught myself the Greek and Russian alphabets that year when I found a table in a dictionary. Some of the Greek had come up in math and science, so I was already familiar with that, and a lot of Russian is based on Greek. But the next year, I took modern Greek, and the next, Latin.

I grew angrier with Christianity as I got older. It seemed to me that the reason I wasn't allowed to have fun was always because of God. I just wanted to be left alone. Later, I was drawn to Eastern religions and psychedelics. We often discussed this topic in school at the time and it was anything but boring. I was a bit young to be involved, but the ideology behind it appealed to me. It sounds cliché, but the Beatles' songs had a lot to do with it. They seemed simple yet profound, terse yet deep. I started getting high after becoming convinced that our health class teacher didn't know anything about drugs and was just repeating propaganda. From what I'd learned, I wanted to try pot, speed, and acid. That was in the spring of '72. By that summer, I just wanted to stay high.

A year later, in the early summer of 1973, I had an existential epiphany in a park. I realized that the search for the meaning of life was futile because there was no meaning. Everything would eventually burn up or burn out, and nothing mattered in the long run. The cosmic joke was on us because we were looking for a meaning that didn't exist. Although I can state it simply, I felt it profoundly. Life was a repeating cycle of temporary conditions. Everything was nothing. I felt profoundly empty.

This meant that life was futilely boring. Supernatural power was a valid distraction in a bleak situation, and satanism was the way to gain supernatural power and get people to leave me alone. I didn't actually believe the devil existed any more than that God existed, but I was convinced that believing in something could cause things that I couldn't explain. In the months that followed, I learned that the devil is real, and I realized there had to be a God to keep the devil from destroying all life.

By the close of the summer of 1973, I was born from above. I literally saw the light. Like a laser, the beam didn't diverge, but unlike a laser, it was white. Every wave in the electromagnetic spectrum in the entire universe seemed to be in that single beam, and nothing else existed at all. I heard a voice and floated into the light, and my mind was flooded with Bible texts I'd learned all my life. The light was Jesus. All I could do was keep saying, "Of course," and I felt incomprehensible peace.

It was like living the book of Isaiah and watching Mark write his Gospel, and realizing that not everything is nothing. I learned that which is eternal is the something in the otherwise nothingness, and the meaning that was absent in the drab diversity of constant change. It all made sense and was completely unexpected. I had never heard of this and didn't know it was possible, but it answered everything for me. The God I didn't believe in was real. Ironically, I'd been a thorn in the side of any Christian who dared talk to me about God all throughout the Jesus People movement. As the movement was ending, I became part of it. Equally ironic is the fact that after these experiences, I still fell for what was to follow.

My first service in a Fellowship church was Victory Chapel in Colorado Springs in 1978. I'd joined the Army in 1977 after two years of college and washing dishes for minimum wage and was finally stationed at Ft. Carson to an artillery unit after a year of military schools and waiting for orders in between. I'd been going to Open Bible Church in town at first, but I had problems with my car, and it was all the way on the other side of town from the base. After missing too many services, I went to Victory Chapel because it was near the bus station downtown, and a bus went past the barracks where I lived.

I loved Victory Chapel, especially Ron Jones, the pastor there. He was from Kentucky, just across the Mississippi River from Missouri, so he was easy for me to relate to. The church reminded me of churches I'd been to in the past. I'd seen churches put on plays for Christmas, but Victory Chapel had a drama team that put on relevant imaginative skits between songs every Saturday. They also played the kind of music I liked. They had seriously talented musicians. (Some were musicians at the Air Force Academy in Colorado Springs.)

But mostly, I liked the sermons. They were gritty and real, not comparisons of different doctrinal perspectives. The pastor stated matters plainly—not intentionally offending anyone but also not afraid to. They pointed out the craziness that had taken a hold in a lot of churches since the sixties, which was an already disturbing trend. They also had moments where everyone would break out praying in tongues simultaneously for a certain period of time, which I really liked. The Fellowship was described almost as a logical continuation of the Jesus movement. I appreciated their roots. And everything had a purpose. The skits, sermons, and music were all part of an evangelistic strategy. They took initiative instead of waiting around for God to move, which seemed like a great idea at the time.

Over time, I grew even more enthusiastic. I was really impressed with the vision. Wayman Mitchell had a vision that inspired him to build a church and then plant other Fellowship churches that would evangelize the world. I took this to literally mean a vision like Isaiah or Paul because of my own experiences. I had also heard about David Wilkerson's vision, which I also took literally. I knew such a thing was possible. I never took his references to the vision as a mere metaphor. It now appears I should have. It never occurred to me until long after the fact, that Wayman would himself abandon that vision a short time after I first heard about it. I thought that it was a good thing The Fellowship had upright leaders, because the shift toward centralization and (Fellowship) orthodoxy seemed vulnerable to abuse. But since Wayman Mitchell and his disciples were upright, it was okay.

I moved around a lot because of the Army. In 1980, I went to school at Ft. Huachuca in Arizona and attended The Fellowship Church in Sierra Vista. Bill Coolidge was pastor there, and I really liked his perspective. There, I locked in—made the decision that I wanted to remain part of The Fellowship.

The church in Sierra Vista was a lot like Victory Chapel in Colorado Springs. One of the things that had bothered me about Assembly of God, Open Bible, or Foursquare (non-Fellowship Foursquare) churches is that even though they were part of the same denomination, the churches varied a lot. The overall atmosphere could be remarkably different, even among different Assembly of God churches in the same town, which I'd seen in Spokane and Virginia. This was usually because of the individual pastors in charge.

But The Fellowship seemed the same no matter what church you were in. Some churches were bigger; they might even speak different languages. But every church I visited seemed the same, consistent in a good way.

I returned to Colorado Springs later in 1980, back to Ron Jones's church, but was assigned to a different unit. He preached fairly often on revivals of the past, how many moves of God seemed to die out over three or four generations at most, leaving dead organizations behind. Tragic.

I'd witnessed this trend already in the years before I came into contact with The Fellowship. Historically, Jones was right. I didn't want to see this happen with The Fellowship; I wanted to do everything possible to keep that from happening.

Europe

But in 1982, I was looking at an assignment in Europe. Although my orders said Germany, I was assigned to a unit in the Netherlands. (The battalion headquarters was in Germany, but my unit was in the Netherlands). Ironically, I received a call offering to get me out of the Army and into school by fall. I could keep my rank and pay if I would sign up for ROTC and return as an officer for four years, but I had no plans to stay in the Army, and I couldn't keep Russian as my major. I hated my job and kept trying to change it. I didn't care much for the Army either but wanted to go to Europe. By this time, I'd had four years of German, two of Russian, and a year each of modern Greek, Latin, French, and Koine (NT Greek), as well as linguistics classes. My Defense Aptitude Language Battery (DLAB) score was 148. The highest score possible is 164. I've never met anyone else with a score as high as mine. Someone even started calling me "sir" after seeing my score. Now I had an opportunity to apply what I knew and learn Dutch on the ground.

So now I was in the Zwolle church, which had just become part of The Fellowship and was one of the only two Fellowship churches in Europe. A year later (1983), Zwolle hosted the first European conference, and then there were five churches in Europe.

That was an exciting time, and for most of the people in the Zwolle church, it was the first time they'd witnessed the reality of church planting and churches working together to evangelize, in this case, Europe. I even played bass in a band.

I took a lot of pictures because I felt like I was documenting something, including of many people who later became pastors in the Netherlands. Many of the other photos were baptism photos. The Netherlands is, in many ways, the hardest military assignment I had. A 55.5-hour work week wasn't enough. We were extremely short-handed and had long supply routes (which I usually had to travel three times a week). I had 24-hour duty twice a week and every other weekend. I once worked 53 hours straight with no sleep, and 110 hours was my longest work week, but 70 hours a week was pretty routine.

My heart rhythm has never stabilized due to lack of sleep. I now have a pacemaker. Still, I extended my tour and ended up staying 4.5 years because I was thinking about getting out and staying in the Netherlands and spending more time in the church.

I met my wife soon after that first European conference in 1983. We were married in the Zwolle church in '85.

In December '86, my wife and I went to the States, back to Victory Chapel in Colorado Springs where I first became part of The Fellowship. Wayman had recommended that I stay in the Army while I was in the Netherlands when I said I didn't feel called to pioneer. I had only asked Rudy van Diermen because I was wondering how difficult it would be. But he asked Wayman who gave an answer that was a major disappointment, but if Wayman himself thought so, what could I say? So I re-enlisted, and we moved to Colorado, this time to an infantry unit. Both our daughters were born there before we returned to Europe, this time to Germany in '89.

That was the first time in eleven years I didn't live near a Fellowship church. For the next eight years, we went to conferences in Zwolle twice a year and tried going to German (or Belgian) churches in our area in the meantime. We also moved eight times in ten years because the Army started closing units in Europe, but I planned to stay in Europe.

Six months after we moved to Germany, we got a letter from a friend that said, "I suppose by now, you've heard about Pastor Jones and The Fellowship." But this was the first time we heard that Jones had left The Fellowship along with several other pastors I knew.

Soon after that, I learned I was going to be deployed to Saudi Arabia for a year. (It turned out to be only 4.5 months.) So I arranged for my wife and daughters to move back to Zwolle in the Netherlands while I went to the desert.

I spent the whole time trying to imagine a scenario where Jones and Mitchell could part ways without one of them being horribly wrong. I ended up deciding that unless I learned otherwise, there was no good reason to leave The Fellowship.

After my unit came back from the Gulf, I was busy turning in equipment, which became my primary job for two years. The US and Russia had come to an agreement, and our unit was marked to return to the US from Germany. I was in charge of all property in whatever unit I was assigned to, so I was the one who had to get everything turned in to the right place with the right paperwork. This involved a lot of time on the road as well as a lot of paperwork. Fortunately, I'd bought my first computer in '83. I kept all my data in dBase and wrote programs to fill out Army forms using that data. This enabled me to generate ninety-nine turn-in documents a day, a limitation of the document number system, not my programs. I ended up closing three units, the first two in Göppingen, Germany.

Every three weeks, I drove from Göppingen to Zwolle to spend four days with my family. Other than that, I worked. I never made the drive in less than six hours, even on the Autobahn.

One time, Mike, a friend of mine I'd been in the Gulf with, came along during conference time. He asked me how I knew Mitchell was okay. I pointed out that he'd just heard Bill Coolidge and Hank Houghton preach. I said, "And if people like that follow Mitchell, you know he has to be on the level."

Mike ended up going back to the States when I went to a military police customs unit in Bremerhaven in December '91. He ended up at a Potter's House Church on the East Coast (near Ft. Bragg). But he summed up his experience in that place as follows: "My pastor is an idiot." He also told me they had special prayer meetings where they prayed judgment on people who opposed the church. I'd never heard of that. It sounded satanic.

Later, he ended up at Paul Stevens's church in Texas, but he was told that the FBI was investigating that church and that he'd have to quit or lose his clearance. He later moved to Oklahoma and took a government civilian job. I took it badly that he was no longer in the Potter's House. I never could believe what he said about praying curses, and I couldn't understand why he left The Fellowship until he told me later about the FBI.

When Bremerhaven closed twenty months after we moved there, I was sent to a unit in Pirmasens, Germany, near the French border that had also just moved there from Wiesbaden.

Actually, at first, my orders were for a cavalry unit near Fulda, Germany, but headquarters saw they were about to lose me and had my orders changed to send me to an ordinance unit under their command in Wiesbaden. People with experience turning in unit property were in demand at that time, and I'd just finished my third unit. My new orders had originally said Wiesbaden, but the unit moved and my orders were amended to indicate Pirmasens. Our son was born while I was stationed there. My unit moved (once again) to Miesau while we were there, but it wasn't far, so we stayed in housing in Pirmasens.

I left Pirmasens when I was assigned to Brussels. I got the assignment in Brussels because I spoke Dutch and had been useful in translating a briefing. (It had a lot of slides, Harvard Graphics in those days, long before PowerPoint.) As it turns out, I was nearly sent to Koblenz for the same position because they needed a German speaker as well. Our

HQ had been looking for someone like me, and I ran into a major who was looking for a Dutch speaker. Even though I hadn't gone to the Defense Language Institute, I took the proficiency tests for Dutch, German, and Russian. I'm glad I did.

I was in an ideal situation in Brussels, a dream job that suited me well. I dived into learning French since I could already speak Dutch to the Flemish speakers and German to the German speakers. I was the junior of two Americans stationed with the Belgian military headquarters. I was even offered a civilian position if I would stay, but I thought the best thing to do would be to return to the Zwolle church and raise my kids here. I thought they'd get to experience an ongoing revival like I had. Unfortunately, revival was already being strangled in The Fellowship, but it would take me another twenty years to figure that out. At the end of 1996, we returned to Zwolle from Brussels. On Thanksgiving Day, I was finally a civilian again.

Rudy van Diermen was still the pastor in Zwolle when we returned from Brussels, but he left for South Africa about six months after we returned. (Maybe it was six months before I heard he was leaving, and he left soon afterwards.) In any case, the church changed pretty abruptly after we returned. He was the one who told me that Bill Coolidge and Hank Houghton had also left The Fellowship.

A couple of years after he went to South Africa, I was told that Rudy van Diermen had plans to take De Deur out of The Fellowship. Horrible. Unthinkable. Just like Jones had done! It didn't make sense. So I rallied behind everyone who was trying to keep that from happening.

I intended to stay with The Fellowship to the end, and I didn't want Zwolle to separate as Victory Chapel had. In hindsight, though, I participated in the coup that Valk and Wayman had planned to wrest control of the Netherlands churches and kick out van Diermen. (I have since apologized to Rudy for that. People hold grudges against him for various reasons, but I don't personally, and I was wrong to back Valk, the usurper.)

After I had become locked in to The Fellowship, I decided to back them with everything I could muster. In my case, that especially meant technological innovation. I learned a lot while I was in the Army that I planned to use in my post-military career and could program in more than one language, knew different database programs/servers, and also built websites.

De Deur needed a website. After bugging Valk a year for permission, I registered the name, found a host, and went to work. At one point, I was generating pages for forty churches from Access table data and uploading them to the server when they changed. I could make updates whenever I was asked to.

But more importantly, I felt like people needed to learn more about the Bible. My dad was an Open Bible preacher. One of the things that Open Bible used to do was have contests between churches. Teenagers answered questions and competed against other teams. The correct answer was always a quote from the King James Bible, not just verses but entire passages. It had to be word for word. *A* instead of *the* would be wrong. Everything had to be exact.

I'd witnessed this and knew many contestants personally. They memorized whole chapters. I had been in the church in Spokane before joining the Army. They had a strong, active team there.

This was a far cry from the level of Bible knowledge in the Zwolle church, which was pathetic. (Nowadays, it's sadly worse in the church at large, even among pastors.) I had brought up the Open Bible contests to Valk as an example of an area where the church could improve, but he didn't see any value in it.

Since one of my goals was to teach people more about the Bible and its background, I started subtitling educational videos and music videos. (Some people in Zwolle didn't even understand the words they sang along to.) My emphasis was on knowledge. But a lot of the pastors started demanding more "entertaining" videos. Think about that.

A lot of my motivation in helping all The Fellowship pastors was a lingering guilt about how I had opposed everything Christian when I was growing up in a preacher's home. I had fought everything Christian as if my survival depended on it. But after being born from above (and as part of the process), I saw how wrong I had been.

So I was determined, once I decided to support The Fellowship, to try just as hard to help afterwards as I had fought against my family back then. I took that mission seriously, and being a workaholic helped. I was constantly thinking of ways to ease the burden on pastors and assist them with information and tech. A lot of them just seemed happy to have some variety because they could fill up time with what I was producing and did not have to come up with something on their own. I was involved in translating the services into English and generally organized translation for the other translators as well. We routinely translated into French, German, Spanish, and Portuguese also, but nearly always, we translated into English. As part of that, I often went into the pastor's office. I made copies of the sermon notes, especially the Bible references, for all the translators to help them get ready for the sermon.

One day I walked into Valk's office while Nomdo Schuitema was talking to a group of pastors hanging out there about diversities of rewards. This caught my attention. He seemed to expect that they, as pastors, would receive a greater reward in heaven than other Christians. I thought that was a strange elitist attitude. It sounded like something they'd earned, which struck me as unbiblical. I hadn't seen that attitude before.

It was my idea to team up with some people to make videos for the European conference, just like Prescott had been doing. I bugged Valk for a year before he decided to go for it, just like about the website.

I had never been a pastor but could appreciate what was involved because of my family background. However, I felt like I couldn't speak authoritatively to anyone who was a pastor. How do you tell someone how to do their job if you've never had that job? That was why I insisted that the text for any film should be written by a pastor. I was the narrator and translated what I read.

The pastor who usually wrote this text, Martin Klok, wanted someone from his church involved, and the person he involved, it turned out, was completely unreliable. This caused many problems.

In the Army, if you have a problem with someone, you go to their superior to deal with it. That is proper procedure.

So I went to Martin Klok, his pastor, who told me he would deal with it. Except he didn't. Not that year. Or the next, in spite of his reassurances. Or even the year after that.

Each year, I was caught up in a very stressful situation doing video conversions that shouldn't have been necessary, but Klok never took care of anything.

I was very much at the breaking point. Right before this, I'd had to go through a couple of chemo rounds with lingering side effects, and the stress of unnecessary deadlines wasn't helping.

Worse, I saw that Klok, someone I had thought highly of, was lying to me. Apparently, he lied more than once and didn't even feel bad about it. I went to Valk about Klok. He wasn't even interested.

The only explanation I could come up with was that relativism had crept into the Dutch churches more extensively than it had in The Fellowship at large. Relativists have a hard time defining right and wrong because there are no absolutes. Valk obviously didn't care about what was right. I figured if I could just force them to focus on what was actually going on, he'd see I was right. For some reason, he didn't seem to want to see what was happening at all. And since Klok seemed to be denying everything I was saying, he was lying and therefore had to be confronted.

A letter had been posted on the bulletin board outside the pastor's office about what to do if you had a disagreement with leadership, just like a commander's open-door policy in the Army. It was a familiar concept, and I'd read the letter more than once while standing outside waiting for the singing to stop. It seemed like the obvious step to take. I'd done it in the Army and knew it was a useful way to try to resolve problems.

So I requested to see the board of elders, which in the Potter's House means the pastors appointed to oversee disputes in the churches, in this case, the Netherlands. Paul Leidelmeijer was the first to talk to me. I thought the conversation went well. I told him what had happened. He seemed to understand.

After that, my meeting with the council got postponed. Repeatedly. Finally, after a whole year, I was told I could see the council after one of the men's discipleship meetings, late on a Monday evening, when everyone wanted to go home.

I didn't go in the discipleship meeting but stood in the hall and looked at everyone gathered there. I decided consciously, "I don't want to be like any of them." I didn't know what was about to happen, but I became aware of an aversion to their self-centered perspective.

Kangaroo court was actually the most apt description of that meeting. Klok hadn't actually denied my account of what had happened, but his position, as well as the council's, was that I had opposed the authority of a pastor (Martin Klok) in one of his decisions. They turned my issue against him into their issue against me.

This disoriented me completely, because I'd thought he'd disputed my account entirely, but actually he didn't. So I thought I was wrong. Even though he'd lied to me repeatedly, he hadn't lied to everyone about it like I'd thought. I was gaslit.

Against my wishes, a friend of mine had also gone to the council to speak on my behalf. This seemed superfluous. I'd known everyone on the board since before any of them had become pastors. Why did I need anyone to speak on my behalf to this group? Besides, I had the truth on my side. But even Leidelmeijer had taken the position that I opposed the authority of the pastor.

So against my wishes, Willem became a witness. When we left, he told me it was a *schijn*, a show. I didn't think it was that bad, but it turned out it was. (Willem left The Fellowship before I did, but my wife told him not to tell me about it at that time. By then, I was really sick, and she didn't want me dealing with that as well. I refer to that time period as my four years in a wheelchair.)

What went wrong? How could the council, people I'd known since they were saved, most of whom I'd taken their baptism photos of, not see the obvious wrong in what was happening?

I thought, *Wayman Mitchell must not realize how screwed up things have gotten in the Netherlands*. It was a big mistake not having anyone in the Netherlands who'd actually been discipled in a real Potter's House Church like in the States. A key early-days emphasis had been on a transference of spirit, the idea that being around someone under the right circumstances taught you to think and act like they did. That's why everyone was discipled by a disciple of Mitchell until we actually started referring to this as third and fourth generation. But that had never really happened in the Netherlands because no disciple of Mitchell had pioneered there.

Rudy van Diermen joined The Fellowship and implemented this pattern of discipleship, but his contact with the States was mostly tele-phonic. The transference of spirit had never really taken root. Even Valk, with his annual two trips to the US, hadn't accumulated as much face-time with Wayman after thirty years as a local disciple would in three years. Somebody never did the math. Ironically, Rudy kept the vision of The Fellowship after Wayman had abandoned it.

Applying their teaching about transference of spirit to Wayman and his disciples, The Fellowship disciples should logically have the same spirit as Wayman himself. That was the expectation and one of the arguments that The Fellowship used to contrast discipleship with Bible schools, which were frowned upon. A very suggestive theme, Elijah and Elisha, made a great illustration in many sermons on this topic as well.

Increasingly, themes about our founder became a safe topic for confer-ence sermons. We had to pledge our allegiance to him and all that. "Where would we be without our pastor, Wayman Mitchell?" Paul Stevens or Richard Rubi (or probably both of them) said this. Mitchell didn't seem to discourage these kinds of statements.

Before I attended The Fellowship, I had witnessed a popular Assembly of God preacher say he wouldn't return the next year if they didn't quit acting like he was special. What a contrast! That kind of humility had no place in The Fellowship.

Instead, there had been a growing trend of competition among certain pastors, one trying to outdo the other, praising Wayman for everything they could imagine crediting him with. It seemed a bit excessive, and the same ones were usually exaggerating. This was all consistent with the Mitchell clone phenomenon. (People often remarked that many pastors seemed like clones in their mannerisms, and this was often seen as a compliment.)

No one in the Netherlands had ever undergone that kind of direct discipleship. There was a break in the chain that until then, had been considered important—at least, that's how it had been taught. But pragmatism had won in the end.

Seeing the corruption that I was uncovering in the Netherlands leadership, I concluded Wayman had no idea how wrongly this mess had turned out. I thought, *When Mitchell finds out, he'll replace the lot of them.*

I had told myself I'd never do another round of interferon treatments. The first had cost me my thyroid, and the second left me in chronic pain and unable to handle noise.

But I had developed blood blisters on my feet that had opened up, and then my Achilles tendon became visible. Hepatitis was thought to be the culprit, so I decided to do another round. It seemed like that's what I had to.

Interferon is like having a constant fever. The first round lasted eleven months. So did the second. Round three would go for two and a half years. By the time round three started, I'd already been on codeine. Then I switched to Tramadol for about five years.

But now I was facing the use of morphine, methadone, oxynorm, oxycontin, and fentanyl in addition to the interferon, ribavirin and the third time, Boceprevir—all at once. During my first treatments, the medicine had been labeled "for research only," and the Boceprevir treatments started on the day it was legally approved in the Netherlands. I ended up in a wheelchair or bedridden for four years. I had carpal operations on both hands from leaning so hard on crutches when I moved around in the house.

It got worse. My leg started rotting away. It stunk for two years. I ended up sleeping for seventeen hours a day.

During my waking hours, I worried about what had happened to The Fellowship. How would it ever be restored?

Even though my survival was looking doubtful, I was aware that God was with me and that people were praying for me. I couldn't make much sense of anything else as it all seemed wrong. God was my only hope and only constant in a universe of variables.

At the same time, it was hard to believe that while I accepted divine healing as a reality, I was in pretty bad shape. A couple of thoughts began emerging during this time. One was from this verse:

"Confess your faults one to another, and pray one for another, that ye may be healed. The effectual fervent prayer of a righteous man availeth much." (James 5:16).

After observing how healing services had deteriorated in De Deur and after seeing that righteousness wasn't even a goal in the leadership in the Netherlands, I decided asking for prayer from leadership would probably do more harm than good. People weren't getting healed as often as they had in the past, and this passage in James seemed a likely explanation.

I also thought, *I'm not helping them with anything anymore.*

When I was really sick, I sometimes couldn't talk well. Sometimes my grammar would scramble. As I mentioned, I've studied languages a lot, and on some basic level my conceptual grammar has become a bit blended. I don't think in just one language because some thoughts can be expressed in one language but have to be described in another. Sometimes, I was just too zonked out to even say an entire sentence, especially if I had to speak loudly enough to be heard. The concentration to speak required a lot of exertion.

During my lucid moments, I thought a lot about what had happened, what it meant, and how things would go on after I was gone. Bigger picture stuff. I wasn't constantly involved in projects to strategically aid The Fellowship anymore. I was now out of the maelstrom, so to speak.

But even though I couldn't always think clearly, I clearly saw that The Fellowship was wrong on more levels than I'd even considered. It wasn't as much their doctrine as it was certain perspectives that had begun to distort the doctrine. I didn't take their preposterous claims of authority seriously—I thought it was all hyperbole. I'm American, and we exaggerate as much as the British understate facts. And after so many years in the Army, you learn to ignore the way it sounds when someone exaggerates. What they say is not meant to be taken literally. But this was something else: ego, self. Selfishness was at the core of the entire culture of The Fellowship.

Righteousness was no longer a guiding principle in The Fellowship and may not have been for longer than I was aware. As a result, unrighteous behavior was being justified. Compromising truth to hide their motivation was as rampant as the gossip culture that was also flourishing. I never saw it clearly until after I left, but being in the hospital a lot actually helped me gain perspective so that I could reevaluate my memories later. People in The Fellowship have a unique checklist to evaluate status. This includes Fellowship principles, standards, and conditions, such as Do you have a tie? or When can you fill in in the nursery? The questions continue to becoming a pastor, planting a church, the number of churches planted, and the number of those that were international.

When my last interferon treatments ended, I got intestinal cancer. This was the worst pain I've ever felt. Prior to this, I thought pain level ten was when you passed out, but I suddenly discovered that a daily level twelve didn't make me pass out. I was screaming and crying for three hours a day from pain. I couldn't hold it back. My doctors have since confided to me they hadn't expected me to survive. This pain continued for three months until they decided they had to operate. I had one operation, and it was gone. I felt better and stronger, and for the first time in years, I was hungry.

Soon, I was looking forward to going to Bible study again. Bible study was always my favorite. It was the one time we could comment on the Bible, and I have a lot I can say on the subject. I had recommended to Valk that he lead Bible studies on Romans and Hebrews when he took over Zwolle. He never got to Romans, and his study on Hebrews had been a serious disappointment. It sounded like he read it in a book instead of studying himself. I told myself he was still learning.

I had heard that Johan Houtman, who had become the assistant pastor in Zwolle, had been doing Bible study, and that it was pretty good. Everyone seemed enthusiastic about the series he was just finishing, and I was looking forward to the start of a new series, the Sermon on the Mount.

But the first week wasn't really about the Sermon on the Mount. Some-how, all he talked about was the authority of the pastor, which doesn't relate to anything in Matthew 5. The second week was a continuation of the first week. Matthew 5 didn't come up. After sitting through the third week, I suddenly realized, "This is worse than what people say about us." It felt like I'd been punched in the stomach. I was nauseous and went home before the morning service.

I quit going to Bible Study then.

I had a friend in the Zwolle church, Isaac, whom I had known since '83. He was the fourth English speaker in the Zwolle church (I had been the third), and he was from Ghana. We had both seen a lot of changes through the years, and both he and I had had lived elsewhere and returned in the meantime.

I heard he was very ill and went and visited him in the hospital after I'd gotten better. Reluctantly, he began confiding in me "how far we have fallen." He talked about how the Zwolle church had been and how it had become. I felt things breaking inside me. I couldn't deny anything he said. He was right. Worse, he had put those feelings into words. He died a couple of months later.

One day in 2015 or 2016, I was outside after a sermon, and Etienne de Sain, the assistant pastor in Zwolle by that time, came outside. He had actually preached what I thought was a good sermon, but, being pretty agitated, I said, "If you'd practice what you preach, it'd be a lot better." (I used the plural for *you, jullie* in Dutch, and was really referring to all the pastors and not only him.)

He responded with "you should talk to your pastor about that." I responded, "He's the problem." At that, Etienne turned around and walked away.

In 2016, before my exit, I also confronted Kevin Foley (whom I have known since he had hair) for praising Valk through the roof. He began defending Valk to me, but I immediately thought, *You don't speak a word of Dutch, and you don't know him,* and then I turned and walked away without a word saying anything. He wasn't listening anyway.

Through the years, I'd seen so many couples come and go. These families seemed willing to serve God but, for some reason, left The Fellowship. I had always thought, *If you want to go for the full one hundred percent, The Fellowship is the best place to do it. All your efforts will be channeled into evangelizing the world.* But still, people suddenly left the church. Solid people, not the kind that seemed afraid to be involved in what God was doing. And I watched them leave. It was disturbing. I wondered what was happening. And it happened too often.

On one occasion, Valk preached an entire sermon on the word *phobos,* using a passage that didn't even contain the word, but he said it didn't matter "because people were helped."

Chris Hart (an evangelist frequently invited to Zwolle) didn't "want to discuss the Bible" with me when I tried pointing out that the Greek in the passage he'd just preached contained some real gems he might not have been aware of. People teaching the Bible who don't care what the Bible says? What's that about?

My wife was getting tired of my sometimes-audible reactions during the sermons. I was once surprised to hear myself say, "I can't believe he said that" out loud after one of Valk's particularly stupid remarks. Many of his sermon illustrations were taken from *Reader's Digest*, or as he called it, "a well-known Dutch magazine."

This was the leader for Europe that Wayman had chosen. Van Diermen had warned Wayman that Valk had marriage problems and wasn't a great choice, but that disaster wasn't averted.

Joe Campbell preached a sermon during conference and told about a preacher in The Fellowship who would visit a stripper when he was out of town. This stripper later got saved and was very excited when she ran into this pastor (he wasn't named in the sermon). He denied knowing her, and at some point, this pastor was questioned about it. Wayman exclaimed, "Don't lie! The Holy Spirit is here.," whereupon the pastor confessed to everything, at least in this sermon.

But over the years, Wayman didn't have enough discernment to know that he relied on a liar to translate his sermons during conference. (Klok nearly always translated for the American pastors.) He actually seemed to like Valk, except he never learned to pronounce his name, so there was no discernment there. In hindsight, Wayman used moral failures as a matter of strategy. He controlled whomever he had dirt on.

I quit going to conferences. I was more disappointed than encouraged. I heard cautionary tales instead of examples and saw people behaving in ways I couldn't justify.

Then one day, Klok showed up in the Zwolle church. He was profaning the sanctuary, and no one seemed to care. After shouting at him and telling him to leave, I saw Valk. I called him a thief, liar, usurper, and hireling to his face. Even worse, it turned out, was true as well.

Greg (the son of Wayman and heir to the Potter's house) had to have heard me. I'd already seen him there, and everyone in the building heard me. I'm sure Greg understood me as I was shouting in English.

After that, I never went back. While I haven't been back, there's more. One day, my wife told me my daughter wanted to talk to me but wouldn't say what it was about. When we arrived at my daughter's house, I met a friend of hers and found myself in what seemed to be a moderated discussion. It was strange. My daughter said that she had something to tell me, but I had to promise to "not do anything about it."

Then she told me about Valk. As badly as I thought of Valk, I had never suspected he was a predator. It explained a lot. It turned out she was also a victim, one of thirty she knew about. After what happened to her, she started asking questions of other girls she had grown up with in the church before she even told my son, who was the first person she told other than her husband.

At first, she didn't want to jeopardize Valk and the church. What if people backslid and went to hell because of her story? She had learned of a few other victims but didn't know how high the number went. But her therapist told her Valk would never stop, that he was like an addict. She knew he had to be stopped, and she filed charges. Valk has a blood fetish and liked filming girls killing fish. Once he filmed a girl with a chicken, and another time, a boy was with his sister. The first time had been when Valk was in Amersfoort, so it had been going on for thirty years. I didn't know about any of this when I exploded at church. My daughter has been personally thanked by women who realized they were being groomed when everything came out, but no one else came forward. The (now ex-) head of the original European Fellowship conference church, Wayman's personal pick, was an embarrassing pervert, and they were going to try to rehabilitate him (redirection is what they called it).

As a result of Valk getting kicked out, his daughter decided to graffiti my daughter's house. This brought the story into the wider world because the police and my daughter's neighborhood were suddenly aware of what was happening. After that, my daughter decided she had to tell us as well, which also led to the police finding out.

My daughter did take him to court, but he claimed what had happened was mutual. There was a year-long backlog of similar court cases, then Corona, and it was delayed a long time. None of the other women wanted to be identified, and the judge never understood the mindset (that the pastor has the final authority) that affects someone raised in the cult, so he was released. Both of my daughters have since taken Krav Maga lessons, but The Fellowship is against martial arts.

My daughter has been haunted by the narcissistic manipulations, Valk's smear campaign and his excuses (it was her fault), and his dark, demonic side. Her therapist had warned her that a narcissist is an addict that keeps looking for victims, so she decided to report it to the police. Therapy has helped her and my son.

My own nightmares stopped after I left the church. I used to cry out in my sleep because I felt trapped and couldn't keep out people who were trying to break in. My wife had to wake me up to get me to stop. I didn't notice for a couple of years that they'd stopped when I left. A lot of people in The Fellowship have mental issues. They're being lied to constantly and told they have to follow the advice of their pastor. I actually found a video of a pastor in Australia teaching that "it's way worse to disobey God than it is to disobey the police. Way worse to disobey God or your pastor."[1] He has since filed a copyright complaint with YouTube because the video of him saying this is online. A darkness comes where the Spirit is unwelcome, and The Fellowship has an evil streak that's grown like a cloud over the congregation, a film on a window, or corrosion on metal.

I had told myself I'd leave everything alone if they didn't try to bring Valk back. Well, six months later, Nomdo let Valk back in the church. He was greeted with tears and showered with sympathy. As I'd planned to if that's what they did, I went to the newspaper about Valk. I told my story to the reporter, as well as the details I'd learned about Valk and my daughter, and contacted as many people as I could find who were willing to talk to a journalist. In the end, the journalist wrote a good series about what had been going on. As a result, Valk closed his online counseling site (where he could look for potential victims). Nomdo also questioned Valk and realized he'd been lying to him as well. Valk had lost count of his victims and couldn't give Nomdo a consistent number, so he kicked him out. But Nomdo's first reaction had been to protect Valk. That's standard procedure in The Fellowship. No one cares about the victims. There are no victims, according to the narrative, so victims are always liars.

I found an old letter online that had been posted in a Yahoo group of ex-Fellowship members that said Wayman always blamed women, and few would argue with that statement. Yahoo groups no longer exist, so it's obviously an ongoing problem with a long history. Pastors get redirected, and pastor's sons undergo discipline, exclusion for six months from everything. Women usually end up leaving. I know of at least one ex-Fellowship women's group online. If The Fellowship had the Spirit of Christ at all, they would help the victims and expose the evil. They should think about repentance, meaning change in thought and action, for a long time before thinking about reinstating a predator to a platform. They should embrace the truth, which they instead actively conceal, ergo, they historically and routinely misrepresent God. God did not send them to do this.

"And this is the condemnation, that light is come into the world, and men loved darkness rather than light, because their deeds were evil. For every one that doeth evil hateth the light, neither cometh to the light, lest his deeds should be reproved. But he that doeth truth cometh to the light, that his deeds may be made manifest, that they are wrought in God." (John 3:19–21).

---

1. The Potter's House Cult, Facebook, November 21, 2022, https://www.facebook.com/watch/?v=1216284752639535&ref=sharing.

CHAPTER 2
THE SON OF A REBEL
JOEL

"For rebellion is as the sin of witchcraft, and stubbornness is as iniquity and idolatry. Because thou hast rejected the word of the Lord, he hath also rejected thee from being king."
—1 Samuel 15:23

I grew up in Zwolle, a small city between the rivers IJssel and Vecht in the Netherlands. There, the grass was always green, the cows were always fat, and the tap water was clean and didn't taste of chlorine. I could ride my bike for thirty minutes in any given direction to leave the city and enjoy the countryside where agriculture thrived on the tulip, corn, and potato exports. Living in such a peaceful city would be a dream come true for most. Had my experiences in Zwolle been different, I would've found it peaceful too. But to me, Zwolle isn't peaceful anymore.

I moved to Zwolle in 1997 when I was three years old and only have vague memories of our life in Germany and Belgium. My dad was a staff sergeant in the US Army and was moved around a lot. He left the army after twenty years, requested a residence permit based on being married to a Dutch citizen, and moved to Zwolle where he'd lived for almost five years when he was stationed in 't Harde. He'd met my mom there in the same church denomination he had been a member of in the States.

My childhood revolved around the church. I went to Sunday school and children's church. I even joined the children's choir despite my stage fright, where my pastor described me as the captain of a sinking ship because I refused to move to the rhythm of the music like all the other children.

Before I went to high school, I started paying attention to the testimonies of older kids in my church. I was afraid I'd lose my salvation and wanted to know what to look out for. Was there a way I could secure my salvation? As I listened to various testimonies, I learned most kids started smoking and drinking to try to fit in—which wasn't allowed in the church. Just like owning a television or going to the cinema wasn't allowed either.

If you did any of those things and got caught, you'd be disciplined for six months and weren't allowed to be in ministry during that period. Our church taught we were supposed to set an example to sinners and other Christians through our lifestyle, which meant we were to take a firm stance against anything we didn't approve of. I was afraid trying to fit in meant I would start smoking and drinking, and figured the best way to secure my salvation was by being proud of being different.

In high school, my classmates noticed I was different right away. I didn't know any cuss words. Pretty soon, the name-calling began. After that, I got into a couple of fights until I was held up at knifepoint by a classmate and was compelled to drop out of school. I went to a temporary school for troubled children before finally going to Greijdanus High School, a Christian school.

I was thrilled to go to this new school. Our previous pastor had a falling out with the local reformed church, and as a result, no one from our church was accepted there. Given my circumstances and the fact that pastor van Diermen hadn't been our pastor for several years, this school accepted me on a trial basis.

I was on my best behavior and took my trial period very seriously. I needed two months to prove myself, and after that, other kids from my church would be accepted into this school as well. But after several weeks, I was bullied again. I punched a classmate in the eye and reported myself to a teacher. Luckily, this didn't influence their decision to accept kids from our church into their school.

I kept getting bullied and occasionally was beat up. I began to hate people, school, and life. I wanted to die rather than live another day. After a difficult day of name-calling, jokes at my expense, and bruises, I went home to my parents. My father's health was rapidly declining at this point, and he relied on three handfuls of pills each day just to stay alive. He suffered with unbearable pain and was bedridden on most days.

He wanted to talk to me, but I was depressed and very angry. I often fought with my sister, who wanted to talk to me as well, but I told her to stop meddling. I wanted to be left alone, to escape the real world, to lock myself up in my room, lie in bed, and play games on my laptop. I didn't want human contact or to go to church anymore either. I didn't fit in with my peers and often felt the loneliest when I was at church. My mom often asked me to keep my dad company while she worked, to which I reluctantly agreed. Other days, she tried to get me to go to church, even when she had to work and I had to go alone.

At church, I was taught to seek advice from my pastor. I requested a meeting and told him I struggled with depression. I also told him about my home life and my difficult relationship with my father. Pastor Valk listened to my troubles until I was finished, and then he weighed in.

"When you feel depressed, just smile," he began. "Smiling releases a chemical in your brain that makes you happy."

I found this strange advice coming from a man of God and had expected him to pray for me or cast out demons instead, but I respected him and decided to do what he advised.

"And about your father," he continued. "Your father is a rebellious man. It would be better for you to look for another father figure in the church."

I had heard people call my dad rebellious before, which often had to do with the fact that he asked difficult questions or publicly corrected the pastor when he made a mistake during a sermon. I often felt embarrassed when he drew attention to himself. Everybody in our church knew you weren't supposed to question or correct the pastor—except my dad. When you did correct the pastor, you did it privately and not before explaining your motivation for correcting him. To hear Pastor Valk call my dad a rebel took it to another level. Now I wasn't just embarrassed of my father's actions; I was ashamed to be his son.

Smiling to battle depression didn't work. And my relationship with my father became strained (just like my relationship with my sister). I tried to spend as much time in church as I could to avoid my father but felt a constant need to prove I wasn't like him. I didn't have the same connection with my pastor that my peers had, despite my effort to establish a connection with him. And I knew it was because my dad was a rebel.

After I graduated from high school and went to college, I got an internship at a furniture store. One day when I rode my bike home, I felt particularly depressed. I didn't want to go home, but I had nowhere else to go. Next to the bicycle path was a train track, and a train was coming. I made a split-second decision to steer my bicycle onto the track, but the train went onto a switch track I didn't know was there. Had that train stayed on course, I don't know if I would've jumped out of the way or not. On several other instances afterward, I tried to drown myself in my bathtub, but I couldn't go through with it.

One Wednesday evening, I went to a church service and sat in my usual spot. I didn't want to be there and sit through another church service alone. I hated sitting alone. Suddenly, a guy I hadn't seen before sat next to me and introduced himself as Ricardo. He asked me if I was new, even though I grew up in this church and he was clearly a visitor himself. He had a deep voice and a loud laugh. He looked and acted like he was my age, but he was ten years older than I was. At the same time, he acted and walked like a seventy-year-old man. He was very peculiar, and I didn't have the energy to deal with him, but I was supposed to be a good disciple, so I was polite. I sat through the service and was on my best behavior. But I intended to leave as soon as church was finished.

When the altar call was over and Pastor Valk finished his prayer, I immediately got up to leave. But before I knew it, I was trapped in another conversation with the newcomer. I politely listened while my thoughts were set on leaving. Then Ricardo began telling me things about me he had no way of knowing. I started paying attention to what he was saying, hoping to catch something wrong, but everything he said was spot on.

How does he know this? I thought.

"And now you're thinking, 'How does he know this?'" the stranger finished.

My eyes lit up, and I burst out laughing. "That's exactly what I was thinking," I sputtered.

From that moment on, Ricardo became my best friend. I learned he was great at reading people, especially when they were different, like me. He'd had a difficult childhood himself and learned to see people differently than most people usually do. When he invited me to his house, he was tidy, but items were out of place. He had two closets but kept his clothes in grocery bags stacked on top of each other instead. His kitchen had pans in the upper cupboard, his studio had a bunch of stuffed animals, and he had a child's bedspread.

Something was very different about my new friend. He was neglected as a child and hadn't learned basic skills from his own parents. I helped him clean up his studio and taught him things most twenty-eight-year-olds should've already known. In turn, he helped me with my social anxiety and depression.

He loved show business—drama, singing, and anything where he was the center of attention—and was a natural performer. He convinced me to join the church's drama team and choir. I suffered from severe stage fright, which he helped me overcome.

Eventually, the choir hosted auditions for soloists, for which I decided to apply. I hoped this would help me overcome my anxiety, and I wanted to be in the spotlight for once. I wanted my peers to invite me to birthday parties, I wanted Pastor Valk's approval, and I wanted everyone to notice how different I was from my father and see that I was a good disciple. I wanted to fit in.

Nobody in the church had ever heard me sing, and the same handful of people usually applied to be soloists in the choir. When the choir leader received my application, his jaw dropped. "If you get the part, you will sing a solo on the Thursday evening of the International Bible Conference," he explained.

Fear gripped me. Our church held week-long conferences twice a year. We would rent a huge building where people from all over the world would come to listen to seventeen sermons by various preachers. And Thursday evening was always the busiest—that was when couples were launched out to plant new churches in other cities. Maybe the founder of our church, Pastor Wayman Mitchell, would come to the Netherlands to preach. If he did, he would hear me sing. Though I was more anxious than ever, I went through with it. I practiced the song over and over until I was satisfied my audition would go well.

The day of the auditions came, and I was called upstairs to an old storage room. The choir leader was there with two other people. They played the song, and as I sang my part, the choir leader was speechless.

"Where have you been hiding that voice?" He laughed. "You got the part."

I was thrilled! After several choir practice sessions, my peers finally seemed to notice me and cheered me on. Then, the conference started. That Thursday evening, I performed "The Power of Christ" in front of twelve-hundred people and overcame my social anxiety once and for all.

Ricardo had been so influential in my life that I could now do things many people told me I could never do. I became more involved in church. I wrote skits and performed them; I was an active member in choir and even started my own rock band called Vanguard where I rewrote lyrics to fit our Christian message. And I finally had friends at church.

The church became such an important part of my life that I was rarely home anymore. I was either at church, in school, at work, at Ricardo's, or at home asleep. My parents often complained I was rarely home anymore, which I couldn't understand. My mom had wanted this; she tried to get me to go to church when I didn't want to go. My dad complained the most; he rarely got to see me, which I was happy about because I was trying to avoid him anyway.

My dad was now in a wheelchair. Something was wrong with his legs. I didn't understand, and neither did the doctors. One of his heels had an open wound, and when he got out of the shower, you could see his Achilles tendon. The carpet in his room had spots from the secretions that seeped out of his wounds. He was like a modern-day Job.

Everything started when the doctors diagnosed him with hepatitis. He got medication for that, which led to another sickness as a side effect. At one point, he had more than ten different illnesses I couldn't even pronounce and had a medication list over three pages long. Doctors didn't know what to do but seemed to agree they needed to get rid of hepatitis in order to address everything else. Over a span of fourteen years, he received three treatments lasting a total of four years of an experimental drug. Doctors warned it could cause suicide or murder as a side effect. They prescribed it in combination with antidepressants and opiates.

On this new medication, my dad became very unpredictable. I learned to determine his mood by showing him memes. If he laughed, we were safe. When he didn't, I had to watch out. Once, the neighbors had a birthday party and, in their drunkenness, made too much noise. My dad was infuriated. Without warning, he got up from the dinner table and nearly climbed the neighbor's fence, waving his crutches in the air, threatening them.

The first time this happened, I didn't do much besides panicking and telling him to stop while I called the police. But I vowed to physically stop him if it happened again. Two years later, it happened again. And since I was the only one physically capable of stopping him, I felt compelled to wrestle him to the ground and restrain him until the police arrived. While the police spoke to my mom and dad, I sat on the couch, staring blankly in front of me. My mind had become static, and the memory of what had happened slowly became a blur. I knew something had happened, but I couldn't remember what it was. The image was gone; all that was left were words.

I was now more angry with my dad than ever. I hated him for what he did. I trusted he would never do this, but he broke my trust. *Pastor was right about my dad*, I thought.

One summer, everyone in my family (except one of my brothers-in-law) went to the United States to visit my grandfather. I hadn't been there in twelve years, and I had fond memories of our previous time there. I was particularly excited that my family was going together; this was one of the first times we were spending more than a day together since both of my sisters were already married. *This*, I thought, *would be the perfect opportunity to try to restore the strained relationship I had with my oldest sister.*

We had been staying with my grandpa for a couple of days before my sister arrived on a separate flight. The whole family went to pick her up from the Bentonville airport in Arkansas, including my grandpa and uncle Gene. But when I saw her, out of the blue, she told me she wasn't going to put up with how I treated her anymore. I had done nothing to provoke her at that point. And since I hadn't given her a reason to be mean and had actually hoped to restore our relationship, I wanted to give her a reason to say that. But I didn't—not at first. I gave up the couch for her and slept on a mattress on the floor. I was nice to her and tried my best to make polite conversation.

One time, during one of our conversations, we were walking down the street to the Dollar General store.

"Have you ever killed an animal?" I asked her.

"Why do you ask me this question?" she replied, looking at me wide-eyed and pale.

"Just making small talk," I responded. "Why, have you?"

I figured she must've gone hunting during one of her trips to South Africa and felt bad about shooting a gazelle or wildebeest or other animal.

"I don't want to talk about it," she responded, making it very clear this was the end of the conversation.

Later that week at my grandpa's house, my sister and I got into an argument. She started screaming in my face, and I pushed her to the ground before locking myself in a bedroom. My mom quickly followed me and asked me to let her in, hoping to diffuse the situation. But right after I let her in, my father came in and slapped me.

This was the third time he flipped out, and I couldn't take it anymore. "You're crazy," I screamed. "And now your family knows it too." Then he slapped me again. I became infuriated at him. I hated him. I got up, threw him on the bed, and pushed his hands onto the mattress. Uncle Gary got behind me and put me in a bear hug. I twisted my body free from his grip and stormed out the door.

"Let him go," my grandpa said. "He'll be back."

I ran as fast as I could. I knew where I was going, and I didn't plan to return. My mom also knew where I was going and tried to catch up to me. We were both out of breath and exhausted, and I let her catch me. She begged me to walk together in any other direction than the one I was going.

"I can't go back," I cried. "It won't get better."

I knew I would have to face everybody again to fly back to Europe, but I couldn't, not after what had happened. I dreaded the unavoidable confrontation and couldn't see any way our family could recover from this. A railway crossing was down the road from where my grandpa lived, and the trains always thundered over it at great speeds. I wanted to jump in front of an oncoming train and kill myself there.

Just as my mom was trying to calm me down, my sister showed up, rolling up her sleeves and provoking me to a fight. I started running again; this time I hoped I would make it. But I quickly got out of breath, and my mom caught up to me again, begging me to turn right into the park. Grandpa and Uncle Gary found us, made us get into the car, and drove us back to grandpa's house.

It took the rest of the day until late in the evening for our family to resolve our differences. I explained my side of the story while my sister explained her side. Though we didn't agree and this wasn't over, we put our differences aside for the remainder of our vacation.

Once we got home, everything went back to the way it was before. I was heavily involved with church activities and avoided my father. I'd attend sporadic counseling sessions with Pastor Valk about the strained relationship with my sister, and he'd advise me to apologize to her in all sorts of ways, even if I felt I wasn't in the wrong.

"God sees your efforts," he'd say. "He will reward you for humbling yourself."

I bought my sister flowers and wrote her letters where I told her things that would've made me cry if I said them aloud. And though it didn't seem like I was getting through to her, her anger toward was me decreasing.

One Sunday morning, I went to church with my parents when Pastor Klok was visiting from Amersfoort to translate for Pastor Greg Mitchell—the son of our church's founder. When my father saw Pastor Klok, he flipped out. This marked the fourth time it happened, and this time it was at church. I felt more humiliated than ever to be my father's son. He started screaming and yelling at Pastor Klok and Pastor Valk for being liars and thieves. After that, my father refused to ever step foot inside the church again.

Several months later, my mother left the church as well. I felt humiliated—my parents were some of the first people in the church, and I was a church kid, which made me proud. But now they'd left, and our family was falling apart. They started talking to former members and reading and watching information outside of The Door–approved sources. One time, they invited some people over whom I refused to greet because they were former members.

I made them miserable for leaving. I was taught there was no legitimate reason to leave the church because God placed you in that church specifically, and he had a plan and a destiny for your life there. If you left the church, you'd be outside of the will of God, and you'd be a rebel. I was used to my dad being a rebel, but my mom? A rebel? That was new.

I fought with my parents more than ever, avoiding both of them. Every moment spent away from home was a win. Once I moved in with one of my best friends for two months in order to avoid my parents. I wanted to move out. Once I moved out, I'd never have to see my parents again. I could be free.

Several months later, my oldest sister was having medical problems and was unable to drive because of the medications she was taking. But she saw a painting online she wanted and asked me to take her there. I was more than happy to do this. The mere fact that she asked me proved there was still a chance for us to resolve our differences.

But during our drive, she began to ask me questions about our trip to the States, something I hoped we could put behind us. "Remember when you asked me that question?"

"Which question?" I responded.

"The one if I'd ever killed an animal," she replied.

"Oh wow." I laughed. "I'd completely forgotten about that until now."

"That question has haunted me for the past three years," she confessed.

At her serious tone, my face paled and my fingers tingled. I had no idea that question was of any significance. But as she went on to explain, she believed the Holy Spirit was urging her to answer my three-year-old question. She couldn't hold off any longer.

She explained our pastor, Pastor Valk, had asked her to kill fish for a drama video he was filming. He planned to use the video at a youth rally. The video was supposed to be about a young man who is seduced by a woman and runs after her like an ox going to the slaughterhouse, as it says in Proverbs 7. "If I wanted to, he needed clips of someone who was going to slaughter a fish, a live fish. I thought that was weird. But he had also done a lot for me. He later said he lost the video because of a crashed computer."

The slaughter ritual had to be repeated at least four times. With each repetition, she became more suspicious. She started asking him questions. "Why do you want to kill fish every time?"

He confessed he found women with knives exciting. Certain objects or rituals, rolling up sleeves, and slaughtering animals, excited him. He asked if she wanted to pose with a knife every now and then and if he could take a picture of her.

Pastor Valk told her he sometimes fantasized about being slaughtered and eaten himself. He associated his first name, Evert, with *evertzwijn*, the Dutch translation for *boar*, and confessed he felt like he was a pig.

"He groped me," she said. "On another occasion, Pastor Valk tearfully talked about his sexual frustrations. He threatened to go to prostitutes and said I could dissuade him by sexually satisfying him."

I was dismayed. I couldn't believe what I was hearing. The man I had looked up to, who had told me my father was a bad person, who had given me advice about my sister, was a perverse sexual predator. "Can't you tell the church board?" I asked.

"They are all men," she responded, making it clear she didn't want to tell any man something so humiliating.

"But one of them is your uncle. Can you at least tell him?" I pleaded.

For the next three months—caving under the weight of my sister's secret—I rarely slept. The stress affected my behavior; I avoided my girlfriend and refused to tell her why other than "If somebody asks you to do something in church, say no." Not long after, she broke up with me. Every time I saw my sister, I carefully broached the subject and implored her to involve the church board in the situation. I couldn't go to church knowing my pastor was evil. Surely, the church board would remove him from ministry. To my surprise, my sister said she would think about it. And three months later, she went to the church council.

The following church service, Pastor Valk preached his Sunday-morning sermon as if nothing changed. After the service, I stood outside with a couple of friends and saw Evert in his office with the church board. The blinds were up, and I could see everything that was happening. But something felt wrong; it looked like a normal conversation. No emotion was involved. Was he being removed from ministry or not? The three men got up and left the office. Pastor exited the church building and caught me looking at him. That's when his emotions surfaced. I had never seen someone look so angry. He quickly got in his car and left.

That Sunday evening, Pastor de Sain preached. Next to me, the church tech guy was working on the live stream from his phone. When I asked him what he was doing, he told me he was going to manually turn off the livestream after the altar call. I immediately knew what would happen. After the altar call, Assistant Pastor Etienne de Sain went forward to announce Pastor Evert Valk had been removed from ministry due to moral failure. I looked at my roommate (who coincidentally was my sister's brother-in-law) who knew about the situation at this point, and he looked back with relief. After the announcement, I got up and walked toward the exit, but everyone remained seated. I looked around as people were crying. I went through hell these past three months. What were these people crying for?

Right after the announcement, my girlfriend told me she knew I had something to do with it, after which I told her everything that had transpired. After that, we started dating again. Several church services later, it was announced Pastor Nomdo Schuitema would replace Evert. (I later learned they were best friends.)

Six months passed, and my sister and her husband were advised not to go to church until the pastors said they could come back. Meanwhile, Evert Valk had returned to church as a member. At his first service back, he responded to the altar call to publicly give his life to Jesus. This had to do with appearances and being an example to the rest of the congregation, but it was special to see my pastor saying the sinner's prayer—that never happened otherwise. After the service, I walked up to him; his wife and he both looked scared and uncertain of my intentions, but I only shook his hand and welcomed him back to church. I wanted to show him I was a good disciple. I wanted him to know that still, I wasn't like my father. But after my interaction with him, I went outside and cried. I felt gross for touching that man.

Nothing changed after that. Pictures of Evert were still on display around the church. *A man that perverted must surely have had some sort of negative spiritual influence in the church,* I thought. The new pastor should revisit the doctrines. But that didn't happen. I became skeptical. I had assumed Evert was a rotten apple on a fruit-bearing tree, but now I wondered: Was the apple rotten or was the tree?

The worst pain I had ever gone through in my life was because of the church. In my opinion, I had saved the entire congregation from a monster. I had done something good for the church, unlike something anyone else at church ever had to do. I felt responsible for the church's well-being. I also felt like I had contributed to a good cause. And for this, I believed I could talk to my pastor man-to-man without fearing consequences for what I said.

I only spoke to the new pastor a couple of times. I occasionally voiced my concern about the contents of Evert's preaching in general, but our sessions were usually about what happened to my sister.

"It was a mutual relationship," Nomdo told me. "Your sister seduced Evert."

How could it be a mutual relationship if he had authority over her? But still, I almost believed him because he said it so firmly and was in a higher position than me. Later, I learned this is a manipulation technique called gaslighting, said to make me doubt myself and what I knew. I gradually lost faith in my pastor. Perhaps Evert Valk was not the only bad pastor of our fellowship. Maybe there were more.

Then Ricardo was the target of some allegations made by Pastor Schuitema toward him. (These turned out to be false.) This was the last straw for me.

"Why is The Door a bad church?" I asked my parents, sister, and brother-in-law—who had all left The Door at this point.

"Show me which Scriptures support your claims." I doubted they could present any biblical evidence at all and assumed they would take verses out of context to justify their rebellion. I was desperate for something to show I was right and they were wrong. They wrote thirty-three pages filled with Scriptures and explanations. They showed me how the pastors had taken verses out of context. Everything I believed fell apart.

Still, I wanted my family to be wrong so badly; I decided to ask my pastors for advice. I wanted to know what ultimate comeback I could give to silence them once and for all. But before I even got around to asking my four questions, Pastor de Sain asked, "Do you still believe in tithing and leadership?"

None of my four questions had anything to do with this, and I thought: *If this is what's most important to them, maybe I shouldn't believe in that anymore.*

The pastor quickly ended our session, leaving my questions unanswered.

I was a sporadic tither. I didn't tithe once a month; I usually paid my back tithe once every few months. After my session with Pastor de Sain, I felt uneasy and wondered if I should pay my back tithe that day. But I decided against it.

I planned another session with Pastor Nomdo Schuitema to ask for permission to propose to my girlfriend. I got his permission and proposed under the Eiffel Tower in Paris on May 25, 2019. We wanted to get married that summer, but Pastor Schuitema didn't reply to my messages when I asked him what date we could pick to get married.

Then, after a Sunday evening service, he called my fiancée and me to talk, first with my fiancée, then with me, and then with both of us together. He told us he wouldn't marry us because I wasn't stable. "If you marry him, you will fall into the pit."

"But what if we marry somewhere else?" my fiancée offered. "Would we still be allowed to come to church here?"

Pastor Schuitema began to laugh. My fiancée started crying, and he then turned to me angrily as if it were my fault. He then turned back, asking, "What do you take from my sermons? How do you view leadership?"

I didn't say a word. I kept quiet. *If I don't say anything, the conversation will be over sooner*, I thought. After his monologue, we rode away from the church on our bicycles.

"Did you hear how he talked about you?" my fiancée cried, "as if you were a piece of trash."

"Yeah," I responded. "I'm used to it by now."

We cycled a little further. Then she asked: "Joel, what are we supposed to do now?"

I had waited until we had cycled far enough away from the church to tell her. I had made up my mind. We would leave the church.

I counted on losing friends when we left the church and only invited four church friends to our wedding. I was certain they would remain my friends forever. Two of them still refused to attend our wedding, telling me I was outside the will of God and they didn't approve of my choices. I was a church kid; I was supposed to know better. I didn't reply to their messages or speak to them again until they both left the church three years later.

One week before the wedding, my fiancée received a phone call from her brother. He told her marrying me was a bad idea and he didn't approve of us getting married. Even her sister, who was supposed to be one of our wedding witnesses, told us she didn't approve—which made us decide to ask my fiancée's cousin instead. We got married on a beautiful mid-September day four months after leaving the church. My wife's brother and sister both withdrew their objections to our marriage, though they remain members of the church.

My best friend, Ricardo, left the church six months after us. He hadn't once objected to our leaving the church, and I've remained (and will remain) friends with him forever. He restored his friendships with the friends he knew before he became a member of the church, started working at Greijdanus (the school I used to go to), joined a Christian choir through his work, and became active in another church's youth ministry.

My sister and I restored our relationship. She fought through her experiences and learned to cope with trauma. She learned she had been manipulated by a narcissist who used emotions and power to get what he wanted from his victims (of which there were about thirty that we know of over the span of thirty years).

When she started therapy, she hadn't told anyone about her experiences aside from her husband and me. She was hesitant to tell anyone else because she was scared Evert would be removed from ministry. He said it would be her fault if revival stopped. Her therapist told her it wasn't going to stop; Evert had an addiction and would hurt others again and again. She didn't know how many victims he already had.

One girl later visited my sister's home to thank her for speaking up; she had been groomed by Evert for half a year already and told my sister about the long messages he would send her. My sister still struggles with the physical violations, narcissistic manipulations, smear campaign, and the demonic side of him that she experienced. She especially wrestles with the fact that such a demonic force could be hidden in plain sight and infect others. Yet she lives a beautiful life, and you wouldn't believe someone like her could have experienced something so horrific. I admire her strength and often wonder how she is able to flourish after what was done to her. I know it's because Jesus watches over her.

We still live in Zwolle, but in our small city, we regularly encounter members from our old church. This is difficult for me. These people ostracized and excommunicated me. The worst pain I've gone through is because of that church. I associate them with the church, and I associate the church with pain. This makes living in Zwolle, an otherwise peaceful city, feel anything but peaceful for me. It's especially difficult when I see the pastors. They always had these terrible sermon illustrations from former members who left the church and met with disastrous circumstances. I was taught that's what would happen when I left because it was God's will for my life to stay there. But my own experience is the opposite. I'm still a Christian, I have a healthy marriage, and I restored my relationship with my sister. I finally recognized I had a wrong image of my dad. He's a great dad. I'm proud of my father, and I'm proud to be his son.

I'm proud to be the son of a rebel.

CHAPTER 3
THE GOLDEN BOY
NATHAN

"For they bind heavy burdens and grievous to be borne, and lay them on men's shoulders; but they themselves will not move them with one of their fingers."
—Matthew 23:4

The welcome was warm, like seeing family that you have not seen for a long time, ushering you in with smiles and singing, praise, and worship. It was like a big show, and my eight-year-old mind was in complete and utter awe. What was this amazing place we had just walked into? It was exciting, new, and lively, and I felt like we instantly belonged. Before, I was brought up Catholic, and we attended a Catholic church, a Catholic service. Hymns were sung, and praise was given, but it was nothing compared to the joy you felt walking into the Potter's House Church. My parents first introduced me to the church; they had a few friends who attended the services who encouraged and convinced my parents to go and check them out. "Come and see what the church is all about. You will love it."

At the time, we had our routine at the Catholic church. Until one Sunday, after attending Catholic mass, we got in the car, and my dad drove us to the Potter's House Church. The one we attended was in East London and is known as the Mother Church, the head church in the UK. At the time, we did not know we had been invited to this one. After mass, my father, mother, younger brother, and I drove to the Potter's House church, and while my mother, brother, and I sat in the car, my father went to check it all out. He said he would only be a minute, but it felt like he was gone at least a good half hour. I wondered what was taking him so long.

He then came running out, excitedly shouting to us. "Come in, come in! You need to come and see this." At the time, I was so extremely excited. I was stepping into this new world that was fascinating and fun. The church didn't look like an ordinary church; it was just a big hall with a lit-up sign out front with the church's name on it. My first impression was a happy one. We walked in and were greeted by a row of ushers with huge smiles on their faces as they shook our hands and told us to make ourselves comfortable. There were smiles everywhere; everyone seemed so happy and welcoming.

"Welcome, welcome." That was all everyone kept saying, I felt like I belonged, so warm and happy. The room was alive with songs and praising, with people singing and smiling. It was magical. I turned to look at my father, and he had the biggest smile. That was my first memory of the Potter's House Church, and from then on, I knew nothing else. We were officially members.

All that I knew were my close family, mother, father, brother, and the church. That was my life. I didn't realize until I left the church that there was a reason it was such a close-knit society. Once you became a part of the church, you were encouraged to stay within the church and to cut off any outside influences, including any friends or extended family not associated with the church. That was the way it was. There were a lot of talks and preaching on "being set apart" and not mixing with "worldly people" and "sinners." They discouraged you from spending too much time with people that are not in the church: family, friends, colleagues, schoolmates, and others. No one was immune. Along with that, a lot of emphasis was placed on church attendance, and there was *always* something to keep you so occupied with church-related activities that you don't even have time for anyone outside of church.

I was brought up in that culture, so it was the norm for me. So I hardly knew my extended family (cousins, aunts, uncles). We were almost never at any family functions like birthdays or weddings. I never really got to play with other kids, and in secondary school, I was somewhat isolated too. We were not allowed to have a television either, which also made my teenage years hard and made me feel more isolated. As a result, the only place I felt like I fit in was in church. To say I was sad about it would be wrong. I wasn't because I didn't know any different. You can't miss what you don't know. Now, looking back, I am sad for that young boy and angry that he missed so much of his childhood and so many other memories.

Soon, that eight-year-old boy became a teenager, and as with any teenager growing up (in or out of church), my hormones were pumping. I began to be attracted to girls, one girl in particular. I had grown up with her; we were always part of the same youth activities. But at the ripe old age of sixteen, I realized I really liked her. We would shyly catch each other's eye, sneaking glances, smiling awkwardly, and look away. My heart pounded at the sight of her, and I often arrived at the sessions early because I was so excited to see her. We couldn't do anything else but simply like each other; anything other than that didn't even cross our minds, as we had a very strict upbringing in the church with a lot of preaching against sin. We were told that we would go to hell if we were a sinner—the teachings were pretty heavy.

"You will go to hell if you do anything wrong." We were taught this and believed it. Fornication or sex before marriage or any sexual activity or contact was forbidden; if you sinned, you would be disciplined, whether that meant being kicked out of the church or put on a disciplinary punishment. This drove a lot of fear into us that we couldn't sin; it was simply not an option. We were not even allowed to be alone with the opposite sex in case we fell into temptation; if we fell into temptation, it would cause us to sin.

Once, we were driving in the pouring rain, and a woman from church was walking, the rain soaking her to the bone. We drove straight past her. He told me that we were not allowed to pick her up because we couldn't be seen with a woman alone in our car. We couldn't even drop her off down the road and give her shelter from the rain as we would be breaking the rules. At the time, I thought it was harsh; this poor woman was soaked. What harm would it do to shelter her from the rain? But you did not question the teachings; you just followed them.

I once got in trouble for being alone in a room with a girl although it was completely innocent. I was much younger, and we were simply just chatting, completely oblivious to the fact that we were breaking rules all because we were alone. I didn't understand why we were not allowed to be alone with women; it just didn't make sense to my young mind. I finally understood the reasons when I got older.

So because of these rules, I couldn't spend a lot of time with the girl I liked. That was unless we wanted to make it official, and at the age of sixteen, we couldn't really do anything to make that happen as we were too young. We were not in a position to get married or have a serious relationship. We just knew that we liked each other and that was all it could be, so we had to keep our distance from each other until we were at an age where we could make it official and get married. People around us put a lot of pressure on us. "You know what you need to do if you like her. You need to marry her."

Young marriage was not just the norm; it was encouraged. You're encouraged to find a partner quickly, get married, and "do something for God," like become a pastor. If you did this, you were seen as an excellent example, a trophy couple. As I said, I felt a lot of pressure at this time to get married, and my future wife did as well. But with the pressure of marrying young comes a lot of other pressures. You can't just marry someone; you must first put other things in place. You need a decent job and a lovely home so that your wife will be looked after.

I had just finished school and started college, but I was very heavily involved in the church. I didn't get much fulfillment from college, so I left within six months. I wanted to get a job because, in my head, that was what I needed to do so that I could get married. My first job was in retail, and I was so proud of myself, my first job. Looking back now, it was a terrible job! I simply worked on the shop floor and in the restaurant section for a few hours. I barely made any money, definitely not enough to pay for my own house or to look after a wife. I soon realized that this job was not paying me enough, and I had to make a change. Luckily, my mom came across an ad in the newspaper for an apprenticeship. It meant working for four days and studying for one day, and I would get paid up to two-hundred pounds a week, which seemed like a lot of money to me at the time. I was over the moon. This was amazing! I was finally getting paid something close to a proper wage.

At only seventeen or eighteen years old, within the first month of working and getting paid, I made arrangements to move out of my parent's house. I moved in with two or three other guys from church. This was another set up and encouraged within the church. They called these ministry houses, which were basically houses where people from the church lived together, like a flat share, but with other godly people. This was seen as the right path to go down and the next right thing to do as a young man of the church.

My relationship with my future wife now began to blossom. I had my own place and a job, and in the eyes of the church, I was now a man. I was closer to the position of being able to marry, to look after my wife and potential family. We began to date, and at nineteen years old, I proposed to her. We were then married at twenty. At the time, I felt like a man. I was doing what men do, and I felt like I was on the right path. Looking back and talking about this with friends, I now realize that I was far too young to be married. I was still a child myself. I thought that I was a man because I was told that I was a man, I had a job, I had my own place. I was married; therefore, I was a man. I felt like I was climbing all the right rungs on the ladder to success within the church. I was praised by the church for the choices that I was making, and they saw me as a success.

I was following the path that had been laid out in front of me and was extremely happy about it. I was a golden child in their eyes of the church, the sheep following the shepherd; the church had trained me well. I was heavily involved in the church choir and music and soon was asked to run the concert scenes. I was known as a talented individual, a man with gifts. Music is the spearhead of the church; we wrote a lot of songs and gave a lot of performances. This razzmatazz helped entice people in, it's what we loved to do. I could reach out and connect with a lot of young people in and out of the church. I was liked and was considered extremely influential. They would say, "Look at this young man. He is a man of God. Look at what he is doing for God. If you do God's will, you can be like him."

I enjoyed being used as a positive example and felt like I was a positive influence within the church. A few of the guys and I were very influential among the youth; we were seen as people who got things done, the movers and shakers. We put on events and concerts and led many outreach projects to reach out to other people to try to get them into the church. I was also involved in creating a youth band that became quite popular and influential. I led many of the youth services that ran alongside the normal services. I was the worship leader for the youth and was extremely proud of that title.

We organized meetings with the Local Authority and Council to get out in the public and the community to show that we were making a difference. We thought that we were bettering the community by getting young people to come to the church because then there would be less gun and knife crime in the community.

I was getting to the age where my involvement and influence were moving from the youth groups to the main service groups, and I was now becoming part of the main service music team. I was quickly made the leader of these groups. The week I got back from my honeymoon, I was told, now that I was married, I could become a worship leader. This was a huge deal and an enormous privilege. I can't even begin to explain how amazing this made me feel. This was the mother church, a huge church with hundreds of people involved in it, so to become a worship leader was a *huge* opportunity.

Looking back, I was praised, lifted up, and put on a pedestal by the church leaders and members. I was glowing with pride and felt like a success. Alongside becoming the worship leader, I also became the choir director and a Bible study leader. The church has levels of privilege as to where people fit in:

- The fringe: These people were just visiting and on the fringe of the church. They were not really involved.
- Regular attenders: They attend all services and events and join the various groups and activities within the church.
- Leaders. These folks, like me, were highly encouraged and really had no choice but to attend every church service, every event, and every activity. We were the inspiration, the encouragement for other church members, and if we wanted to stay in leadership and continue to inspire people within the church, then we had to attend *everything*.

This sounds like a lot, and looking back, it was so much pressure to put on someone. But at the time, I felt like I was thriving. The church was my life, so I gave up my own life for the church. This included going to prayer sessions every single day, services four times on Sundays, midweek service on Wednesdays, Bible study on Fridays, and outreach on Saturdays. As a leader, you were expected to attend them all. Although they didn't say it in so many words, you didn't have a choice. If you failed to attend, you could be rebuked. You might be publicly told off, embarrassed, shouted at, or mocked. This was sometimes done supposedly in jest, but you and everyone else knew the intention behind it.

Once, a guy was performing a song during a baptism service, and his mic cut out (turns out the battery died). I was standing next to the sound desk and so was the pastor. He turned to scowl at the sound man. (I guess he thought the sound guy did something wrong.) But I said, "Oh, it's just the mic. It's cut out."

He shouted back, "Well, why has the mic cut out? Fix it!" I was scared and shocked as others were around. Plus, it wasn't my fault or within my capability to fix the problem. But this was part of the culture. When the pastor speaks, you listen; when he wants something done, you just make it happen.

Another time, we had a team meeting for the music ministries, and the pastor came in to take over the meeting. He started indirectly digging at me. He talked about how we should be "spiritual and not carnal" about these decisions. He was dissing certain songs that we did sing. It was all very personal as everyone in the room knew that I was solely responsible for choosing the songs. People even came up to me after the meeting to ask if I was okay.

Rebukes can go as far as turning into discipline so that you could be stripped of your position and made to sit down for a period of time. This could happen if you failed to adhere to the rules. I once confessed to the pastor that I had watched pornography when I was younger. I had to endure a grueling one-on-one conversation with him and divulge specific information about exactly what happened, when, where, and how many times, etc. By the end of it, I was told that I could not be in ministry for three months. Obviously, people noticed that I wasn't on stage singing or actively doing anything and asked why. I had to explain to them that I was under discipline.

For others, the discipline could be worse (e.g., kicked out of the church). Looking back on it, I can see now that this was all fear tactics to maintain control. I definitely felt fearful about making any wrong decisions lest I be publicly shamed or demoted. Image was everything, and there was a lot of pressure to have a perfect image. No one likes to be told off or publicly humiliated, so it worked to force you into being this perfect godly man. I tried my hardest to do that. I wanted to be a shining example. My goal was to be a man that everyone looked up to and inspired to be like.

I was part of the Purple Circle, which meant that I was very intricately connected to everyone who was high up within the church. I was involved in church leadership and was very close to the pastor. My wife and I were the first people to ever be invited to join him at his home for Christmas celebrations outside of his family. This made us feel incredibly special.

"Wow, we get to go to pastor Brown's house for Christmas!" We were stepping through the pearly gates. Nobody ever had this privilege, and look at us!

One of the pastor's friends said to us, "Well, you must have done something right because he really likes you if he is inviting you to his house for Christmas."

We felt elevated, special, well-integrated, and liked. We were on a high, and everything kept going right for us. I soon became a pastor myself. Similar to when I got married, I felt a lot of pressure to become a pastor. This was normal and the next step on the path within the church. I wanted to please the leaders, so I kept climbing the ladder and eventually became a pastor. Did I want this? At the time, I guess I did because I loved how integrated and how liked I was within the church. But I did feel a lot of pressure to be successful and to do the right thing or what the church taught was the right thing. The church always says that the way of the church is to go out and preach about the will of God. The goal was to become a pastor, and even many of the wives encouraged their husbands to do this.

"Don't you feel the call to preach?" My wife at the time said these things to me even before we got married. I guess I did feel that call at the time because I wanted to do what I loved within the church: all the music, choir, and events. I loved all of this. I loved being a leader, so surely if I felt called to do this, then I felt a call to become a pastor because that was the next step, right? I had a falling out with myself and my wife because she called me out on the fact that I had told her early on in our marriage that I felt the call to preach, so not only was I getting pressure from the church and from the pastor, but I was also getting pressure from my wife. Although I technically had a choice, did I really? If I wanted to continue being successful, liked, and influential within the church, then I had to take this next step whether or not I felt ready for it. That was just how it was done.

I got sent to the south of the UK to become the pastor of a small church there. The objective was to replicate everything that I was taught in the mother church, bring it to this new church, and teach it to the people in this congregation. We hosted a lot of events and outreach projects to entice people to join this new church. The aim was to build, grow, and draw people in. When I took over the church, only ten people attended. A lot of the Potter's House churches are smaller, which I wasn't used to at the time because I was from the largest branch. I was only used to the huge number of people that attended my home church; a small church and congregation was new to me. At this church, I created a relationship with two local universities, and the students who attended there began to come to church. They loved it!

When you become a pastor, your mother church will give you money to move and set up your life, and then you are expected to make it all work. In my case, that meant that I had to find a job to take care of my family; my wife, and my two children. I had to make this new church that I was now the pastor of grow, evolve, and become successful and influential. I was under a lot of pressure and a great deal of stress personally, and this put a huge strain on my marriage.

Back in our hometown of London, we felt comfortable, and we had friends and family there. We had both grown up there, and now, we had been shipped off to another part of the UK, miles away from home with no friends, family, or other support. I was working full-time while trying to build a successful church. Creating this church was not the hard part for me; I thoroughly thrived in this area. The church started out with only ten people, and I grew it to ninety-plus by the time I left. That wasn't what I found hard; what I found hard was navigating my marriage. My wife and I, just the two of us, were in a foreign city. I saw more of her than I have ever seen and spent a lot more time with her. In London, I was at church every night of the week, attending different events, services, and rehearsals and fulfilling my responsibilities as a leader. Now, as a pastor in this new city, I had none of that. There weren't as many events or services to take me out of the house and away from my family, so I was with my wife a lot more. We found that unfortunately, we got on each other's nerves.

Our marriage started to crumble. My wife had some mental health issues that we—and certainly I—didn't know about, which were probably exacerbated after we had our second child. In hindsight, she probably had post-natal depression, although, at the time, I didn't understand or know this. Post-natal depression can cause a person to go into a deep depression. But in the Potter's House, you do not talk about or discuss mental health issues, and they are never preached about. The topic of mental health was hush-hush. If you were suffering from any mental health problems, you either had a demon that needed to be cast out, or you were under spiritual attack. That was how the Potter's House church approached matters.

After the birth of our second child, my wife was on her own, away from her family. Due to the teachings of the church and the lack of correct information, I didn't understand what was going on with her. We argued a lot. She became very paranoid about the young girls who attended the church and thought they were laughing and talking about her. I tried to defuse the situation by telling her that she was wrong, but this only made the situation worse as she then believed that I was protecting everyone else but her.

We had so many arguments that just escalated; arguments began small and got bigger and bigger. At different times, we ended up reaching points where we were both stormed out. After one argument, she took the car and drove off. I had no idea where she was going until her mother phoned me saying that she was outside their house. She had driven two-and-a-half hours back to London to get away from me and to be around the people whom she needed at that time. It was a really tough time for both of us.

My wife called the pastor at the mother church in London and told him that she didn't like it where we were living and she didn't like the way I was treating her. I asked her what I could do to make things right and better. I just couldn't figure it out until one day, her mother called and said she thought her daughter had a mental health illness. I struggled to accept this as I didn't notice any signs to suggest this. I just saw that my wife, who had been fine and normal until now, was suddenly difficult and argumentative. But more was going on with her that I didn't know about.

One morning before I was about to go to work, she told me that she urgently had to go to the hospital but was reluctant to say why. When I asked her why, she eventually told me that she had swallowed a load of pills. Her health declined to the point where she attempted suicide. I was in a complete state of shock. She told me that she wanted to go to the hospital alone, so she drove herself there, and I called in to work to arrange emergency leave and stayed home with the children. We never talked about this incident because she was terrified that if we told the pastor back in London, they would pull us out of this new church. So we never spoke of it again.

My head started to become so messed up because of this. All I could think about was that I was supposed to be a pastor and supposed to help people, yet my wife was trying to commit suicide. It wasn't registering in my head. Things weren't right and just kept getting worse between us. Eventually, she called the pastor back in London and told him that she couldn't take it anymore. She wanted to come home, and I was to blame.

I got a call from the pastor, saying that we had to come back home to London. I didn't have a say in the matter. When I asked him why, he said that I needed to work on my marriage. So we were pulled out of the church, and I was no longer a pastor.

So now, I was back in London and, with that, came such a sense of shame. Not that long ago, I was the golden boy: successful, married, influential, an example, and a pastor. I did everything right and was constantly praised for it. I was put on a pedestal, and to be honest, I loved the view from the top. Everyone had been aspiring to be like me, but now, I was back in London instead of being out there doing the will of God. In my head, I was now a failure, and the church probably thought the same.

The Potter's House church kept the whole situation hush-hush; they didn't want people to know that my marriage was failing, so they pretended that everything was fine. They told people that we had come home for redirection when, in fact, we had come home because my wife wasn't happy, but I didn't know how to fix it. I asked the pastor for help, direction, and guidance, and he just told me to speak to my wife. But she did not want to speak to me; every time we spoke, it turned into an argument. I didn't know which way to turn or what to do. I was getting no help from the people who were supposed to guide me. It got to the point where I just shut down. I couldn't deal with the arguments anymore, so I chose to just ignore her. I ignored her calls and texts and just went to church. But how can you fix a problem if you just ignore it? You need to communicate to fix matters, but I didn't know what to do at the time. I didn't know how to handle it, so I just blocked it all out. This was how I coped.

When I got back to London, the pastor also told me that I wasn't allowed to be involved in any ministries any longer: not a Bible study leader, not the worship leader, not a choir member, not an usher, or any other position. So the church life that I was so used to had now been taken away from me. I was told that this was because I had to work on my marriage. I was so frustrated because I didn't know how to work on my marriage. I wasn't given any guidance and didn't know what to do. I felt brushed aside and left to deal with problems alone. I couldn't speak to the pastor because he just told me to speak to my wife. When I spoke to her, we just argued. I felt trapped and put in a corner. It felt like they stuck me in a little box to keep my problems out of sight.

My wife wasn't happy with the church because she felt the same way I did: We were just left on our own. We weren't given any counseling; we were told to go our own way, sort out our marriage, and then come back. But we didn't know how to do that. We felt alone, isolated, and abandoned by the church. We had no help, and in the end, my wife had enough, so she decided that she was going to leave the church. Our marriage had gotten to the point by now that we weren't even talking. She had stopped attending Sunday services and was slowly fizzling out even when she did attend. The pastor caught wind of this as well and called me into his office. I sat there with him and the assistant pastor, and he said, "It seems like your wife is leaving the church, and if she decides to leave, then you must leave as well."

I didn't understand this; it didn't make sense to me. First, I had been brought up in this church, independent of my wife. If she decided to leave, I thought I would still be able to attend. And second, we weren't the first pastoral couple to have marriage issues and be called back. I knew of several couples like us whose marriages failed. Some even got divorced, but in their situation, one partner had left the church while the other stayed. Why was it okay for them but not for me? This church was meant to be my refuge and where I felt at home; it felt like

I was clearly being set aside, marginalized. Those words echoed in my mind. "If she leaves, you leave."

This seemed to be his way of managing the deterioration of our marriage. He could probably see the writing on the wall, that our marriage would end, and he did not want such a high-profile case to blow up within his church. That would ruin the squeaky clean and wholesome image the church tried so hard to maintain. A failed marriage would tarnish that image. If our marriage fell apart outside the church, however, then they could label it what they wanted. "They lost their way." "They lost sight of God." "Their marriage fell apart because they left the church and God." But they couldn't do that if we were still a part of the church.

After that meeting, I eventually felt like I didn't want to be a part of the church either. I sat there and listened to him preach, this godly man, perfect in every way, preaching about a perfect life. But I felt like he had kicked me out and left me in the dirt with no care and no conscience. I used to attend every service, every event, and everything the church did, and now, I found myself starting to leave church earlier and earlier until I eventually stopped going altogether. I lost all faith in the pastor and in the church. Older people had rallied around me, persuading me to get married and telling me it was the right thing to do, guiding me in the good times and pushing me forward. Where were those people now? Now that my life was falling apart, where was my support? Where was my guidance?

To leave church was the hardest decision I have ever made; I had been so extremely involved in the church up to this point. The church was my life. Obviously, leaders and members did not speak well about you when you left the Potter's House. Leaving had such negative connotations due to the strict teachings in the church. People who had previously left were usually labeled as backsliders, sinners, and rebels and were often used in sermons as examples of what not to do. As such, I didn't want to leave, but I really didn't feel like I could stay. I felt like if I left, I could no longer be a Christian, that my relationship with God was over, and that I had no faith. Leaving the Potter's House Church meant leaving my faith; there was nothing else to it. At the time, I couldn't separate God and the church, so if I decided to leave the church, in my head, that meant that I had decided to leave God.

I no longer feel that way, but at the time, it almost killed me. All my friends were from the church; I didn't know anyone outside of church or have a life outside of church. So leaving meant I was leaving everything behind and starting life all over again. It is hard to fathom how difficult it was for me to make that decision. When you are a part of the Potter's House church, your whole life is about the church. You are congratulated and patted on the back if you refuse to associate with people outside the church, whether they are your family or not. Leaving meant that I had nothing and no one. In their eyes, the church should always be your highest priority; it came before anything, including family and work. That was what we were taught, and that was the culture. In fact, the founding pastor of the Potter's House didn't even attend his daughter's funeral because he chose to be at church instead. That was the way it was with the Potter's House; the church came first.

As you can imagine, this decision about leaving caused me extreme anxiety and stress. But eventually, I did leave, and now I realize that it was the best decision I have ever made. Now that I have left, I feel a great sense of freedom. I am now living outside the little bubble that the Potter's House Church created and liked to keep you in. Being out of this bubble has made me realize things I couldn't see before, and I now view everything from a completely different perspective. Now I see things for what they are. I've had to unlearn some things and learn new things all over again. Until I told people about my experience, I didn't realize that what I experienced was not right. I've been told countless times that although it presented like one, what I was involved in was not a church but was definitely something else. I am happy now that I left, but it has taken me a long time to get to this place. So many people warned us and said we should leave the Potter's House. But I brushed their concerns aside; I told them that of course, we had free will. But did we?

I had a lifetime of experiences in the Potter's House church—growing up there; being the golden boy, leader, and influencer; being successful and even worshipped; being pulled down from that ladder, shoved aside, and pushed out the door. It broke my heart and made me lose faith. Now that I am out and on the other side, I see that it was the best thing that ever happened to me.

I am now what the Potter's House would call a sinner. I am happily divorced and have an amazing relationship with my children. I have fallen in love again and am now in a same-sex relationship, happier than I have ever been. Love is not a sin, even if they made us believe this kind of love was. In fact, when I was a pastor for the Potter's House Church, a lesbian couple attended a service. When I mentioned this to the pastor in London, I was told to preach on particular stories and Scriptures that would stop them from ever coming back again. They did not want people who are different to attend their church. They didn't fit their wholesome image. I know how this church and the pastor operate. It was their intention to isolate me. The way that they pushed me out of the church was very well orchestrated. If you didn't fit the squeaky-clean image they portrayed, they did not want you in their church. They didn't want someone in their church who had a failed marriage and who fell from the top of the ladder. I didn't fit the perfect image anymore, so they fixed the problem by making me leave.

You must ask yourself, What kind of church is that?

CHAPTER 4
A WEB OF LIES
NICK

"Stand fast therefore in the liberty wherewith Christ hath made us free, and be not entangled again with the yoke of bondage."
—Galatians 5:1

In 1995, I was lying in bed, an axe gripped tightly to my chest. My hands were shaking uncontrollably as I scrunched closed my eyes. My heart was beating so fast I thought it would explode out of my rib cage as I struggled to even my breathing. No matter how much I tried to calm my anxiousness, it would not leave. I told myself over and over that I was safe. No one was coming for me; no one was here. I was alone, and I was okay.

I didn't believe those words because they weren't true. I was in a lot of danger. If they came through my door again, they would kill me. The axe was my feeble attempt to protect myself if I needed to, but let's face it, if a gang of men tore through my house with the sole purpose of making me pay, this axe would barely do a thing. Due to this deep-seated fear, I did something I had never done before. I closed my eyes and I prayed: to God, to Jesus, to anyone who would hear me. I needed help. I just spoke the word *God*, and my whole room suddenly filled with the brightest white light. A hand came down and rested on my chest with a touch like a mother caring for her baby. All I could hear was, "It is going to be okay. Everything will be fine."

It was so strange. The words were not spoken aloud, but it was like they filled my mind. Even so, I knew that they weren't my words; my mind hadn't spoken them. I instantly felt such comfort and peace envelop my entire being. I closed my eyes, and the bright light still blinded me with its beauty. No matter what I did—cover my head with blankets and close my eyes—I could still see this amazing bright light. The minute I prayed, it was like my life changed in an instant. From that moment, I constantly heard the voice of God. He told me not to worry, that nothing would happen to me, that he was there for me and would protect me.

I started to read the Bible. I quit drinking, I quit smoking, and I had a powerful motivation to be a better man.

I wasn't raised as a Christian but was raised in an atheist household. I was anti-Christian in many ways; if I met a Christian, I would mock them. I thought Christianity was stupid, but I was interested in spirituality. I was looking for answers, for a purpose, for something; I just didn't know what. I read a lot of books on Scientology and spiritual matters to try to find some meaning in life.

I had a lot of bad people after me. I knew deep down that I didn't want to continue living life the way I was living it, but I didn't know any other way to live. I didn't know how to step away from this path. My life was filled with sin, evil, and crime. I lived every day, working to party and take drugs and fight. I was a rough guy. My friends were rough, and my life was heading on a downward slope straight toward a prison cell. I couldn't care less about it. Our group of guys loved heavy metal and going into the city looking for fights; we wanted to party, we wanted to smash things up, and we didn't have hope for our future. We were depressed. We didn't have a purpose in life, so we filled it with partying and crime.

One day, we went to the house of a drug dealer, pretending to buy drugs. He lived in a small caravan parked in a field, and when he least expected it, we bashed him and stole all his drugs. This man had a broken leg; I did not for one second think that he was going to chase us. This was an easy run, a laugh; we would steal the drugs and easily get away with it because he couldn't chase us with a broken leg. He would never catch us; he would never know who we were. Yet as we walked away, drugs in hand, chuckling at the ultimate robbery we had just pulled off, I turned around. He ripped the cast off his leg as he began to hurtle toward us. He caught me and bashed me. He was followed by ten of his friends who also came out of this caravan and bashed me.

Indescribable fear gripped me as I saw these ten beefy, rough men race toward me. I thought I was going to die, that surely, they would beat me to death. I don't know how, but I managed to escape. They could have killed me, and they would have without a second thought. But I found an opening, and I ran.

Even so, one of the guys knew who I was. That was the beginning of the end, the start of what led me to leave all this behind for fear of my life.

They came for me, thirty of them at once. They came to my house and smashed my windows, threw bricks, and came inside, destroying everything I owned. They had poles and baseball bats and just walked through my whole house, bashing and smashing anything and everything in sight. I could do nothing but stand there, frozen, terrified. I thought they would kill me. My friends managed to climb out the back window and run off, but I couldn't, so instead, I was left there by myself with these guys. I rang the police; it was the only thing I could think of doing, and they managed to get there before a baseball bat ended up wrapped around my head. But after that, I feared for my life. These guys would kill me at some point.

I used to deal drugs, and my dealer came around to see me and said that I needed to leave town. He said he had been hanging out with the guys who had come to my house, and he heard them all talking about me. They got so angry that they took a baseball bat and started to bash a table until it was nothing but a pile of broken wood. He bluntly told me, "They are going to come around to your house tonight and kill you."

He wasn't the only person who was relaying these types of messages to me. I started sleeping with an axe, just waiting for these guys to come around. I was miserable, exhausted, and scared for my life. I did the only thing left that I knew how to do: close my eyes and pray. My experience awakened me, and from then on, God was speaking to me.

The truth is, I was new to all this, and I did not feel safe. I was freaked out. I walked down the road at night on edge, terrified that any car driving past had someone in it who was going to kill me. If I was alone and heard a car, I jumped into a bush. God's voice would tell me that I would be all right, that I didn't need to worry. I began to reply to him, it was like we were chatting with each other as I began to form a relationship and trust with God. This lasted for around six weeks. I was trying to read the Bible, although I struggled with where to start. I wasn't attending church. I was now a Christian, I believed in God, he had my full trust, I just didn't have the guidance to know how to serve him properly. I didn't know where to go from here. Then, my sister reached out to me and introduced me to the Potter's House Church.

My sister had recently started attending a Potter's House Church two-thousand kilometers away near Byron Bay. She encouraged me to move there and join the church. I wanted to escape this life that I was leading, become a better man, and leave the drugs, gangs, and violence behind, so I moved. I packed up all my belongings and journeyed from Melbourne to begin my new life and join the Potter's House Church.

The people in this church came from very similar backgrounds to mine; they had changed their lives from one filled with alcohol and drugs to one where they didn't even touch a drink or a cigarette. They had a new and fresh start, which was extremely attractive to me. If those people could change their lives, then I could too. I was already fully committed to Christianity before I even moved from Melbourne; the Potter's House just made me feel like I had direction. They gave me something to pour all my energy into, an outlet for all the good I wanted to do. They helped guide me. One minute I was hanging around drug dealers, druggies, and alcoholics, and the next, I was hanging around these same kinds of people who were now clean. They had changed their lives around. I thought, *Wow, this guy used to be a heroin addict, and now he is clean. He has a beautiful family and a good job and is doing well.* It spoke to me and was massively inspirational.

The first time I attended the Potter's House Church, a pastor from New Zealand was preaching; he was telling a story about a boat sinking in South Africa. He described how on this boat, unlike the famous story of the Titanic where all the women and children were evacuated first, this boat was like a parallel universe. The captain said, "Every man for himself," and all the men jumped on the lifeboats first, leaving the women and children behind, causing them to perish. He used this as an example of today's men, saying how men are not really men anymore; they are selfish and only look out for themselves. This challenged me. I thought he was right; on many levels, I was that kind of man: selfish and only focused on myself. The pastor encouraged the congregation to lift their hands for an altar call, and this story encouraged me to do that. So I lifted my hand and went up to the altar. Someone prayed with me, and that, to them, was meeting God. They said, "You have now met with God."

It wasn't a matter of, "Now you have joined the church;" it was, "You have met with God now." My testimony became that this first visit to the Potter's House was the day I became a Christian. That was what I would say. I actually became a Christian when I had my experience with God in my bedroom, yet I began to tell everyone that I came to the Potter's House, and then I became a Christian. I am unsure why I did this, but I do know that the day I joined the Potter's House was the day I finally felt safe. I had joined a church, so subconsciously, I felt safe because on my own, I could have ended up anywhere. I was okay now because I was in the Potter's House boat; I was part of something, part of the Potter's House family.

When I joined the Potter's House Church, I jumped in with both feet. I wove myself deeply within the fabric of the church. I went street preaching, outside nightclubs, everywhere. I wasn't afraid of confrontation, I wanted to spread the Word, and I believed that I could help people change their lives. They could start fresh just like I did, and the church would help them do that. I went on mission trips, I did everything the church expected, and I truly believed that I was living the right Christian life. My influence brought a lot of people to the church. We were like a big family, all of us together; at one point, around a hundred people were a part of this church. I became very close friends with many people in the congregation. Some became pastors, and we always supported them; I would have given some of them the shirt off my back.

During my time there, I set up a website called The Potter's Club, that focused on doctrine and what the Potter's House believed. We focused on fundamental Baptist teachings with a Pentecostal flare. I had a lot of books and information against the Toronto blessing and other similar occurrences. I argued that the Potter's House never got into the drama of falling in the Spirit, laughing, screaming, or shaking—that is why it was good. These other churches do this (and were overly emotional), so we were the correct ones.

In hindsight, just because our services weren't full of these kinds of practices, didn't make us right. I was passionate about this and was online constantly, getting questioned by former members who claimed that I didn't understand, that things weren't right, and I was fighting against them, proving them wrong. Unfortunately, some were wrong, and some did lie about the Potter's House, and I called them out. But when I look back at this time, I might have listened if someone were to have approached this differently or told me in a different way. I may have come to the realization a lot sooner. I was 100 percent–pro Potter's House. I was the main voice against all the former Potter's House members. They claimed that the church was a cult, and I threw all the facts and figures at them. I asked, "Well, what makes a cult a cult?" As far as I could see, we were just following the Bible.

I was a part of the church for thirteen years; a lot of my friends became pastors. I lived for the church; I believed in Christianity, in God, and the power of faith. I listened to the pastors preach and soaked it all in as if the words came from an almighty guru. It wasn't until I stepped away from the church that I realized how toxic it was. I didn't question any of it when I was in the midst of it. On reflection, I subconsciously noticed a few areas that made me uncomfortable, points that I didn't always agree with. Still, my faith and belief in the church far outweighed these little hiccups that I was witnessing until these little hiccups became too much for me to cope with.

My eyes were opened when our leadership eventually installed a bad pastor who was constantly lying. We often caught him in a lie, and when the issue was raised to those above him, he didn't face any consequences. They wouldn't resolve the issue; they made me believe that I was, in fact, the issue. No matter who we contacted up the chain, no one dealt with this guy; they didn't do anything about it. So I lost trust in the church and decided it was time to leave, but just until they sorted out the leadership. Once that was resolved, I had every intention of returning.

I had a friend who was to become a pastor; he was told he would go to Papua New Guinea to start a new church there; he was extremely excited about this new challenge and adventure. So he gave the church, this pastor, eighty-thousand dollars to start his new church. He believed this was going to happen and began preparing himself for this new life. Then, out of the blue, the pastor pulled the plug on it. With no explanation, he said, "Sorry, this is not going to happen anymore." The money? Well, he seemed to just keep all that to himself.

My friend was a very successful businessman and the sudden loss of a lot of money made him question, "Well, where is this money going? How come he has just reallocated it somewhere else?" We began to question this guy; what was going on didn't sit right with us and made us query a lot of his actions, making us wary of his intentions. He seemed to come into the church like a whirlwind but didn't seem to have a heart for the people. He told racist Aboriginal jokes, so twenty Aboriginal people left the church. I confronted him about this, and he lied to me, telling me that he didn't say this. At first, I gave him the benefit of the doubt; maybe there was a miscommunication, or maybe those people left for no valid reason.

A year and a half later, I was talking to a former member of the church about the situation. They confirmed that they were present when this happened and that he did tell racist jokes. This got my head in a spin, and so I contacted everyone who was there that night (about six or seven people), and they all had the same story. So once again, I confronted the pastor and gave him the evidence. I said, "You told me that this didn't happen."

He immediately replied, "You have to forgive me."

"I don't have to do anything. I am not the problem," I replied. "You must repent. You lied to me. Why did you lie? Why did you tell these jokes?" People had left as a result of those jokes, and I had been defending him blindly. I thought he had a kind, genuine heart. I was embarrassed and annoyed that all along, he had been lying and he did tell these horrible offensive jokes. He did not have a good heart, and I began to question everything, including where the money went. Everything that had happened came back up, and I had to rethink it all with this newfound knowledge that this pastor was a liar. What else was he capable of? I began to go around the church, asking the congregation if they had a bad experience with this man, and they all said, "Yes, he has lied about me."

The more we investigated, the more we realized that this man had to go. He was no good for the church. With him at the pulpit, our church went from a hundred people to thirty-five; people were getting offended and leaving. I decided I needed to do something drastic: phone the Australian leadership. It's funny. The minute I thought this, it was like a sign came to me. During morning prayer, I happened to look up and on the back wall was a sign: If you have a problem with leadership, phone this number.

This was amazing! I thought, *This is exactly what I need. I will phone the Australian leadership, and this will work. Everything will be sorted. We will get a new honest pastor. Things will go back to the way they were, and we will continue to do God's work.*

It didn't work.

As I was walking down the stairs to phone the number, another member of the church stopped me. "Did you hear? The Australian leadership of the Potter's House quit this morning." My jaw dropped. I was just about to phone him, and he had quit. The whole church was in a huge upheaval; many leaders and churches had up and left the Potter's House. The problems in our little church now became insignificant. Compared to the big split that was happening across Australia, our problem was nothing. Still, I knew I couldn't just give up; this pastor was bad and needed to go. I was going to sort this problem out, so we flew the pastor over from our mother church and got him to sit down with all the leaders in our church. We all told him that the pastor was the problem, and we needed to fix it. Immediately, without a second thought, he called us all rebels—every single one of us who spoke out. We were angry; we knew that we were seeing matters clearly; how could we be rebels? We then spoke to the pastor in another church; this pastor told us that he would sort the issue out and get us a new pastor. Yet, when the conference came around, he didn't bring up the issue or speak to Wayman Mitchell. When I confronted him and asked him when he was going to sort the issue out, he told us he wasn't. He let us down too, and more and more people were leaving the church.

The last straw came when I confronted our pastor at church. I wanted answers and asked him why he had been lying. He told me that I have demons.

"You are the one lying, you are the one stealing, yet I have a demon?" I said calmly to him. This situation was just getting ridiculous. I wasn't even angry anymore; I just found it laughable. "You are a hireling. You are off the wall, and you need to repent."

He stormed off upstairs. A few minutes later, during service, he asked me to do morning prayer. I could only laugh at the absurdity. *If you think I have demons, then why are you asking me to do morning prayer?* That evening, I went home just feeling that the whole situation was getting even crazier.

At the next service, the pastor started bad-mouthing the people who were leaving, the pastors and the congregation who were pulling out of the church. It was like something switched in me. I had enough. I stood up mid-service and said to everyone, "This man is a liar and a hireling. He is lying about me and about everyone. If anyone wants to know the truth, then contact me, but I am leaving. I will not come back until this man is gone." I turned and walked out.

I contacted Wayman Mitchell and told him everything that had gone on, and he replied that they have over two-thousand churches, and he can't get involved with every fallout. I was to keep praying to God and keep doing right by God, but there was nothing he could do. I decided it was best if I just stayed away.

I didn't leave the church because I thought it was bad. I didn't leave because I thought it was toxic. I didn't leave with the intention of never returning. I left because I wasn't happy with the situation at the time. I left, intending to return once things improved. I didn't know that leaving would open my eyes to the truth.

When I left, I started to question their idea of authority. They were teaching the notion that pastors were like Old Testament kings, like King David. If King David clicked his fingers and said, "I want some water from that well," the soldiers just ran down, broke through the enemy camp, retrieved the water, and brought it back to him. Pastors saw themselves as these kings; they thought that they could command their disciples, asking them to do whatever they liked. It's an old covenant idea of kingship that they were bringing back to apply to their own lives. They ruled and control what job you got, who you married, where you lived, and how you raised your children. You did what he said because you believed he was higher than you and superior to you. He was your king, the great pastor. Some pastors had their whole church running around after them, doing everything that was asked of them and more, fulfilling every beck and call.

Wayman Mitchell was seen as some sort of anointed class, like a guru in the eyes of the people of the church. Herein lies the problem. The Bible teaches us that we are all the same; we are all equal. No one is above us or below us. We all have Jesus in us. The Potter's House has a pyramid structure of hierarchy. Wayman Mitchell sits at the top, followed by his chosen board of elders, national leaders, and area leaders. Then the structure works its way down: Bible study leaders and people in charge of the offering to just members of the church. I was told it was like the anointing that goes down Aaron's beard and flows down his clothes. In the same way, this anointing goes from Wayman Mitchell and flows down The Fellowship. The problem is, Jesus didn't teach this. Jesus is supposed to be the head of the church, is he not? The Bible declares that the idea of hierarchy is a worldly concept. It should not be like that in the kingdom and should, in fact, be in reverse, with he who serves being the greatest of all. But this is not how the Potter's House Church serves.

One of the key doctrines that I picked up in the Potter's House is tithing, giving your money for your salvation. This keeps people in the Potter's House and aligns their hearts with the church. They often bring up Malachi 3:10 in their sermons, claiming that if you don't give to God, then you are robbing him. But the Bible says this is pure legalism. They advertise that becoming a Christian is all free, a free gift of eternal life. But once you come through the Potter's House doors, they say it is free for a fee. Once you are in the church, you must start paying. It is like you are paying off your salvation.

I began to give 10 percent of my income, which I was happy to do because that is what is expected and that is what everyone does. If I didn't, then I would be taking from God and wouldn't be serving him in the right way. It was okay to begin with, but after a few years, I began to realize that I was giving a lot of money. But I had to support the church, right? They still had to pay for the building, the lighting and heating, and all the others bills. I needed to support this because I was a member. They teach that if you don't give to the church, you are robbing them. Wayman Mitchell teaches that if you don't give to the church, you will go to hell. So giving to the church is not something you do because it is right. You do it because you fear the wrath of hell; you fear that you aren't being a good Christian.

This means that the Potter's House Church is purely work-based salvation. If you come to Jesus, then all your sins are forgiven and all your debts are paid. The Potter's House says that yes, this is true, as long as you keep up your tithing. Keep your salvation by making the monthly payments. This clever method ends up affecting who you become. You are paying your hard-earned money into the church to support missionaries and pay for salvation, so your heart becomes knitted to the church because you have invested into it. This was how I felt, and I began to defend the Potter's House. My money was in that church, and I wanted it to continue and thrive and be a success. I was invested, hooked, and anchored into the church because my heart and money were there.

A lot of things about the church didn't sit right with me. Once I started to notice these things, more and more things became apparent. For example, the Potter's House doesn't like it if people come to them who are already Christians. They want you to answer an altar call because then you and the church are intimately connected because you met God there. They like you to meet God and the Potter's House at the same time.

I didn't do this. I met God outside of the Potter's House while I lay in bed, terrified for my life. After my encounter with God, I joined the church. This could be considered dangerous. I had a friend who did street preaching. He often found someone on the street, preached about God and the church, and prayed over them. Our pastor called him in and rebuked him for doing this. He was told that he needs to bring them to church and pray for them there because then they are connected to church.

When you joined a Potter's House Church, they believed that you should stay at that church. Once you are saved at a church, you can't leave unless the people above you say you can. Whether they allow you to marry a person from another church or send you to preach somewhere else, you must get permission every step of the way. You cannot just decide to leave or attend another church even if it is another Potter's House Church. If you do, you are considered a rebel.

This is not in the Bible, so why do they make it a church doctrine? Yet Wayman Mitchell left the Foursquare Church. He saw that there were flaws there, so he packed up, left, and set up his own church. Why was he allowed to do this, but we aren't? If I saw flaws in my church, why can't I leave and set up my own church without being called a rebel and an outcast? It is like they believe they are the only church in the world.

The Potter's House Church amalgamated themselves with God; when you become involved with the church, you become involved with God. If you leave the church, then you are leaving God. They preach that when you give money to the church, you give your money to God. But you aren't—you are giving your money to the church. It is preached so often that the members truly feel in their souls that they cannot leave, because if they do, they are giving up on God. I felt this too. I was terrified when I left that I would be seen as leaving God even though I knew I wasn't. Leaving the Potter's House is like leaving the Mafia. You are leaving all your friends and family and letting everyone down. You could leave the church and go on to have a very successful ministry away from the Potter's House, but it would never be acknowledged. They would never talk about how well you were doing, whether you were ministering in Africa or doing street preaching in the Philippines. They would tell everyone that you were a rebel, no matter how much good you had done and no matter how much you lived for Jesus. All the good would be tainted and even nothing because you had committed mutiny. You are seen as part of the enemy. It is considered rebellion in their eyes because you are either with them or against them. When I took a step back, I could see them more clearly and it worried me. Was this how a church was supposed to act and treat its congregation? It didn't seem right.

All the people who inspired me years ago, all those drug addicts who turned their lives around, all those alcoholics and heroin addicts who were clean, 95 percent of them are not Christians anymore. They've gone back to whatever lifestyle they chose to live because this perfect world that the Potter's House made you believe you can live in is not sustainable. If you fall from grace, they don't want to know you. They won't support you because you no longer fit their squeaky-clean inspirational image, and they don't want that, so they brand you a rebel, a person with demons, and cast you out.

I do believe that all the supernatural experiences that happened not only to me all those years ago (when God came as a bright light to me in my bedroom), but also to all those people who were a part of the church were real. You cannot fake the things that have happened to people. I truly believe they were real, and I witnessed a lot of supernatural healings within the church that I cannot explain. The Potter's House never took part in any overdramatic, televangelist, wild healings. They boasted that they did not do any of these fake healings and that their miracles came from God himself. The fact they didn't dramatize healing like these other churches made them more superior, more real. Although I do not believe in a lot of the things that the Potter's House did and believed, I do believe that I witnessed real miracle healings while part of the Potter's House.

When I left the church, I didn't leave God. I still hung around with Christians, I still preached on the street and lived a Christian lifestyle. I've travelled to many different countries and worked in Bible translation. I go to hospitals and pray over people. Upon reflection, I do much more now than I ever did when I was in the Potter's House. There, I was very limited in what I was allowed to do. They restrict a lot of what you do; for instance, you are only allowed to go away for two weeks at a time.

When I left, I decided to write a list: the good, the bad, and the ugly. I wanted to get things straight in my head to decide what to do moving forward. Under the good, I wrote that they evangelize and pray for the sick. I agreed with this. Under the bad, I wrote tithing and the authoritative leadership. I looked at how I was treated compared to my friends. I was single the whole time I was in the Potter's House and although I was restricted in many ways, I was nowhere near as restricted as some of my married friends. The church had a hold and a say in everything they did, from who they married to how they raised their children and where they went to school and lived. They even gave them marriage counseling. I did not have these same restrictions.

I also did a lot of things that would have probably been frowned upon, but because of my nature and personality, I was never really questioned about those. When I set up the Potter's Club online, a lot of people did not like it. I did not have permission to do this, and it broke many of their rules, yet no one stopped me. When I look back, I am sick at how much money I gave to this church. I was encouraged to give; I was told that the more money I gave, the more blessed I would be. When I stopped tithing, it was the most liberating moment. I am no longer paying for my salvation.

When I left, I suddenly felt free. I didn't realize how restricted I was until then. The lid had come off. I didn't have to wear a suit all the time to pray, I could go off and set up my own ministry if I wanted, and I could preach in other countries without having to have it approved first. I wanted to successfully leave the Potter's House, I wanted to keep my faith, and I wanted to still be a good Christian. I have seen many people leave and revert to their previous lifestyle, a life filled with alcohol and drugs, and I did not want to do the same. I was determined to carry on as a good Christian. Leaving liberated me. It didn't hit me straight away, but the longer I was gone, the more liberated and the freer I felt. I didn't realize I was so trapped in my faith when I was a part of the Potter's House.

I sometimes pass people who still attend the Potter's House, and they don't even acknowledge my existence. I have known these people for many years, yet they walk past me like I don't exist. I am saddened by this, but I know that their heads are getting filled with tales of how demons are within me; they cannot bear the idea that someone might be a good and successful Christian outside their church, so they talk badly about them. I know they have tarnished my name. I am not angry about this; in fact, I feel bad for the people who are still deep in the clutches of the church. I hope they eventually see the truth and are set free.

It took leaving the church to see how toxic they really were, and it was the best thing I could have done. It was like a weight was lifted. I feel free and liberated, and I have spread more good outside the church than I ever did when I was a part of it. I know this is not the same for everyone who has left the Potter's House. I am angry that I was so blinded. I cannot deny that they helped give me a purpose and that a lot of good is within the church; it is unfortunate, however, that the bad and the toxic far outweigh the good.

CHAPTER 5
ANSWERING GOD'S CALL
LINTON

"These six things doth the Lord hate: yea, seven are an abomination unto him: A proud look, a lying tongue, and hands that shed innocent blood, An heart that deviseth wicked imaginations, feet that be swift in running to mischief, A false witness that speaketh lies, and he that soweth discord among brethren."
—Proverbs 6:16-19

I helped her rip up the only picture I had of my father and watched as the tiny pieces of photo paper flew through the air and scattered on the ground in front of me. She cursed his name. The importance of what I helped my mother do was lost on my young mind. I never knew him, had never even met him. That picture was the only thing I had of him, and now it had been destroyed. All I knew about him was that he was an abusive man; he locked my mother in the house when she was pregnant with me until, one day, she escaped through an open window.

"You were an accident!" she often said, as if disgusted by my presence. I guess I was the result of an abusive relationship. She fell pregnant to a man she did not love, but I felt rejected, unloved, and like I didn't belong. I was born and raised in a single-parent home in Newtown, a rough neighborhood in Birmingham, United Kingdom. I was raised in a broken home with no male influence other than the string of men my mother brought home after a night out who had little interest in their lover's child. I longed for a father figure, but none of my mother's boyfriends ever stayed long enough to make an impression. Even if they did, they were never around. My mother left me in my grandmother's care for days while she stayed with her boyfriends. Her parental priorities were misaligned.

My mother was the fourth oldest of her nine siblings. My grandmother had her first two children in Jamaica at a very young age. She came to England in 1960, where she gave birth to the rest of her children. My grandmother struggled to raise all ten of her children, so they all grew up in different households, which caused a lot of friction, rivalry, and upset feelings between the siblings. Some of her siblings lived with family members, some were moved to children's homes, and some went into foster care. My mother was the only sibling who lived with her mother.

The friction in the family resulted in both verbal and physical fights. My mother had a temper; I experienced this many times as a child myself. She was extremely protective of my grandmother, so she would constantly fall out with her siblings over matters I was too young to understand. She would curse, bang on the walls, and throw things, and then we wouldn't see or hear from my aunties and uncles for a while. I hated this. I was so desperate for a proper family unit, yet their fallouts made this impossible. My mother wouldn't let her siblings get close enough to form a bond with their own mother. A lot of them, including my mother, struggled with mental illness. She was very emotional when I was a child; I watched her cry. Seeing her cry and hurt traumatized me. Now, as an adult, I find it hard to show emotions; I resent wanting to show any feelings, so I keep them to myself.

When I was growing up, social services got involved, and I almost went into foster care. My younger sister did go to foster care. My mother gave her up, saying she could no longer cope emotionally and mentally with her. My mother treated me more favorably. I never understood why. Shouldn't her love for us be equal? It was clear that it was not. My sister was a lot younger than me, so it was my duty to be a father figure to her. Neither of our fathers was around, so I was her only chance at having any kind of father figure. This was too much for a young teenager to cope with, and I never could form a sibling bond with her; this has affected our relationship to this day.

Money was always tight growing up, but my mother did her best to raise me. She cared for my grandmother full time, which she had done since she was a young teenager, so she couldn't get a job. But this didn't stop her from trying to give me a good life. She taught me solid morals and showed me love and affection, and despite her shortcomings, she was a kind mother. Unfortunately, she had a tough upbringing too; these experiences can be passed down through generations, causing secondary trauma. It is a pattern of life, one that only you can break.

I was bullied in primary and secondary school, so I struggled with rejection. I became depressed and developed behavioral difficulties. I was an intelligent child but always struggled to do my schoolwork and found it hard to focus. I also struggled with self-confidence, low self-esteem, and especially with building genuine friendships. I always tried to win their friendship by giving them toys or acting out of character so I could be liked, not knowing this would never help. In the end, I did manage to make a few genuine friends in school; some I still talk to today. However, in school, I struggled so severely with social relationships that I ended up attending a boarding school similar to a PRU (Pupil Referral Unit). Social services agreed to this when they asked me what I wanted. All I knew was that I did not want to go into foster care.

I really enjoyed being at my school because the classes were smaller, and I managed to connect wonderfully with some of the care staff and teachers. This worked out just right for me.

The school had some born-again Christian teachers, teaching assistants, and care staff who always had a positive attitude: They were always easy to talk to. I liked their calm and positive energy, maybe

77

because it was so different from what I was used to. They discussed the Bible among themselves, piquing my interest.

They played reggae music in the school van, which brought me so much joy, reminiscing about the eighties and nineties music I listened to and danced to with my mother. She had a passion for reggae, and I thought she would love this music. The minibus driver explained that it was gospel music. I had no interest in Christianity until this point as the music reached deep into my soul. I asked the man for a copy to listen to. Other than that, I had no Christian influence in my life, but when I listened to this music I connected with it on a deep level, deeper than I ever imagined. From this point, my journey to salvation began.

I appreciated these Christian workers who showed me the love I was so desperately looking for. There was an emptiness in me caused by the absence of a father figure in my life and no proper family unit; this first interaction began to fill the void inside me.

One Saturday, I was riding my bike home from my mother's house when a Jamaican man with a strong accent from the city of Bristol called me over from across the road. He looked to be in his forties, was casually dressed, and friendly. His words of Christian faith made me stop in my tracks and listen; his energy made me want to hear this talk of love and forgiveness. He then shared the gospel and told me about Jesus. "Do you know how close you are to hell right now?"

He handed me a flyer and invited me to attend his church; a sudden feeling of being compelled to attend overwhelmed me. I had nothing to lose. I was searching for answers and looking for some kind of love; maybe this was God's way of answering my prayers. The next day, I attended this church in a community center in Newtown down the road from me in an area called Lozelles. The short travel distance really appealed to me; I could ride on my pushbike.

It was a small church of about twenty people, nice and cozy. The people were genuine and showed they cared for my well-being, even helping me when I was in need financially. I was not used to this; I grew up facing rejection in every area of my life, even from my own family. This welcoming and loving feeling from these people was alien, but I wanted more of it.

I caught sight of the Jamaican man who invited me the previous day, so I sat next to him in the service. A Nigerian man, who was in his early thirties, invited everyone to stand. I followed the direction of the others, not knowing what to expect. I joined in with the uplifting worship songs, thinking how smartly he was dressed in his suit and tie as he played the keyboard with the built-in beats. Then the young Nigerian man got up and preached. I was shocked to discover he was the pastor; I expected the pastor to be old and gray, yet he was young and lively.

Through his preaching, the Holy Spirit reached out to my soul. I didn't understand this feeling, but I knew it was meant to be. He spoke to my soul, and I was finally understood. I belonged. I soon attended a church concert; the room was alive with music and drama. The young pastor was preaching, his arms raised in praise as he passionately proclaimed the gospel. I was hooked on his words, and my heart filled with so much joy and passion. Here, I decided to give my life to Jesus.

My Christian journey began with a newfound Christian family that appeared like an answered prayer. Joy was spilling from every inch of my body as I finally felt accepted. These people were there for me, listening to my concerns about faith as a new believer and answering all my questions. The excitement coursed through my veins at the thought of attending church as I met so many new people, young teenagers like me, who were as equally keen as I was to be in this church. I attended church once a week on a Sunday morning for a few months and then eventually was encouraged to come to a midweek service. From there, I began to attend regularly, joining in more and more activities. I now knew that God was calling me to preach the gospel. I was happy, I was accepted, and I was home.

Every Saturday afternoon, they had evangelism where they reached out to people on the streets and shared the gospel. I loved going along and watching how the members approached people, speaking the word of God and encouraging them to attend a service. Some members were aggressive while others were gentle; each worked in their own way and helped the church expand. I was overjoyed to be a part of something that was doing so much good.

The church held an International Bible Conference twice a year back then, where various pastors from the Christian Fellowship Ministries preached seventeen sermons in a week, starting on Monday evening and ending on Friday night. People came from all over the world, and pastors from several countries preached on various topics and shared what God was doing in their churches. These sermons included what the Christian Fellowship Ministries organization and its vision were about. Every preacher had different preaching styles; some made me fall asleep with their monotone voices while others gripped me in my seat with their charismatic sermons and high energy.

One sermon inspired me; it made sense to me. The preacher spoke about the journey to start your own church, which they called "getting sent out." I couldn't take my eyes off him as his words buried themselves into my heart. This was my journey; this was what I needed to do. I wanted to be ordained to be a pastor and to start my own church. This became my dream. They called this discipleship. Imagine if you were working in a supermarket and learning everything from your branch manager to eventually become a branch manager yourself and follow the company standards explained during training. At this point, I had committed to become a devout member of the church and expressed my desire to preach to my pastor. I was determined to get sent out and start my own church, and I would do anything to prove that I was worthy. My journey began, and my pastor started discipling me. Little did I know what this entailed.

Immediately, my pastor's behavior changed. Instead of being this nice man who was easy to approach and talk to, he became cold, no longer that loving father figure I once thought he was. He was now controlling and manipulative. Whenever I got anything wrong, I was humiliated in front of others. He said he was making an example out of me, calling it rebuke, and even having a biblical justification for hurting me. I felt so worthless and unappreciated. In the early days, I helped set up the equipment for church and concerts, so when I forgot a lead for the microphone, or to add petrol to the generator, or any time during an open-air concert on the streets, my pastor yelled, "You must think!"

When I was late to church or when I missed evangelism or church services without a valid reason or when I forgot to wear a tie to church or didn't dress according to the standard of a disciple, then my pastor would yell at me. He was a hypocrite! He made many mistakes himself. When he was late to church (which was quite often), I wouldn't dare question him, but since I was a disciple, pillar, senior member, or whatever they called it, they held me to different standards. I was yelled at both privately and in front of other disciples. They found it funny and laughed while I remained degraded and humiliated.

My pastor and other visiting preachers emphasized through their sermons that attending more church activities equaled being a better disciple of Jesus. The more you prayed, studied, and attended church, the better. I was told it was good discipline to come to church for morning prayer before work; apparently, this meant I was more serious about God. Deep down, I felt like I was doing it for show and to get my pastor's approval. When I was late or did not attend morning prayer, I was questioned or even rebuked.

It did not take long before church began to consume my life. I attended church activities three or four times per week. I attended morning prayer as many times as I could during the weekdays. Morning prayer was simply a time when you would come to the church building in the morning to have your devotional time with God; I struggled with this as I always believed this should be in my own home, but the church believed that if you did this as a disciple, then you were leading a more godly lifestyle by example. If you were a leader in the church, this was compulsory and if you ever expressed that you wanted to be a pastor, then you had no excuses.

They emphasized coming to church one hour before the service started to pray; this showed that you were hungry for God. My time was so stretched that I would rush from work with my church clothes, quickly changing out of my uniform so that I was dressed appropriately and smartly enough for church. It was hectic. I did not have much time to make myself presentable, and the only place to change was the men's toilets.

Outreach was Saturday, starting at 11:00 a.m. We traveled all over the UK for a whole day event to help new churches and always arrived home very late, yet we were still expected to be in church on time the next morning, especially if we were in public service ministry like an usher or worship leader. If you drove the church van, it was worse, as you were always the last one to go home but still expected to be in church early the next morning, no matter how tired you were. There was a little grace at times, but it was a trend, and if others made it to church before you, then you looked bad and would be rebuked.

I found myself struck with fear each time my pastor called me, wondering if I had done something wrong. Sometimes he called me to have a casual conversation before asking me to take up extra responsibility in the church or to do him a favor; other times, he rebuked me for something I wasn't doing right in his eyes. Maybe I wasn't fulfilling my ministry to the standard of how it was done in the organization, or he found something off about me and reprimanded me.

"You're not fulfilling your ministry properly," he scolded and then continued lecture me about something else that was not up to his standards. I feared him when he called me; I never knew what to expect. I was genuinely scared of him. He feared his pastor in the same way I feared him. His first pastor gave him the same treatment when he was younger, which just filtered down to me. Now, he was in his thirties, and I was an eighteen-year-old young man; he was in the position his pastor was in when he was younger. He intimidated me. I was young and vulnerable and had no family to protect me; in a way, he was my family. The pastor took it upon himself to be a so-called father figure to win me and a few other young people over, so that was all I ever wanted, a father figure. I did not know any better; I did not know that his treatment of me wasn't right.

"Men need to be teachable. If your pastor rebukes you, you must take it on the chin and be a man! Do not be a coward who cannot take correction!" A visiting pastor preached this. Being teachable is one thing, but being publicly humiliated, shouted at, and ridiculed is a whole different story. If you showed any emotion, then you were labeled, so you just bottled it up, saying nothing, even though it killed you inside and made you feel worthless. Nobody dared to challenge the pastor. If you did, you were accused of being rebellious and treated as an outcast. In some cases, you were even ostracized from the church and made an example of from behind the pulpit. It was a scare tactic. They told horror stories about you and how you were now cursed because you were out of the will of God.

The Potter's House was very legalistic. When I got involved in ministry, I was not allowed to miss any church services unless I had a valid excuse. There were also other rules: don't own a television, don't be on social media, and don't look up information about the church online because people might make negative comments. The people who wrote or said things about the church had issues, were rebellious, and were cursed by God, and if you read anything or listened to what they said, then the rebellious spirit would jump on you. They controlled my life to the point that I needed permission to apply for university or to move to another city or country. Yet even if I'd ask, I would not get permission. Only certain jobs were allowed for church members, jobs that did not require you to work on Wednesday evenings or on weekends; those days were reserved for church services and outreach. Even if I wanted to date, my pastor had to agree and approve of the girl.

It wasn't just the control that was difficult; the men in the church were all competing for the pastor's approval, especially when you were asked to lead ministries or preach in church. It was similar to the workplace; everyone was competing for a promotion. When you get a promotion, you gain status. If you didn't, you were looked down on. I questioned myself, "Am I doing enough to get noticed?" I usually didn't think I was doing enough, so I worked harder and did more to stand out.

The more competitive men got the types of positions that gained status while I was overlooked. I was treated differently than the other men. The pastor was harder on me. I was publicly humiliated for every little thing I did wrong.

"He loves you like his own son. That's why he's harder on you," people said. But I have two sons of my own, and I would never do to them what he did to me. This was not real love; he did not treat his own children like that. How could they say he loved me like his son?

My relationship with my pastor was fear-based. I never felt good enough. At times, I laughed with him, but I usually didn't know what to expect. He had a narcissistic personality and never admitted when he was wrong. He was incredibly difficult to deal with and to trust, even though I had known him for over fifteen years. He never opened up to me about his personal struggles and difficulties in an attempt to encourage me; he always made himself seem perfect and flawless.

Everything I did in church was to please my pastor and not God. I loved him like a father, and if he needed anything, I was always there at every beck and call to help. I even ran personal errands for him: dropping him off or picking him up from the airport and taking his children to school. When I served in church, everything I did, I did without complaining. It was exhausting. He rarely showed gratitude except occasionally, depending on his mood. Sometimes he gave me money to cover gas, but that was it. Eventually, I stopped letting it bother me.

Once, when I was on hiatus and the building the church rented needed renovation, I was expected to help paint and decorate the building. Despite my financial situation and employment status (or any lack thereof), I was not paid for my labor. "It is for the kingdom," the pastor said.

I was nearing my mid-twenties when I was pressured to get married. Unmarried men over the age of thirty were questioned and even mocked. "If you're not married by thirty, you are either involved with pornography or you're hiding something," a visiting pastor said.

Rubbish, I thought. I knew many single men who lived exemplary Christian lives.

"You must wait for God to bring your wives to church," pastor said in the early days of the church. "You don't need to look anywhere else."

Trying to date in the church was difficult, and I made many mistakes. When I approached girls, I did not realize I needed pastor's approval. Whoever I liked had to go through the pastor first. He had a way of making me feel like I did not know what I was doing. If my pastor had given me general advice, it would have been fine, but instead, he took every opportunity to belittle and manipulate me. I wish it would have been different. It should have been up to me whether I wanted to approach a girl.

I mentioned one girl to my pastor, but he did not approve of her. What a horrible experience! He called me one time to rebuke me. "I've washed my hands of you," he said angrily.

The mixed messages were hard and confusing. On one hand, the pastor pressured me to get married, but on the other hand, I could not approach who I wanted and needed his approval. Then, my eyes began to open, I began to question matters in the church. Deep down, I knew his treatment of me was wrong. Yes, I had made mistakes, but pastor went too far and acted as if he didn't want anything to do with me. I wasn't allowed to pursue girls he didn't approve of. Everything was on his terms, and if I disagreed or did things differently than how he wanted them, I risked his disapproval. He told me he would not perform my wedding ceremony. I was one of the last men in my friend group to get married. I was still only twenty-seven, but most men in the church got married around twenty-two years old. Despite joining the church at the young age of sixteen, I still hadn't found a wife. This was unusual, and the pastor wasn't happy about it. But I couldn't see why there was such a huge rush. It would happen when it happened, right? Why was there so much pressure?

I met my wife in 2011, and we got married in 2013. I started praying for God to bless me with a wife who was on the same page as I was, especially with what I knew deep down about the church. I did not agree with so many of the church practices, but I kept quiet. If they knew what I was thinking, I would face backlash and they would accuse me of being rebellious. Such accusations had been made against people before, so I was scared it would happen to me.

My wife and I faced many challenges in the beginning because we came from different churches. She was from The Potter's House in London, and I was from the Potter's House in Birmingham, Digbeth branch. When I met her, we started talking to each other before telling our pastors. We soon realized that we wanted to be married, and for this, we had to let our pastors know. Her pastor had known her from a young age and wanted her to stay in the London church under his leadership. When she told her pastor she desired to move back to her hometown in Bristol after she graduated from university, he became cold and distant and made it difficult for us to court.

I needed to try to make it official. I made a five-hundred-mile round trip from London to Birmingham to meet with my pastor first, then from Birmingham to Bristol (another one hundred miles) to meet with the pastor there, all in one day. We were then expected to get engaged and marry quickly; this wasn't a problem as our love was strong.

With dating came another set of rules we had to adhere to, especially since we had an inter-congregational relationship. My pastor was the most controlling and would not allow me to spend a whole Sunday in Bristol because I was in ministry and was supposed to be an example. I was only allowed to visit her every two weeks on a Sunday afternoon because I had to be in church in the mornings to count the offering. Her pastor was more relaxed and allowed my girlfriend to see me on Sunday morning until the evening.

Courting didn't just come with a new set of rules; it came with a lot of gossip. People were nosy and inquisitive about our relationship, but we didn't answer anybody's questions. It was none of their business; we were adults. Sometimes people made false accusations or ran to the pastor behind our backs, and we needed to explain ourselves. In church, we couldn't show any affection to each other. We couldn't hug, hold hands, or kiss. These behaviors were believed to be sinful and wrong. Keeping ourselves from showing affection was difficult as our feelings for one another grew. Needless to say, sex outside of wedlock was considered a terrible sin, which is why the church manipulated people into purity culture to prevent them from falling into sin.

When we got engaged, the manipulation and control escalated. We were told that marrying on a Sunday would honor God more than if married any other day of the week. By marrying on a Saturday, we would not be honoring God, and the people we invited would not want to hear preaching. On a Sunday, people would probably expect preaching, which was good marketing for people to join the church.

Despite this, my pastor convinced me to get married on a Saturday so he could be there himself. I honestly didn't mind. I wanted as many people as possible to attend our wedding. If we married on any day other than Saturday, people with ministry positions would not be allowed to attend the wedding, including some of my groomsmen. The leadership dealt with a lot of contention about holding our wedding on a Saturday. My fiancée especially felt the frustrations of her pastor in Bristol as he was being rebuked by the pastor in London, the head-quarters of Bristol, for allowing a marriage to happen on a Saturday, even though it was my pastor's idea. The politics caused tension between the churches.

We got married and went on a three-week retreat from Birmingham. We needed a break from all the politics. My wife moved to Birm-ingham because the church rules required the women to submit to their men and join him in his church. You were frowned upon as a man if you didn't follow this pattern as you would be accused of not leading your home. When we returned to church after three weeks, pastor slyly complained we were away for too long. After a while, church got a little better, but then my wife noticed people's behavior. She saw them for who they were and was vocal about it, which people did not like. So they treated her differently.

In January 2014, God told me I would be a pastor that year. I just prayed, "God, you let it happen." I couldn't understand where this was coming from as I never felt good enough. Despite my influential and successful efforts at outreach for new people to join the church, my pastor never saw me as influential. Other men came to his mind instead when he thought of people to send out to become pastors. I still didn't have any experience preaching, but after getting married, I did start leading a Bible study group. Shortly after that, I led new believers and church attendees, something the church called follow-up. Both were amazing experiences; they taught me a lot about organizing and leading classes, which I had no prior experience with. God put me into these positions to make me ready to become a pastor. As the conference drew near, the pull from God to preach the gospel grew stronger, but my wife and I prayed. "You let it happen." We left it in God's hands from there. I had such a strong belief that something was going to happen at this conference but wasn't sure how.

We were thinking of not going to the conference as money was tight for us since we were newly married. Then, a few days before the conference, our pastor randomly called us, saying that he had put us up for the conference at a hotel. I knew this was God's will as we were not planning to go. The conference came and the pull from God grew stronger, but we weren't sure what to do. After praying, God spoke to us to approach our pastor about getting sent out. I told him God had called me to become a pastor. We prayed together and were at peace about taking a step that neither of us would have taken lightly.

In October 2014, I answered the call at a Bible Conference to move to Newport, Wales, UK, to pioneer a church. In the conference on a Friday night after the preaching, they announced couples to come up on the stage to be prayed for and ordained into pastoral ministry. You must have had a meeting with your pastor before this during that week of the conference to confirm this. However, for us, this meeting never happened as when we agreed on a time to meet with our pastor, we ended up missing each other, so by the time the conference came around, we hadn't been able to have the needed meeting. At this point, we weren't sure if we were going to be announced that Friday night, but I knew in my soul that it was going to happen. Even so, to my surprise, our names were announced as a new work to Newport,

Wales. This was one of the most exciting yet scary moments of my life. This was a dream that I desired, and it was finally here.

I was excited about this new adventure. The nerves were pumping through my body, the butterflies in my stomach fluttering manically away as the senior pastors and church council prayed over me and my wife. I received two words of knowledge from two pastors. One was about my brokenness and how God would use us both as we had both come from broken families. The second word was about studying the Word and that God would equip me. Both made sense. This was one of the most memorable moments of my life. Those words are still coming to pass now even after leaving Potter's House.

The response from the people in my church was mixed; some were happy for me, and others thought I wasn't good enough to pioneer a church. Moving to Newport was not easy. When I got into the ministry as a pastor there, I was saddened to see some problems I did not expect. I was disappointed by the amount of corruption in the ministry. A lot of these so-called men of God that I once looked up to were not what I expected them to be. They were actors and did not reflect the preaching from the pulpit. My wife and I both had to find employment and housing within a set timeframe because we had an opening date to work with. On top of that, we were expected to organize back-to-back promotional events for our new church.

The motive for evangelism was different; it wasn't simply sharing the gospel and whoever came, came. I evangelized more than I did before so the church would grow. I was under immense pressure to make this new church grow, but despite all this, I enjoyed pastoring and preaching. Even so, the control and politics involved behind the scenes disheartened me. I didn't realize evangelizing nonstop made me an annoying pastor who was pushing people to come to my church and events.

There was also a lot of insecurity among the leaders and competition of whose church was bigger. The fact of the matter was that in order to make it as a pastor, you had to have a decent amount of people in your church, be arrogant and cocky as a pastor, and pay good tithe money to your mother church.

I was also saddened by how much money was billed as a church expense but spent by the pastors enjoying their lives. At times, as a disciple, I would put my last dime in the offering, hoping that God would bless me. Instead, I faced more financial hardship. Sometimes I couldn't even pay my electric bill as I used that money to pay my tithe, yet these pastors were spending large amounts of money on expensive hotels and restaurants and many other luxuries that I believed were wrong. When visiting preachers came to preach, the amount of money I had to spend was ridiculous. It was a self-employed career path for some of these men.

The numbers were not showing in my church, so I was treated as if I were not fruitful. Yet God began to use me and my wife in different ways than what The Fellowship believed was effective. We both developed the spiritual gift of prophecy where we prayed and prophesied God's word over people. The more we prayed, the more the presence of God led us supernaturally to approach church differently from what The Fellowship was teaching, but in the process, we were getting a lot of persecution for it. I was always compared to my peers (other pastors) who had more people join their church. I was under a lot of pressure to organize back-to-back events, write two sermons and a Bible study each week, follow up with new people who attended, work a full-time job, and be a newlywed husband with a child on the way.

When my first son was born, I told our pastor that I was going to cancel an event where my home church was planning to come for an impact team. I pleaded with him not to come, but my pleas were ignored, and I was expected to organize the event anyway. Even my wife, who was still recovering from childbirth, was expected to evangelize and build the church. I was expected to be at every event The Fellowship organized from men's meetings to pastors' conferences. Nearly all of my work holidays were scheduled so that I could be at these events as it was important as a pastor, despite any family commitments.

Continued pressure was put on us while we struggled to hit numbers in the church. Sometimes, God stirred us to do things differently than the tradition and pattern of The Fellowship, but we kept getting persecuted for it. The more we obeyed the Spirit of God, the more fruit we saw, but this was against what The Fellowship believed. I was rebuked for this and was told not to do what God had led us to do. I was told I needed to pray longer and press into the presence of God. To stop organizing different events than what The Fellowship was used to. The control from others made me lose my zeal as the Spirit of God in me was being starved.

People flocked to follow many charismatic preachers in The Fellowship. This was how the church was built, but I wasn't like them, and I had no intention of being like them either. I just preached the Word of God and wasn't worried if people came to church or not. Simply because of my pastor's pressure, this was an issue.

During this storm of pressure, manipulation, and control, I wanted to leave The Fellowship. That desire grew stronger and stronger, but I prayed to God because I didn't want to leave. I enjoyed pastoring and preaching, but the politics and manipulation were taking their toll on our mental health. Our pastor kept organizing meetings between me and my other pastor peers to discuss church growth, but it was unnecessary. All the pastor cared about was making himself look good to the head pastor who had just taken over the mother church in London.

My pastor organized one particular meeting during a Christmas banquet in Birmingham that we were forced to attend. Before this meeting, I wasn't planning to go to the banquet. We had a meeting two months prior at the conference to talk about similar issues. I didn't see the point of another meeting, but I knew deep down they had their motives for this.

It was an attack from the enemy, causing us to become heavily oppressed by it all. This happened after I prayed for the situation to get better between my pastor and the pastor peers due to all the tension between us. God, answering my prayers, challenged me, and told me he hadn't given me a spirit of fear. He gave me wisdom as to how to share my feelings and challenge the pastor respectfully. With everything that was going on, frustration was boiling in me. As predicted, the meeting that took place during the Christmas banquet was about the same issues as the previous meeting. When I respectfully confronted the pastor, it backfired. "If I sent somebody else to Newport, the church would grow," he answered. "I was reluctant to send you out in the first place, but I sent you because you had a good wife."

I drove away, confusion clouding my mind. Did the pastor not think I was good enough and that I wasn't fruitful? I didn't like the way he made me feel. I was not at peace. I needed to pray and seek God; my family and I were in distress.

God told me to confront my pastor's pastor in London about everything that was going on. But when I did, he didn't listen. I told him how I was being treated. He pretended that it had nothing to do with him; it was between me and my pastor. I continued to pray. Next, God told me to leave The Fellowship. So I sent a text, blocked all Potter's House contacts, and left.

Immediately, peace filled my body. I knew we had made the right decision, and the chains had been lifted off us. However, we faced a lot of backlash and lost many of our close friends for leaving. I was shunned by the church; The Fellowship believes that shunning is a form of discipline for an unrepentant person living in sin in order to restore them.

"But now I have written unto you not to keep company, if any man that is called a brother be a fornicator, or covetous, or an idolator, or a railer, or a drunkard, or an extortioner; with such an one no not to eat." (1 Corinthians 5:11).

But I was none of these things, neither was I living in sin. I was living for God as best as I could, and I was the victim in all this. Even if I wasn't a Christian, being treated this way was in no way a biblical reflection of God's love.

I lost people I cared about. I became lonely and depressed. I had given over fifteen years of service to this fellowship without complaining. I had a solid reputation in my branch and among other district branches and enjoyed preaching the gospel. I didn't plan to leave the church, but God moved me on.

The text message I sent my pastor was respectful, but he took it the wrong way and deliberately targeted my friends and family. He painted a very negative picture of me so they wouldn't want to be in contact with me anymore.

As a man, it was difficult to be vulnerable, and I struggled to be open about my personal hurt. But the pain was so deep as if someone had stabbed me and stood there, watching me bleed to death while gaslighting me into believing they didn't stab me. It was one of the deepest pains I have ever faced in my life. I was lied about to friends and family by people claiming to be Bible-believing Christians. I just could not understand how that was possible. What hurt me the most was that these people had known me for over fifteen years and ostracized me without ever calling me to hear my side of the story. They just took the pastor's word. My character, my reputation, came to nothing.

Now, six years later, I have found healing and a happy family balance. We are in a much better place mentally, spiritually, and physically. I am still serving God and have truly learned how to worship him in spirit and in truth. There is freedom in Christ—freedom to live the abundant life that God has called us to. We must not let religious institutions rob us of our freedom, destiny, happiness, and mental health. True healing comes from talking about my experiences to help others and helping myself.

After leaving the Potter's House, I released a podcast entitled *The Refuge Centre Podcast* where I share my experiences and preach on various topics. I have had emails from people from different parts of the world confirming that my story was encouraging, and I continue to hear good reports about this.

For a while, I was in denial about my hurt and pain; my ego pretended that life was great, but it was doing me more damage than good. In addition, I went to professional counseling, which helped a great deal. The counselor herself had a son who went through similar experiences, which connected us so that I felt less alone. Since leaving, I have also read two articles about two different pastors who ended their lives due to depression. That could have been me. I came from an environment where men were taught to just be men and deal with their problems. This built unhealthy egos so that men couldn't talk to each other. If you did, what you said was used against you, making you trust no one.

This has been in my heart for a while, needing to be shared. Jesus is a healer, and it is not his will for us to be hurt by people we trust and love. I was hurt while I was part of that church.

Once I left, I welcomed peace and healing.

CHAPTER 6
THE MIRACLE BABY
HELEN

"Before I formed thee in the belly I knew thee; and before thou camest forth out of the womb I sanctified thee, and I ordained thee a prophet unto the nations."
—Jeremiah 1:5

My birth, my parents told me, was a miracle prophesied by one of the visiting Potter's House pastors. He proclaimed during a healing crusade that my parents would have a baby girl in the next year: me. Now that I am older, I know the more likely truth: My parents sought medical assistance, and my mother had a small invasive procedure that subsequently increased her fertility. I am sure a metaphor is to be found somewhere in this, but this nicely sums up the mindset of the Potter's House. Pastors were direct links to God, and through sheer prayer and faith, anything was possible.

I am not sure what would have happened if I had been a boy or if I had not been born at all. Sometimes I like to imagine that it would have been a wake-up call for my parents and that they would have left the church and lived happy lives. Instead, I was born into the Potter's House Christian Fellowship, which wrecked misery upon us all for over a decade.

My first proper memory of the church at about three or four, is nothing special. I was running riot around the church after the service. We were all gathered in the upstairs hall of a community center with huge ceilings, massive windows, and a pale wooden floor. The adults sat on folding chairs, holding white polystyrene cups of tea made by the church women, while I skipped and jumped around the empty space at the back of the hall. My dad sat there, wearing a shirt and suit trousers. Sometimes he wore funny ties that I selected for him, loud colorful ties emblazoned with Mickey Mouse or Wallace and Gromit. Even though he was now a pastor himself, he still sometimes wore those funny ties for me. Like always, I was wearing a dress. As a pastor's daughter, it was required. My hatred of dresses was so strong that during the break between the two Sunday services for a few hours, I changed back into dungarees.

I saw most of the members of the congregation at least four times a week: on Wednesdays, on Saturdays for street preaching and flyering (also called outreach), and twice on Sundays. This, combined with the fact that my parents had moved to a new city in order to take over the church, meant that the congregation was like my family. I saw them fifty-two weeks a year, at every major holiday, and celebrated every birthday with them. I would like to think that I was sad when we shut down the church and moved back to our home city, but I don't actually recall much about that. However, I never saw or heard from most of them again. We left one Potter's House church (my dad's) and moved straight to another Potter's House—because it was absolutely essential to stay within The Fellowship—and began all over again. "If ye were of the world, the world would love his own: but because ye are not of the world, but I have chosen you out of the world, therefore the world hateth you." (John 15:19).

Cults, I am told, work primarily through isolating their members while warning them of the outside world. The aim is to make the cult seem like a safe space and to discourage all outside forms of information that could potentially influence the member to leave the cult. All these signs were present in the Potter's House, and as an ex-member, I am staggered by how obvious the warning signs were. I was only a child, yet I was subjected to such strange and odd rules, all under the guise of being directed by God himself.

Adults of the Potter's House were strongly discouraged from having outside friendships, especially with people who attended other, non-Potter's House churches. For some reason, the latter was seen as worse than simply being friends with nonreligious people. The word *religious* was used as a derogatory term in the Potter's House, used to refer to Sunday worshippers and to those who were not fully dedicated to spending every waking hour with God. We called these people luke-warm Christians who were not on fire for Jesus.

Looking back, these measures were clearly intended to isolate members from other Christians and those of other faiths, no matter how similar their beliefs were to ours. Protestant, Catholic, Jewish, it didn't matter: All of them were wrong, and they would all go to hell. When I was young, I though how empty heaven must be if it were only filled with people from the Potter's House. With this in mind, I asked a lady in our church what heaven would be like. She didn't tell me who else would be in heaven, but instead replied, "We will get to worship God all day, forever."

That seemed so boring. However, I know I was supposed to be really excited about this due to her tone, so I played the part. I don't remember exactly what I said or did, but I responded satisfactorily, which was relayed to my parents. They were very happy at the idea that their daughter loved God so much.

As a child, I was allowed to have friends outside of church. This proved difficult at times due to the sheer number of restrictions placed upon me, some of which were truly baffling. Karate was forbidden and declared to open up my soul to evil spirits. The same was said of Halloween and Harry Potter. Many of the restrictions were harmless, but they affected my ability to live a normal childhood.

How was I supposed to talk to other children about their favorite TV shows when the Potter's House forbade me from having a TV? How was I supposed to sing along to songs at school when worldly music was prohibited? How could I explain to my best friend that I couldn't attend her birthday party because not only was I not allowed to go to the cinema, but I was also supposed to be outreaching on the streets on Saturdays? I somehow managed to maintain friendships outside of church and clung to these semblances of normality when I could. I quickly learned what to say and how to act and tried my best to blend in.

A key point in my childhood at around eight or nine years old was getting into trouble for the first time during a religious studies class. Previously, the class had learned about either Sikhism or Hinduism (I can't remember which), and my parents had angrily demanded that I be removed from all further religious lessons after I came home proudly sharing my new knowledge. With the exception of Christianity and Judaism, I was to learn about no other religions. One of my teachers mistakenly removed me from the Judaism class despite my pleas that I be allowed to stay because Jesus was a Jew. My teacher said I was rude, and my parents believed her and forced me to apologize even though I knew I was right. Despite my adherence to my parents' and the Potter's House wishes, I had been let down and betrayed. All I wanted was to feel normal and not feel weird or ostracized. In hindsight, this was all part of the cult. It encouraged closed-mindedness and obedience to authority from parents to teachers to pastors. I quickly learned not to advocate for myself and to keep my thoughts to myself because, otherwise, I would anger my parents. "There is no fear in love; but perfect love casteth out fear: because fear hath torment. He that feareth is not made perfect in love." (1 John 4:18).

For a church that was so adamantly against magic and witchcraft, the Potter's House delighted in preaching about Satan, spirits, and demons. No matter which pastor delivered these sermons, they all followed a similar presentation style that was truly a performance to behold. They paced the stage like a pious pendulum, clutching a wired microphone in one hand as their suit jackets flapped around their waists like bat wings. Despite small audiences of thirty or so people, they bellowed and sweated into the microphones, pausing only to check their notes or swig some water to fuel the remainder of their sermon. Sometimes the pastor stared straight into my eyes as if God told him my thoughts. As an adult, I fully believe that this was done to spook members of the congregation; some pastors claimed to have the spirit of discernment that allowed them to read peoples' true characters. Sometimes they delivered words from God at the end of a sermon. They talked about how God had placed a message on their hearts for someone in the congregation, and I sat there as a bottomless pit of anxiety grew in my stomach like a sand timer, fearing that I had done something sinful.

The unfortunate consequence of a church so obsessed with demons was the effect it had on children. Most children have wild imaginations and believe in magic, fairies, and ghosts, and I was no different. However, as a child at the Potter's House, I was also told by adults that there was a spiritual realm to the world that I could not see, and that demons and angels were literal, real beings. I was told that God was everywhere, watching me at all times. This presented me with some conundrums. Did Jesus watch me while I showered? Were there demons under my bed? Could I be possessed if I misbehaved and forgot to pray at night? I developed this state of paranoia that at times, left me afraid to turn off the lights or be alone in case some malevolent being took hold of my soul.

According to the Potter's House, the only way to go to heaven was to be saved or born-again. This involved saying a very specific prayer in the Potter's House only, as well as giving money to the church and also seemingly constant repentance for sins. What was not explained to me, however, was exactly how this worked. As a child, my understanding was that God kept a list of everything much like Santa and that if I died with unrepented sins, I would go straight to hell.

I have no idea if this was accurate to the church's teachings as I don't actually remember how this understanding came about. All I knew is that you couldn't just say the special prayer and be saved forever; you had to continuously participate in your own salvation. As a result, I became terrified of falling asleep at night in case I died in my sleep and went to hell. I routinely tried to pray for forgiveness for every single wrong thing I had done and then added in something along the lines of "I'm also sorry for anything I've forgotten about" just to cover my back.

Rather bizarrely, this fear intensified after a fire safety talk at my school, in which I was told about how common house fires were. I then became mildly obsessed with the risk of house fires, far more than any child should be, in case I died in literal flames and then was also sent to fiery hell.

On top of this, I was also terrified of the rapture or second coming of Christ. I once sat in the car at a petrol station after church while my dad filled the car. I was in the back seat with my mum in the front seat. In the shadowy light, I told my mum that I had a red dot under my skin on the back of my hand, and that I was initially afraid that it was the mark of the beast, which was the sign of the Antichrist. She stared at me in the wing mirror of the car, fixing me with her gaze, and asked why I thought that. At the time, I worried that she was accusing me of being a sinner. Now, I wonder if that was her inkling that perhaps this church was damaging to me. Then my dad sat down in the driver's seat and we took off for home, never to speak of the matter again.

I often felt as though I couldn't talk to my parents about church matters because the church came first. Members of the church were very proud in sharing how they loved God more than their spouses and children, which stung quite a bit. I was openly told that God came first, always, before me, and I absolutely believed this. A large portion of my childhood was spent in fear: fear of hell, of demons, of judgment, and lastly, of my own parents.

My dad had an explosive temper. When he was angry, he made quick, unpredictable movements like a striking snake. Out of nowhere, he grabbed at, pulled, or lunged toward me. Despite this, my mum physically punished me. My parents argued about the best way to discipline me and twisted Bible verses about discipline. The verse about not sparing the rod was taken literally because, eventually, I was hit with objects and cried in terror of my parents. The beatings didn't stop until I was a little older and could confide in the current pastor's daughter.

She told me this was wrong. I relayed this to my parents, and magically, the beatings stopped.

To this day, I don't actually know what happened, and I don't know if the pastor's daughter told her father. Because of this, I truly cannot say whether the church stepped in to stop my abuse; perhaps the fact that I had simply told my parents they were committing a crime was enough, or perhaps the pastor had indeed found out and had spoken to my parents. Regardless, I know of multiple Potter's House children who were mistreated by their parents—I was not the only one.

One Sunday, a member of the congregation tearfully asked some of the women to pray for her because a teacher had noticed a bruise shaped like a hand on her daughter's arm and had phoned social services. The woman in question was often rough with her children. She and her husband were part of the worship team, and so they brought their children to the church for hours before the service in order to set up, and they stayed behind after the service with their children to help tidy up. These children were not allowed to run around the church like I had been permitted to when I was younger. They were made to sit still on their seats and be quiet, and they were often treated as though they were misbehaving when, in fact, their behavior was perfectly typical for their ages and could have easily been explained by boredom. The news of the bruise and the visit from social services did not shock me, even though I was still a child myself.

To this day, I wonder what the church members prayed in this case. Did they pray for healing of the bruise? For God's forgiveness for this blatant case of child abuse? Or did they pray for a miscarriage of justice and for social services to step away? I never did find out, but whatever they prayed wouldn't have surprised me in the slightest. "The tongue of the wise useth knowledge aright: but the mouth of fools poureth out foolishness." (Proverbs 15:2).

Prayer requests were always interesting at the Potter's House, especially on Sundays, and occasionally produced gems of entertainment. A sheet of paper was placed on the notice board for the congregation to write prayer requests on, which were duly read aloud from the pulpit by whichever up-and-coming male member of the congregation had been selected to lead the song service. The requests were usually fairly monotonous and unchanging: the thrice weekly prayers for Mrs. Smith's whole family to be saved, the continuing prayers for Mr. Brown's sick nephew, and an occasional illegible scribble that could not be deciphered ("but it's okay because God knows what's on their heart").

What followed was two or three minutes of praying, which varied in intensity between church members. Most people stood unless they were unable to. Some prayed quietly and discreetly with their eyes gently closed. Others took a more flamboyant approach, adopting a wide stance with their arms outstretched and their fingers spread, swaying on their feet like some strange evangelical palm tree caught in a fervent wind, their brows furrowed as they beseeched the heavens.

I must admit, I didn't really pray at all. When I did pray, I preferred to think my prayers; God could read my mind after all, I reasoned. I didn't enjoy the circus of prayer, and I especially didn't enjoy speaking in tongues. Although the whole church had prayed for me to receive the gift of speaking in tongues, I never did. I merely pretended and spoke whatever nonsense syllables came into my head with no direction of thought and no otherworldly compulsion behind it. I performed this once in order to satisfy the congregation and then never did it again. It occurred to me that this made me a liar and that perhaps no one truly spoke in tongues in our church. It didn't seem to provide any benefit or so I believed. Private matters could be prayed for privately, so there was no need to babble furiously in a purely performative way.

One particular Sunday, after weeks of identical prayer requests, a new request caught my attention. It had required lengthy description from the pulpit in order to impress upon us its urgency. A young man in the church had recently acquired a weekend job at a local supermarket and desperately needed the Lord's help. Despite applying for a weekend position, he was asking his manager to give him every Sunday off so that he could attend both the morning and evening church service. Additionally, he was being mandated to wear latex gloves (which he was allergic to) for hygiene purposes, and his hands were suffering badly with huge red welts and blisters, which flaked off his skin like Parmesan. Nevertheless, he needed the congregation's help to petition God to allow him to work only one of his contracted days per week and to allow him to break hygiene codes.

The service leader explained all this with a steely gaze. He gripped the microphone and proclaimed, "The devil is working through Morrisons."

"Amen!" came some voices from the crowd.

A few years later, the same young man was getting married to a woman in the church. Their wedding was arranged to take place in our dingy church building on a Sunday afternoon, and a full sermon was planned for after their vows. Our church was fairly sleepy, and so this wedding had taken our full attention for months and had been subject to intense debate. The pastor's wife had taken over most of the planning and ruled the entire affair with an iron grip, which had deeply upset the bride's mother. The wedding was to coincide with a visit from an evangelist (thus the Sunday date), and the reception would be held in a restaurant a few miles away with absolutely no alcohol for any members of the wedding at all and no organized transport. And of course, the ceremony absolutely had to take place in our church building.

Despite putting on a show for the visiting evangelist, on the actual day of the wedding, the church building itself was plain and undecorated as always: no pretty flowers, no chair sashes, no candles or other ornaments. The bride and groom exchanged vows under the harsh fluorescent lighting of our ex-office building, shared a kiss, and sat down for the sermon. Afterwards, the newlyweds left the down the dirty steps of our building and onto the pavement outside, which faced a flea market.

Apparently, a last-minute flower girl substitution had been made for the wedding that very morning: one of the little girls in the congregation. I didn't learn the full story until later. In protest, the majority of the bride's family had chosen to not attend the wedding, meaning that a shuffle of the bridal party was in order. The pastor and his wife sat at in pride of place at the head table where the bride's parents should have been, along with the groom's parents and a few other close friends. What should have been a happy day was instead fraught with difficulty. *What a shame*, I thought, *that the devil ruined this man's job and also his wedding.*

Weddings (and relationships as a whole) were a complex topic in the Potter's House and contributed to my departure. Even though we only had thirty or so members, we were required to date within the Potter's House church. No other forms of Christianity were acceptable. In theory, one could try to convert their partner to the church, but this would have resulted in raised eyebrows about how exactly you had come into contact with an unsaved person. You could also date a member of the Potter's House from another city; however, this would have required entering a long-distance relationship from the outset and was fairly difficult.

Without exception, all relationships had to go through the pastor. The pastor, after all, had direct access to God and could make these decisions. I would not get married for many, many years as I was the only teenager in the church, and so I did not concern myself with this too much. However, the restrictive nature of dating in the Potter's House gave me some pause, particularly after I saw its effect on other people I knew.

One afternoon, my dad called me downstairs. He handed me the phone and said, "Alan wants to talk to you." Alan attended the Potter's House. He was a close family friend who had known me since I was a child. Although at the time, I imagined him to be in his mid-thirties or forties, he was probably younger than I thought. He was kind and good-natured with an easy-going attitude and a brilliant sense of humor. He was renowned for bringing the same snacks to every church event: Pringles, cheap lemonade, and custard creams. Whenever he hosted church events at his house, he let me escape into another room to watch movies on his laptop while the adults mingled downstairs. Not many adults had this kind of patience for children in the Potter's House, and I was grateful for something fun to do.

In the phone call, Alan told me he was leaving the Potter's House. I don't recall the reason, and he probably didn't tell me. But he made sure to say that in essence, he was still a good person and that he would still be at church, just not at the Potter's House. He was still the same person I had always known, and nothing would change with him. He probably knew that the church would turn against him and that perhaps I might too.

I can't begin to describe how this shift felt. It was like my mind was a dark, dusty attic, and someone had just cracked the window open by a millimeter. It wasn't a surge of inspiration, but it was enough to swirl some dust clouds around. My whole life, I had believed that the Potter's House was an oasis, some secret club to heaven, and that we were the only truly good people in the world. Alan's departure collided with almost everything I knew, and I grappled with this. How could such a kind person leave?

A few years later, Alan married a woman from a non-Potter's House church in a lovely ceremony. Their church was airy and light with a proper steeple, stonework, and big glass windows. The Potter's House didn't believe in fancy church buildings; they were for religious people, and we were on fire for Jesus, after all. We could shout our prayers loud enough anyway.

I had never been in such a relaxed service before. In fact, I had hardly been to any other church services in my whole life aside from the Potter's House; mixing with other churches was forbidden. So I had only attended a handful of services from other church bodies, usually for funerals or school services. Alan dropped his bride's ring, and we all laughed as it clanked loudly down the stairs of the altar. There was not a single mention of hell throughout, and the service radiated with a happiness and peace that I had never felt before. The bride and groom left the church and beamed under a gigantic white umbrella as rain poured from the sky.

The only drama came from the Potter's House itself. Alan's best man still attended Potter's House, which was a huge concern. Ex-members (who we also called backsliders) were to be shunned and put on the prayer request sheet, where they were fervently prayed for over the next few weeks. The best man faced considerable pressure to back out of the wedding, which he refused to do. I was shocked. I had never seen someone take such a strong stand before. The congregation whispered among itself between polystyrene cups of tea to determine whether we should attend. In the end, a few of us did, although we were under the watchful eye of the pastor and his wife, who came at the last minute.

There were no such qualms about attending the funeral of the groom's father a few weeks later, who died after a long battle with illness. The pastor and his wife, who discouraged us from celebrating Alan's wedding, were quick to attend the funeral of a man they had barely met once. I never discovered their motivations for this. But in the background, with every injustice, the window in the attic of my mind cranked open a millimeter more.

Another main reason that contributed to me leaving the church was the church's attitude toward the LGBTQ+ community. The Potter's House had an extremely closed-minded view of anyone who wasn't straight or cisgender, and they took great pride in this view. Common phrases included, "God loves the sinner but hates the sin," and "It's Adam and Eve, not Adam and Steve." The latter always got a laugh from the congregation.

During one particularly notable sermon, my pastor took great pride in sharing a story about an intersex person who also did not have a fixed gender identity and who had attended his church many years ago. From behind the pulpit, in front of the entire congregation, he boasted about how he told them to get scans of their "waterworks" to see what "plumbing" they had, as if it were any of his business in the first place. His justification was that if they had ovaries, then they were a woman. The person quite rightly refused and left his church. Instead of taking time to reflect on his inappropriate behavior, my pastor decided to turn this into a sermon, which he told with glee. Even now, I remember how his eyes shone with religious fervor and how the corners of his mouth rose in a smirk. I cannot remember exactly why he chose to deliver this sermon or what its relevance was to our congregation, other than to boast about his own holy actions.

Earlier, I mentioned that I sometimes wondered what might have happened if I had been born a boy. Sometimes I also liked to wonder what might have happened if I were gay or trans. I am quite certain that I might not have survived. My whole life had revolved around the church, and all the influential adults in my life shared homophobic and transphobic views of varying intensities. When paired with the belief that God was more important than your family and children, my life probably would have been hell. These were the only views I had ever been told, and people took great pride in following them.

I had dinner with my friend's family one evening after school, and discussing the LGBTQ+ community. I said that being gay was wrong, and her father gently challenged me. My jaw dropped. No one had ever done this to me before. He said that the Bible could be interpreted in many different ways, particularly because of the passage of time and multiple translations, and that actually it was important to examine the verses in the historical context that they occurred. I was stunned. Not a single adult had challenged these views until now, which caused a seismic shift in my thinking. I was lost for words—was this true? And if so, did this mean that my entire belief system was a lie?

From then on, I approached the church with fresh eyes. What was once gospel truth was now uncertain, and I began to see inconsistencies in their preaching. All the small pieces began to fall into place. I kept on returning to the same point over and over again: How could we preach love and kindness when the kindness was only reserved for members of our own church? "But whoso shall offend one of these little ones which believe in me, it were better for him that a millstone were hanged about his neck, and that he were drowned in the depth of the sea." (Matthew 18:6).

Leaving the church was extremely difficult and highly traumatic, particularly as a teenager who still lived with my parents. I wish I remembered more of the details to be able to share them. I have large memory gaps and uncertain memories, and I often remember broad situations instead of the exact words that were spoken. Sometimes this makes me angry, because crucial turning points in my life have been reduced to a blank in my memory, and I can't speak to my parents about them to get their memories. Although I can't remember much, I do remember that I began my escape by slowly pulling away and trying to transition to a more normal life. I lied and said I felt unwell so that I wouldn't have to go to church. I told my parents that I didn't want to go. This worked for a while, and I felt a huge relief when I stayed home.

Eventually I had to tell my parents that I didn't want to attend at all anymore. I was tired of returning to church and having people ask me where I was, and I was tired of lying. The small taste of freedom hadn't been enough, and I wanted to be truly free at last. The reaction was as bad as you would expect. What people often don't realize about cults like the Potter's House is that their beliefs are so strong that you often cannot use reason.

For decades, the Potter's House had told my parents to value God more than their marriage and more than me, their own child. For decades, we had been told that the Potter's House was the best—if not the only—way to heaven. If I left, my parents would genuinely believe that I was condemned to hell. Their daughter was a godless backslider, a lukewarm Christian, and they had failed. Another part of the puzzle was that children in the Potter's House were not christened or baptized as infants. Instead, they were dedicated in a ceremony that involved both parents promising to teach their child about God, much like a normal christening. However, because things were never simple in the church, the caveat with the Potter's House is that the parents promised to be responsible for the child until they were sixteen—at least this was what my parents told me.

I bargained with my parents to let me leave and eventually they relented, but not before they had threatened me with homelessness and we had many explosive arguments. At times, I was truly afraid of what might happen to me. I had never heard so much shouting and anger, and I had never felt so unwanted and alone. Our compromise was that I would attend another church while my parents continued to stay at the Potter's House.

One Sunday morning, I attended the new church for the first time. I wore jeans and a Beatles T-shirt, something I hadn't worn to church in years. At the Potter's House, I had to beg to be able to wear formal suit trousers, because women on the ministry team were told to only wear skirts and dresses. Wearing jeans would have been unheard of, and wearing a T-shirt depicting worldly music would have been out of the question. I watched the younger children play during the service and thought about how children in the Potter's House would have been admonished and told to behave. I listened to the modern hymns and marveled at how different they were and how truly happy everyone seemed. Finally, I was shocked when a female pastor approached the stage and gave a sermon. This would have been blasphemous by Potter's House standards as female ministers were considered taboo. My head was reeling. I could not believe that something like this was possible.

Unfortunately, by this point, it was too late. I had experienced too much religious abuse and trauma, and I was at the stage where I no longer believed in God. I attended the new church to appease my parents, and eventually they, too, left the Potter's House to attend a more relaxed and welcoming church. A few years later, I left my new church and left behind the new friends I had made there too.

Now I am a grown woman and not a Christian any more. Even the word makes me feel physically sick because of the memories it conjures. It caused arguments, fear, sadness, and isolation. My family turned against me, and I'm angry when I think about how different my life could have been. To this day, I am still trying to undo all the damage that my upbringing caused: my subservience to authority, my lack of critical thinking, my fear of death and dying. I am angry that I did not get to experience a normal childhood like the majority of adult converts to the Potter's House did. They chose to join the church. I was forced, and I resent the fact that this freedom was taken away from me.

Some days are harder than others, and it's really easy for me to forget how far I've come. I have a wonderful partner who supports and loves me, and we plan on living together soon (without being married). My weekends are my own, and I often spend them surrounded by friends from many walks of life. I can listen to whatever music I like, and I can have a few drinks whenever I want to. Despite being raised to be ignorant and closed-minded, I have overcome all the problematic beliefs that the church taught me. I am often struck by how horrified my younger self would be if she could see me now.

In the end, I am proud of myself. I did what many adults could not do. I left the Potter's House Church, even though it was all I knew, and eventually my parents joined me. I am stronger than my parents ever will be, and I am a better person now than they ever were. Despite what the Potter's House may preach, I know in my heart that I am a good person. My goodness comes from within myself and is not based on the instructions from the pulpit or outdated, mistranslated stories from a book written thousands of years ago.

My pastor once spoke about how people come to God and that everyone is given an opportunity to come to God at least once in their lives. This also applies to people in cults like the Potter's House. Every Potter's House attendee is given insight. Perhaps it is a moment of doubt that builds over time, or perhaps it is a sudden realization that what their pastor is preaching is wrong. For a moment, their eyes are opened, and they have a choice—to continue as part of a judgmental, hypocritical, hateful cult or to leave and be free. Ignorance cannot be an excuse forever, and I say this as someone who was born and raised in the cult.

I chose to leave, and I am proud.

CHAPTER 7

I CAN'T CHOOSE MY OWN UNDERWEAR

CLAUDIA

"Shall I not visit for these things? saith the Lord: shall not my soul be avenged on such a nation as this? A wonderful and horrible thing is committed in the land; The prophets prophesy falsely, and the priests bear rule by their means; and my people love to have it so: and what will ye do in the end thereof?"
—Jeremiah 5:29–31

In mid-December 2014, I was long-boarding at the city center of Veenendaal together with a friend when a bald man suddenly started talking to her. I figured he must be religious. I boarded over there quickly, thinking: *That's gonna be a fun conversation!*

As a seventeen-year-old metalhead, I had always found Christians utterly boring. I'd attended a Christian school, and I knew I'd done everything that God had forbidden, but I didn't really care. If there was a God, he probably wasn't that good. Where was he when I went through tough times? When I was a kid, I had to deal with sexual abuse, which still weighed heavily on me. I was also bullied and had undiagnosed ADHD. I didn't believe there was a loving God.

The three of us spoke for a while, and when my friend left a little later, we continued the conversation. He was the third person to talk to me about faith that week, but with him, it was different. He genuinely looked like he was happy with his God, like he knew him personally, almost like they were friends. I don't remember much of the conversation, but he asked me if I had ever had suicidal thoughts. Wow, that hit me. Even though I had a solid home and my parents were the most loving people, I had suffered from depression as a teenager. I was burned out due to hard times at school and my parents' divorce, and on that very day, I was going through a vulnerable stage.

The bald guy, whose name was Hendrik, invited me to a church service. Because of the burnout, I suffered from a lack of energy and didn't want to go at first. When I realized, though, that the church was just a three-minute walk from my home, I had no excuse. Don't ask me why, but I went to church, attired in sweatpants and a band T-shirt, probably a Hailstorm band shirt (my favorite band).

When I walked to the church, I was so nervous! I'd never been to church before. What did they do there? And what was I supposed to do? When I stood in front of the building, I began having second thoughts, but the building had glass doors and a woman spotted me. Too late! I couldn't leave now. The woman named Petra greeted me kindly. She was the wife of the pastor, the bald man I had met on the street. The church service was held at a community center, and there weren't many people inside. When Petra started talking to me, I didn't pay much attention to what was going on around me or who was there. I assumed everything that took place there was normal. I didn't notice the fact that only a handful of people were attending, and I did not yet understand that this church was new, what they called a pioneering church.

They showed a Christmas movie called *Nativity Story*, and at the end of the movie, the pastor prayed. When he finished, he asked everybody to keep their eyes closed and their heads bowed. He started talking about a new life, a second chance, a chance to start all over.

Because I'd been burned out and depressed for a while, his words sounded great. Who wouldn't want the chance to start all over and find healing? The pastor asked people to raise their hand if they wanted this. I decided to raise my hand, and he called me to come forward, which I did. He prayed, and I repeated the prayer after him. When we were done, a burden lifted off my shoulders. I felt great and refreshed.

For the next two weeks, I attended the Sunday evening services. For some reason, I was scared to tell my mom where I was going on Sunday evenings. It felt a bit fragile. How could a metalhead like me be a Christian? My parents aren't religious, and they always spoke negatively about faith. Finally, after two weeks, I decided to tell my mom after all. She was somewhat surprised, but we didn't really talk about it much. When I started to go to church more often, my mom noticed a change in me.

The church had a strong culture; most people looked and acted the same. They shared the same convictions and knew what to expect of the church and what the church expected of them. I thought that was what God wanted. I quit smoking, cursing, and a lot of other supposedly ungodly activities. Mom probably noticed this but did not say much. When I started wearing skirts, she got very suspicious and wanted to meet the people in the church. The pastor invited us over for tea. "I got forest fruit tea, especially for Claudia because she likes it so much," Petra said.

My mother thought it was strange; why would people make this much effort just for people in the church? I felt embarrassed, of course, when my mom clearly stated she didn't believe in God. I really wanted to be good and do the right thing. I was a people pleaser and talking ill about God wasn't pleasing to the people of the church.

Because of the burnout, I was still extremely tired, so I didn't go to church every Sunday. That changed when I decided to move to Ede, a small city nearby. I thought it would be a smart move. I studied in Ede, and I did not really enjoy my daily fifty-minute bicycle ride to school. When I innocently told my pastor about my happy plans, he asked me why on earth I wanted moved to Ede. He had such a concerned look on his face, almost as if it were dangerous. I could not understand why this was such a big deal. Why should I keep biking from Veenendaal to Ede five times a week? Wouldn't it be much easier to bike from Ede to Veenendaal a few times a week for church?

He said: "What if you can't move back?" But I could not see any reasons why I couldn't return to Veenendaal if I wanted. People moved from one city to another all the time. Right? Even if I could not move back immediately, why could I not just wait for a suitable accommodation? Honestly, I didn't understand what the problem was, so I moved to Ede after all.

Little by little, I started to discover more unwritten rules and restrictions about where a church member was supposed to be at any given time. One day, when I was late for church, I decided to visit a church in my hometown Ede that was part of the same fellowship as my own church in Veenendaal. It was only five minutes from my home, and I was eager to hear from God. I had even been to that church before with the people of the Veenendaal church on a Saturday evening music night, but when I went there on my own for a Sunday morning service, people looked at me, surprised. "Don't you go to the church in Veenendaal?"

Nobody had told me I was not supposed to attend church services in Ede. I thought this was very strange because the Ede church was the same type of church as the one in Veenendaal, and the churches worked together. I then discovered there was an unwritten rule never to attend another church, not even when you move to another city. Because, as I later found out, the church is not happy when you move away from where God has placed you.

My pastor also lived in Ede. He had, in fact, been a member of the church in Ede and was sent to pioneer a new church in Veenendaal. I learned that the church in Ede was part of a group called Christian Fellowship Ministries that continuously expand their fellowship by sending out married couples to pioneer churches in new cities. Pastors are expected to move to the city they are pioneering, but my pastor had some trouble selling his house after he was sent out to Veenendaal, so he was still living in Ede. I might have asked or he might have just offered, but he started to pick me up with his car.

I was shocked when he told me we would leave at a quarter to nine because the service started at eleven. Since the church assembled in a rented community center, a lot always had to be done before service started. We had to put up the projector, make coffee and tea, set up the chairs, tables and music installation, clean the floor and toilets, and decorate the walls with church flyers and pictures. So every Sunday, I helped to set up the church. We were encouraged to attend every service (three times a week) to experience more from God.

Because I was asked, I took upon more and more duties, such as cleaning, evangelism, and helping with the coffee and tea after services. The pastor even asked me to play the guitar. I owned a guitar but didn't know how to play it. I tried to play but had a scar from surgery, so it hurt too much. I told my pastor about it, and he prayed and asked God to heal my hand. And miraculously, it did heal. Because I was healed, I felt obliged to play the guitar, but I still had to learn how. I practiced at home and, soon after, started playing simple songs during the services.

Before I could really start to play the guitar in church, I had to visit the pastor for a short semi-formal conversation about why I wanted to do it. *Uh, I wanted to play the guitar because he asked me to*, I thought. But I had recently learned in Bible studies that the correct answer would be to "serve the church and the people," so that's what I said. I also learned about a contract you needed to sign when you wanted to be involved in any ministry. The more prominent responsibilities in the church were called a ministry. According to this contract, you were not allowed to own a TV or go to the cinema. You also needed to have an internet filter on your computer that prevented you from visiting adult websites, and as a girl, you were expected to wear a skirt to church. You were also expected to be present every time the church doors were open or for any church activity.

Okay. What dedication! So that's how I rolled into church activities: Bible study on Wednesday, evangelism on Friday and Saturday, and two Sunday services. Four times a week was the minimum; sometimes we also had extra activities, such as revival meetings, on other days.

Even though combining the church with school, work, and internships was so incredibly busy, it was also rewarding. I felt pretty good about serving at church. It's hard to describe, but when people keep reminding you how long your skirt should be, and they congratulate and praise you when it's finally the right length, it really does feel good. You feel affirmed and accepted.

Maybe it sounds petty, but the pastor and his wife were micro-managing everything. Not a detail escaped their eyes. The pastor even told me I folded a cleaning cloth wrong because his wife always folded it differently, so I had to do it the same way in church. I wondered if he was joking, but no, he was dead serious, so I folded it the right way. I was very zealous for God, and I really wanted to do what was right in his eyes. I also really wanted to do what was good in the eyes of the pastor and his wife.

I was the only teenager during my first two years in the Veenendaal church. A few young people came on and off, but the rest of the congregation were forty years old and above. There were never more than twenty people at a service. After two years of being the youngest, I was very happy when another young girl named Veerle joined. We soon became close friends. A short time later, a young guy named Geert also started to attend. He came after being invited on the streets for a revival meeting and decided to check it out. Our pastor spent much time with Geert, who soon became involved with all the church activities. The three of us did many things together: set up before service and break down after, play in a band in various formations, and evangelize. Geert had a driver's license, so Veerle and I often rode with him when we went to revival services in other cities.

Geert and I both lived in Ede, so we always biked home together after church. We started to become friends and always had nice conversations. One day, when we were biking, he asked me what I thought about dating in general and if I was open to dating. He didn't ask if I was open to dating him, but I felt a bit shy. What did he mean by this question? I told him I was focusing on my studies right now. I only had a few more months to go, and I really needed to focus.

After that, Geert started dropping subtle hints that he was into me. For example, he told me that I looked very nice that day and then smiled a little bit longer than usual. Once, when we were driving to a revival service in Amsterdam, we were talking about Geert's date with a woman from another Fellowship church that hadn't gone well. I thought he wasn't into me, but when Veerle asked him what he was looking for in a girl, he said: "Someone with sporty brown curly hair and brown eyes," and then he smiled at me.

Butterflies fluttered in my stomach. Was he really into me? Veerle and I ran off to the bathroom as soon as we arrived and giggled and talked about what happened. I was ecstatic.

During a church conference a few months later, he finally asked me on a date. He sent me a message via WhatsApp, saying he was out for dinner with friends. So I jokingly said, "Food? Without me? How dare you!" He said that he would love to take me to dinner. I asked him if he was joking, but he said he was serious. When I saw him the next day at conference, he walked up to me and said he wanted to ask me something. I was so nervous. He asked me if I wanted to help him put some flyers on the chairs. He nervously laughed and then asked me if I wanted to go out.

I had been thinking about it all night, and of course, I wanted to go out! I said yes, and then he said, "I mean just you and me. To dinner or something like that." I said yes again. I was so happy! The pastors often preached about asking them for advice and wisdom, so I asked my pastor for permission. He was happy for us. The first Saturday after the conference, we had our first date.

Geert was, and still is, a funny and loyal man. We enjoyed our dating time, and our love for each other grew more and more. After almost one year of dating, he proposed.

When we started to prepare for our wedding, I began to have mixed feelings about our church. I had been involved there for five years already, and I thought I knew them well, but suddenly, we started to hear about all kinds of rules we didn't know about.

Personally, I think it is okay for a church to have some rules, especially when it comes to dating, relationships, and marriage. If you believe in God, you should keep his commandments. The closer we came to our wedding, though, the more rules we became aware of and the stranger they seemed to us. For example, we *had* to get married either on a Sunday or a Wednesday. Those were the days for church services, and all the members of the church were supposed to be invited to the wedding. I didn't want to get married on a Wednesday, but we didn't have any choice. We were not allowed to get married outside Veenendaal because church members might not be able to travel to our wedding.

Because of the pandemic, the government had placed restrictions on the number of guests at weddings. I really had a tough time with this; because we *had* to invite everybody from church, I didn't have any room left to invite some of my dearest friends. Don't get me wrong. I loved most of the people, but for example, a sixty-five-year-old man had recently joined the church, and I didn't even know his last name. I had to invite him instead of my own friends while I hardly knew him.

A few weeks before the wedding, our pastor also told us we needed a few counseling sessions with him, sessions that were very odd indeed. We didn't talk about marriage or loving each other or serving God together as one would expect. We needed to know, however, if the other person had (student) debts or STDs. Yes! A knowledge of those things is a great foundation for a marriage. It still bothers my husband to this day that we didn't have proper marriage counseling or any type of wedding preparation course. We were told, however, that French kissing equals sex, so we could not do that. It's quite strange for a pastor to be so involved in these petty details.

We personally strived for purity, which made for some funny moments. When we were still dating, Geert used to drop me off at my house. Then we said bye and gave each other a handshake. My neighbor saw us once outside and started to laugh out loud. He thought we were joking. Nope, that's how we were supposed to date, and that's how we did it.

Later, when we had been together for a longer time and our relationship was stable, some side-hugging was allowed. We abided by these rules because we wanted to obey God. I thought it was strange, however, that just three weeks before the wedding, our pastor suddenly announced that if we had had sex, he wouldn't marry us. He had told us before that we couldn't have sex before our wedding because that was a sin, but he had not told us there was a church rule about it. Why let us know this just three weeks before the wedding? But fine, we had no intentions of disobeying the God we loved.

Just like any young woman who is preparing for her wedding, I wanted to have a lovely wedding dress. I wanted to get some ideas and inspiration, so I looked at magazines and catalogues like any bride would. When I found pictures of dresses that I liked, I showed them to the pastor's wife, but she thought that they all showed too much skin. Oh, bummer! What a disappointment!

Once, when I was shopping, I finally found the dress of my dreams, but she wouldn't approve. With a heavy heart, I decided to choose one that was more suitable for church. Later, after I had already bought my dress, I learned that if the pastor (or his wife) thought your dress was not modest enough, he would refuse to marry us, and he might even do that in the middle of the church service. How crazy! Can you imagine walking down the aisle on your wedding day and not getting married because your dress was not modest enough? What a stressful time I had!

Three days before we got married, I called Geert and told him I was done with the church. He could hear that I was clearly upset, so he came over, and we met outside my house. I didn't dare tell him I wanted to leave the church because I was afraid he wouldn't marry me. Not because he didn't love me but because the church was very strict about who you could marry. You were only allowed to marry somebody from your own church or at least someone within the same church fellowship. I cried a lot. Geert was very sweet and understanding; he held my hand, and we laid on the grass, staring at the sky.

We survived the wedding! I was now married to the love of my life, and we moved in together, a new start. We could continue our Christian life as a couple. Unfortunately, from then on, things only got worse at church.

Married life was awesome but also very busy. When I told the pastor's wife how tired and exhausted I was, she suggested I take an occasional Friday night off. That was like putting a Band Aid on an open bone fracture, but all right. We were at church at least twenty hours a week: cleaning, preparing, translating, playing guitar, evangelizing, and performing other duties.

More and more, things weren't right. Geert was just as involved in the church as me, and he also thought it was too much. Some Spanish-speaking people were attending, so Geert translated the verses on the screen to Spanish (thanks to Google translate because Geert didn't speak a word of Spanish). The pastor always sent these Scriptures very late, the night before the service. Geert struggled to find time to translate them on time. Geert told the pastor that it was too much pressure to do it in such a short period of time, but the pastor glossed over his complaint and acted like he should have plenty of time. He always downplayed any problem we had, like it was our issue, like we didn't try hard enough. He acted like working twenty hours a week in the church was not enough. He often made statements that life will only get busier when you have kids. So he did not take our concerns seriously or offer to help or comfort us.

After a while, Geert didn't want to translate the Scriptures anymore. It took a lot of courage for him to go to the pastor and tell him he wanted to quit. At the next service, the pastor announced that there were no longer translated Scripture verses on the screen. He said that since the pandemic was over, everybody could come back to church, and we didn't need a translation on the screen anymore. I was astonished! That was not the reason there was no more translation but because Geert didn't want to do it anymore (because he already did too much at church).

I asked the pastor why he said that (because it was a lie), and he explained he had done it to protect Geert. What nonsense. So it was better to cover for someone and tell a lie than to speak the truth? I thought it was a sin to lie. After this incident, I noticed that my pastor and his wife spoke dishonestly more often than I had thought, especially about other pastors. If I asked a question about a pastor, they always covered for them and never spoke the full truth.

Then something major happened. Our pastor told us that our overseeing pastor in the Netherlands had a moral failure, but he recommended that we not read the newspapers about it. We weren't allowed to have social media, so we didn't have any way of knowing what actually happened. I decided to read the newspaper anyhow. When I asked the pastor what he thought about it, he said that when two people are involved, there are two guilty parties. I was so upset!

How could he say that? This pastor involved clearly had a lot of power over people, and it was completely wrong to say it was also the victim's fault. I walked away and cried. Our pastor did apologize to me, but I still can't get over the fact that they tried to protect the overseeing pastor after all he had done. The pastor's wife even tried to make me feel sorry for him: "You don't have any idea how bad it is for this pastor. Now he must work an actual job."

I was astonished. As if working a job were really punishment after all the harm he had done to his people. When I asked her if she had lost her faith in The Fellowship, she said no because at least the leading pastor in Prescott was still on the right track. Well, before long, that pastor started to exhibit some peculiar behavior too. Now I didn't know him that well, so this was not about him. But when I asked questions about him and what had happened when he was basically kicked out of ministry by his own son, our pastor just told us not to speak ill of the dead because by the time I asked, he had already passed away.

When the person who warned the church council about what happened in the head church of the Netherlands wanted to get married, he wasn't allowed to get married in that church. My husband was supposed to go to his wedding, but because he was kicked out, our pastor advised us to not attend. My husband still regrets this and has apologized to this person. Because of this person's efforts to show the world the real Fellowship and helping people that have left, I am now writing my story to be part of this book.

One day, our good friends from a Fellowship church in Vleuten came over for some tea. We had a nice chat, but after we had been talking for a while, they became serious and finally told us about some odd happenings in their church. It was a long and complicated story, but I was just happy to be a friend and listen.

When I went to our church, the pastor's wife came to me. She had heard that they'd come over, and she started asking me all kinds of questions about what they told me and what I thought about it. I was puzzled. Why did she want to know? She asked if she could come over on Thursday because she needed to pick something up from my house. I said no because those friends would be visiting us again. She didn't listen and came anyway. I thought it very odd that she wanted to come over on the very day our friends were there. She almost seemed to want to spy on them. When I asked her about the situation in Vleuten that she obviously knew about, she was very protective of the pastor in question and covered for him.

It was almost sickening to me how they praised other pastors, almost as if they worshipped them. But I always felt like I was not good enough, not holy enough. I don't know exactly how they managed to achieve it, but I was living in so much fear: fear of not doing things right, fear of not giving enough money, fear of not living holy enough. If I talked to my pastor about it, he always flipped the issue back on me. Are you tired? Pray more. Are you busy? Wake up earlier. No matter how much I did, it was never enough.

Because of the pandemic, we had to do things a bit differently than usual. Pastor asked one day, "How should we do the service?" He gave us two options. We could start the service earlier than normal (and this was very rare because we would never change the schedule), or we could do a livestream.

We said, "Option two. We can help with that!"

Then he said, "Great, but the church is going for the first option." What? Why ask if you have already decided what to do? That day, I clearly saw that "the church" was the pastor and his wife. I started to see more and more things that weren't right. For example, they are called Evangeliegemeente De Deur, but they are, in fact, a Pentecostal church. They didn't want to call themselves Pentecostal, however. When I wanted to know why, they explained it was because Pentecostal churches had such bad reputation.

That might just have seemed like a little white lie, but it was one of the many small lies they told. You might excuse it, thinking that everybody makes mistakes. Of course, nobody is perfect, but a church, as far as I know, is supposed to fight against sin. And if there is one thing that is called a sin in the Bible, it is lying.

I started to realize how the way they worked was based on false intentions. They looked for vulnerable people, told them to repent, and promised everything would be all right. It did not matter what kind of sins they had committed before they repented, but as soon as they had repented, they were expected to change little by little and become more holy. They used the boiling frog method, and they were constantly gaslighting people. If they had told me from the start what I know now, I would not have joined their church. They say God loves you as you are, but he loves you too much to leave you the way you are. If you proclaim that you are the only right church, but you are legalistic instead of focusing on God, then something is very wrong.

The pastor commented on my guitar-playing skills, even though he didn't know how to play the guitar himself. And still, after all those years, he didn't even know how to clap his hands on the right beat. I kindly tried to tell him he was doing it wrong all that time. Now clapping on the wrong beat is one of my pet peeves, but if people in the church had any questions or feedback, he always ignored it and said that they were wrong. Or he might say okay, but never do anything about it. He was not open to feedback at all, and we had no church council at our local church.

As I mentioned, the pastor and his wife often lied, or at least did not tell the truth or the full truth. During the pandemic, they tried to continue with business as usual and to keep activities running as much as the restrictions allowed. They stuck to the rules just enough to make them look like law-abiding citizens, but they didn't care about the health risks and damage if people got infected. The pastor said these exact words to us: "It's just a mild flu. It isn't even that bad. I don't even stick to the rules. It's important that people go to church and hear about Jesus."

Personally, I didn't really care what people thought about the virus, but I was shocked when he spoke to an elderly man and said something completely different than he had told us only two minutes before. He put on an empathetic face. "The virus is really serious. I don't even go out that much." You don't? Really? You just told me two minutes ago that you ignored all the restrictions and were as busy as ever.

I worked at a gym, which was closed along with many other businesses. But the church stayed open with many people gathering at the same time. It was so irresponsible. Once, after a Sunday evening service, we were cleaning up the church building together. My best friend suddenly coughed and said, "I am not feeling well." I was slightly afraid and told her to go home. She said she couldn't because we still needed to clean up. I told her she should go and that we would take care of it. But because she had such a sense of duty, she stayed to help clean up. Unfortunately, two days later, she told me that she had the virus and I needed to get tested. I tested positive for the virus too.

The pastor also had double standards. A woman was banned from the church because she lived with her partner, but they weren't married. Another woman, though, who got pregnant without being in a relationship was allowed to stay. The pastor's wife even told me it was good she got pregnant because now she could quit her studies and start coming to church more often.

I was also surprised when the pastor's wife talked about her daughter having dyslexia. She said that it was very difficult and they were looking for the best way for her to study at school. I was surprised because when I told them I was diagnosed with ADHD, they told me they didn't like labels and that I was just a bit busy. I was diagnosed a few months after I joined the church and was so relieved. I finally understood what was wrong with me. The diagnosis was supposed to help me navigate through life, but the church didn't believe ADHD even existed. ADHD impacts every aspect of my life, so my jaw dropped when they told me her dyslexia was a real problem. She then soon said, "But I don't really believe in labels."

One day, I was done. After many more incidents, I finally told Geert I couldn't continue like this. Because we had already talked to our own pastor without any improvement, we thought that talking to someone in a higher position might help. We went to the pastor of our pastor (in Christian Fellowship Ministries, everyone has a pastor, even pastors and their pastors!) who confirmed that some of what had happened was wrong. But when we asked if we could go to The Fellowship church in Ede, he said he wouldn't allow us to change churches. Some pastors were just more legalistic, and we just had to deal with it.

So we tried it again for a while. We even went on an evangelism trip to Paris, a city I had been to before. I knew how the metro worked and where to find the Eiffel Tower. But the men were talking about the best way to go and what ticket to buy. I tried to help them by telling them how to get there, but they wanted to discuss it between themselves. "Just leave it to the men," the pastor's wife told me. Finally, after only two days, they figured out I was right. Very frustrating. I couldn't really take one of the men seriously because he had to find the Eiffel Tower with Google Maps, although you could clearly see it while walking.

One evening, we had a music night, and something had gone wrong with the venue. We had to wait outside for an hour, and I was pretty done at this point. When we could finally enter the building, it smelled like pee, and it was horrible. But we needed to pretend to have a good time. That day, I was done pretending. I waited outside until the miserable evening was over.

I thought, *Why not honestly express my feelings this time?* I was used to putting a smile on my face and just pretending I didn't mind. I had never expressed my true feelings about the church because I was taught to be an example and be happy for God. But after all the mess, I thought that I might need to be honest for a change. I could not imagine how a visitor would enjoy this venue with the smells and stains. I frankly told the pastor's wife that I disliked it. She said, "How can you say that? You just have to make the best of it. You have to be an example and pretend to have a good time." Pretend to have a good time? I had done that too many times before, and I could not do it anymore.

Standing outside, I had plenty of time to think. My conversations with the pastor's wife bothered me. When I had told her that I never speak ill of the church, she told me I always kept my cards close to the chest, like it was a bad thing. Apparently, she had noticed that I didn't like certain things, even though I had not complained before. I had not been open, and that was wrong. On the other hand, when I expressed my feelings and told her I did not like it, that was wrong too. Something began to dawn on me. I was not wrong for disliking the evening. It wasn't nice to wait outside for an hour and then enter a smelly, dirty building. Why should I pretend to like it? The fact that I hadn't been able to express my true feelings didn't sit right with me. I hadn't been able to express my true feelings for a long time. On a side note, a lady made some really tasty doughnut balls, which was the best part of the night.

At the next conference after these sordid events, the pastor from Paris came forward and gave a report about our evangelization trip. He told the audience about the great time we had and the many visitors that came! I was stunned and could not believe my ears. What visitors? I was there; there were no visitors. Yeah, the people who were present were his family and us and maybe two actual visitors. He made it seem like it was such a great time when, in fact, not that much had happened. In these churches, obviously everything was about numbers, about more converts and more people. And if there were not that many people, it should at least look that way. The only reason they evangelized was because they wanted more people.

After a church service, I went to my pastor with a very serious problem. I had finally mustered up the courage to go to him with this, and I told him, "Pastor, I have a serious problem I want to talk about."

At that moment, he said, "Okay, go on. *Wait*, Alina is leaving, and I need to speak to her!" and he ran off. He had to speak to this recent convert because he was afraid she would leave and not come back or something similar. New converts were clearly always the top priority until they were what was called locked in. That meant that they were no longer new converts and were now part of the church and regularly attending. After you're locked, your only priority is to be a perfect holy example.

Even when I told my best friend Veerle that I was having a difficult time and how much I needed a friend, she said, "I don't like to stick together too much. I want to focus on new people." As soon as she finished talking, she walked over to somebody else. That same day, after the service, she asked the pastor's wife about her skirt length and whether it was okay. The pastor's wife said it wasn't okay. Out of the blue, she told me I could not wear thongs (underwear). Well, excuse me! Only I can decide what kind of underwear to wear. How would she even know when my skirt was long enough? I had not asked her permission to use any item she could not see. She just gave her opinion as if it were in the Bible: Thongs were not allowed. This kind of involvement in people's lives was not only ridiculous but also unhealthy. And what does it have to do with God?

After our trip to Paris and this bizarre conversation about thongs, I was ready to leave the church. Our pastor thought, however, that visiting us at home would help. It was very unpleasant. He accused me of not praying enough and not praying out loud during prayer meeting. I had to be an example, and the source of all my problems was not praying enough and not praying the right way. I was so upset that he intruded in our home in this way. I was almost ready to throw a brick through the church's window. To give the church one more chance, I called my pastor's pastor, but this was not helpful at all.

Finally, I realized I had to leave the church after I went to the doctor with very acute and serious physical problems. The long list of symptoms included chest pain, nausea, shortness of breath, poor eyesight, panic attacks, and much more. The doctor told me how seriously my physical and mental health were affected by the stress I was suffering from. I knew she was right, but I was so scared! I was afraid that something terrible would happen to me.

I was afraid to lose my covering. All the time I had been at the church, they preached about a covering, both financial and spiritual. If you just stayed close to your pastor, tithed to the church, and did everything they told you to do (like always obeying your pastor), then you would be under God's covering. I didn't even dare tell the pastor or his wife in person that I was leaving the church because I was so afraid they would turn things around and blame me. So I texted them. I later learned that some people at church asked the pastor's wife why we left. She told them it was because she no longer had a grip on us. She also lied and told them that Geert and I were fighting. When we confronted her, she denied everything.

After I left the church, I was still terrified. I had nightmares about meeting the pastor and his wife, and I was afraid to go downtown when I knew they would be there. I was physically and emotionally drained. I didn't dare be angry or bitter, but I was. I was always told that these emotions were bad and sinful, so I never expressed those feelings even when they were there. I had always worked hard in the church and kept a smile on my face. But I had eight years of bottled-up feelings, and I didn't find healing until I went to a therapist and psychologist. I had a hard time understanding what exactly had happened, and others also struggled to understand what was really going on.

One year, we had given more than eight thousand euros to the church, yet it felt like we never managed to give enough. From the outside, the pastor and his wife looked so nice, but their manipulation was subtle yet intense. Reading *Reli Detox* by Reinier Sonneveld was most helpful; this book exposed all the ways in which our pastors worked to manipulate us, and I really understood what had been going on. *Reli Detox* discussed many examples of manipulative situations and churches, and I was shocked to see that the church I had been attending was mentioned in that book!

When I joined that church as a teenager, I was in a vulnerable position. They love bombed me and offered a solution for all my problems. Little did I know, they would manipulate, gaslight, and take advantage of me.

It's been a year since I've left, and I just recently found happiness again in my life. The past year has been the hardest year of my life. I know leaving was the right thing to do, but it was still very difficult. I had no life outside the church, no hobbies or friends. My former best friend is still in that church, and she doesn't want any contact with me. I now only have a few good friends left who also left The Fellowship.

I'm still married to my lovely husband, and we attend a different church. When I first visited there, I was a bit hesitant because it was so different than what I was used to. A female was leading the song service, *and* she was wearing pants. *How wicked*, I thought! When she announced we were going to chill with God, I thought I would fall off my chair. This woman singing on stage was so open, and she radiated love for God. Many other women in the church were wearing pants. At my new church, they didn't two complete sermons, one before the offering was collected and another one after; they didn't even take an offering at all.

After the service, I spoke to the wife of the pastor. She said that I didn't have to give money because I was a visitor, and I could come as I was. She was genuine. I had to get used to the lack of extra rules. I could see the love of God through the congregation despite the way they dressed. In the sermon, the pastor even said that it was okay if we struggled or didn't see eye to eye on certain subjects. He just told us what the Bible said, and if we had questions or disagreed, we could always talk to him. All kinds of people were visiting the church, and they all seemed to be there out of their free will and not out of fear. There was no toxic manipulation, no legalism, and no hidden rules, just people worshiping with a big heart and a love for God.

Before, I didn't know what a healthy church looked like, but I'm happy I have found one. I love my new church now, and I am happy I'm finally free.

CHAPTER 8
MY WORTH AS A WOMAN
VALERIE

"But if thine eye be evil, thy whole body shall be full of darkness. If therefore the light that is in thee be darkness, how great is that darkness!"
—Matthew 6:23

We were wanderers, people from the wrong side of the tracks. My father was a jack-of-all-trades and worked a lot of odd jobs but occasionally had steady work. He was also an alcoholic and physically abusive, especially when drunk. He was from a very dysfunctional home himself, abused and abandoned by his own father. I don't fault him; alcohol was probably his only escape from the harsh realities of poverty. So the bars were his second home, maybe even his first. We moved constantly, mostly because Dad hadn't paid the bills or rent. More than once, I was awakened in the dark to load up the vehicles and trailer and sneak away under the cover of night. In a two-year period, my sister and I tallied up more than sixteen moves.

My mother didn't get along with her step-mother and yearned to leave home. So when she became pregnant by a man already married, she married my father. She always seemed angry to me, or maybe she was just angry with me. I couldn't tell. I somehow never measured up and couldn't figure out why. I felt like an inconvenience: unwanted, unloved, unseen. Only when I was an adult did I learn about narcissism. Life must be really hard when you think the world should revolve around you and it doesn't.

My parents' marriage was never good. My most vivid memories were of them coming home drunk and fighting violently. They would throw and break things and hurt each other. During those times, we kids stayed out of the way. I spent a lot of time hiding, making myself as small as I could. Don't be seen. Don't be heard. Years later, I found myself physically freezing in the presence of angry people and had no idea why.

They drank increasingly and later began smoking pot. My father eventually moved to cocaine and my mother to Valium she got from her doctor for her nerves. At home, there was no room for mistakes, just being in the way, or even having the wrong hair color. What passed as discipline, I now realize was actually severe child abuse. As a child, I didn't know this, of course. I assumed everyone lived that way.

My half-sister, the firstborn, was two years older than me. Blonde-haired and blue eyed, she was the favored one, the princess. She was the beauty, and I was the brains, but clearly, beauty was valued. Mom always doted on her. The contrast between how the two of us were treated was clear to me even at a young age.

My sister was usually cruel to me, but she has no recollection of this. It was classic narcissism. She believed she helped raise us. Instead of two, I had three abusive parents. She could get away with anything. Even when we were caught doing something together, she turned the situation around and say she'd caught us doing such and such. I couldn't understand how my parents always believed her. I do understand now; it was a choice.

My brothers, one older and one younger than me, were trouble. Well, at least that was the consensus. Honestly, they were probably just being boys, but in a home where parents were so dysfunctional, there wasn't room for children to have problems. One day, Dad caught my older brother playing with matches. Dad heated a skillet on the stove and burned my older brother's hand in it. Another time, he was caught smoking, and my dad made him eat a cigar. And there were always plenty of beatings to go around. Lucky me, when my brothers misbehaved, I was rounded up with them for a beating. I was actually compliant and timid as a child, but they didn't have time to think about who did what.

My very earliest memory when I was about three years old was of abuse. I had brought home some beautiful purple irises for my mother. The priest followed us home to tell my mother not to let us pick flowers from in front of the church. Oops! I had no idea. After he left, my mother flew into a rage. I huddled in a corner with a belt flailing at me. Only a few years ago, I learned my then-five-year-old sister, was also there. She probably said she saw me doing it and told me no. You never knew what was coming in our home. There was no rhyme or reason to it.

I was a heavy sleeper and was even known to walk in my sleep. A sleep walker appears to be awake, eyes open and speaking, but they are in their dream state, making little sense. One night, I had forgotten to do the dishes, which wasn't uncommon. They called me forgetful, always in my own world. The truth was, I had begun disassociating to avoid a world that was beyond my ability to process. On this night, my parents came home from a night of drinking and awakened me. Except I wasn't actually awake. I awoke in the middle of being beaten with the coffee pot cord to my parents' drunken rage, to bright kitchen lights, to feeling terrified and disoriented. I was only eight or nine, but I quickly learned to be hyper-vigilant. I learned to read people well. I had to be sure everyone else was okay so I could be okay. I learned to be a co-dependent, always thinking of others in order to survive. Whatever me there was, well, there was no room for her.

The first four of us were born one year after another, but my youngest sister was born almost eight years after me. We didn't spend a lot of time together. When I left home early, we'd only had about seven years together. As the youngest, she managed to escape much of the physical abuse. But she did experience the same abandonment, neglect, and emotional abuse that we all did.

When I was eleven or so, my parents were breaking up, not for the first time. My dad was taking us to his sister's home, except for the princess. The favored one was always with Mom. Dad had said he'd be back in a few weeks when he found a job. Unable to find my dad, after three months, my uncle drove us to my mom's aunt's house where she was staying. It was late at night in the middle of winter in upstate New York. Snow drifts higher than the car were across the back roads. After trying several routes before arriving, his temper was understandably short.

When we did arrive, my mom and aunt came outside, and an argument started. They said my dad wasn't there. My uncle replied, "They aren't my kids to raise!"

My mom shouted back, "Well, we don't want them here either." My jaw dropped. In spite of a decade of abuse, I was still shocked to hear my mother say those words.

I grabbed my four-year-old sister's hand and said, "Let's go. They don't want us here." That obviously wasn't wise; we probably would have frozen in a snowbank.

My aunt heard me and said, "Oh, no! You girls come inside." Soon after, I was sent to live with my father, who had fled to another state.

There was one small ray of sunshine during this time. When I was in the third grade, a classmate invited me to an after-school Bible study. A wonderful woman named Wendy was leading it. She told me I had a God-shaped hole in my heart. At eight or nine, I took it quite literally. I felt so cared for when I was there and eventually accepted Jesus into my heart. I believed Jesus came in there to stay.

She probably suspected we had problems at home. At the time, in 1969–70, Child Protective Services (CPS) didn't yet exist. People didn't usually call the authorities, and she probably didn't know the details anyway. But she did invite me into her home occasionally to stay overnight with her two daughters. It felt peaceful there. I began attending church with them and really believed that Jesus loved me because He loved all the children, not just some of them. I also began to realize that other people didn't live the way we did.

A couple of years later, we moved away, and my parents had no reason to find a church, so that ended my church-going years. I still believed in Jesus for a long time, but through years of abuse, I eventually abandoned Him. I felt like He'd abandoned me. I lost my faith, becoming hard and angry instead. How God could be good and yet allow so much misery? It would be many years before He found me again.

As I grew older, bitterness and hatred became a way of life. I became outwardly tough and wore my rage for all to see. The meaner and angrier I appeared, the more likely people were to stay away from me. I didn't realize it was a protective mechanism. By twelve years old, I started drinking and smoking pot. Some of my siblings had started much earlier than that. It was really all we knew.

Right before my sixteenth birthday, I left home. My parents were divorced by that time, and I was living with my father. It was one of the rare occasions I stood up for myself, and I ended up being kicked out, along with my older sister, who was now eighteen. She called Mom, who had moved to another state, and was told, "You can come live with me." When I spoke to her, she said she didn't have room for us both. So not surprisingly, I was out of luck.

My father changed all the locks and nailed the windows shut. Since I was underaged, he reported me as a runaway. I spent that night in a laundry mat. I couldn't believe my life had come to this. I quickly began using hard-core drugs like I had a death wish. People handed me drugs, and I took them without asking what they were. I just wanted to escape my life.

I spent the next couple of months going between friends' homes, and sometimes crashing at parties until I was sixteen and could legally rent an apartment. I hated myself, my parents, and life. I didn't yet realize it, but I was beginning a lifelong struggle with depression and anxiety.

I still struggle with reckoning with some of the abuse I grew up with. It's hard to believe parents can be so self-absorbed and uncaring. Now sixteen, the only relationships I had known were narcissistic, abusive, and abandoning. Abuse that I realize now set me up for later spiritual abuse. I didn't see the signs when they appeared in the structure and functioning of the church where I later found myself. Sadly, it took me over thirty years to see that, and by then, the damage that was done.

In 1980, I had just turned nineteen when I found my way down to Tucson. I was running away from myself, but I had no idea what I was running to. I had found a job, and while hitchhiking to work one day, a woman picked me up. She talked about Jesus and invited me to a music scene the following night. It sounded fun, so I agreed to go. She picked me up the next night, and for the first time, I entered The Door Christian Fellowship, Tucson. I did enjoy myself; it felt like a bunch of young people hanging out minus the drinking and drugs. There was contemporary music, short drama skits, and testimonies of how people had found Jesus, followed by a short message.

The woman asked me if I wanted to pray. I really wasn't ready for that, but suddenly, people were speaking in tongues, something I'd never heard of. I had heard from my grandmother about holy rollers and swinging from chandeliers. It freaked me out, and I decided then and there that they could do their thing, but I would get out as soon as possible. By some twist of fate, however, as I was praying, I felt God's presence. I thought about when I had first accepted Jesus. How I missed him! I prayed, and when I left, I felt like I was home for the first time.

All of this was happening at the tail end of the Jesus People Movement. The Potter's House Fellowship was barely ten years old. People were genuinely kind and accepting. It was strange that people actually seemed interested in me, but my heart had been so starved for love and kindness that I drank it in. It really did feel like a family. It was a whole new culture. The outreaches, music scenes, and fellowships were exciting, and to top it off, we were winning the world for Jesus. We were special. I could not have conceived, at the time, how that special feeling that we experienced would morph into elitism.

I readily entered the discipleship program although we were told, "It isn't a program. It's a relationship with God." But it was most definitely a program. Coming from a home that was so unstable, the simple, clear rules felt comforting with structure and a sense of safety. I soon moved into a girls' house. I was learning a lot and making friends along the way. I still had a lot of internal struggles, but when I brought them up to others, they either didn't know how to respond or told me those were my BC days, before Christ. I guessed the past no longer mattered, so I buried it.

It wasn't the last time I would bury my problems. As time went on, that feeling of being home changed. What began as "come as you are. You are loved" became following the rules and looking good on the outside. We rarely discussed what was happening on the inside unless we were trying to find some sin to root out. We didn't talk much about our struggles. We became disciples, all doing and saying the same things.

So we learned to hide. We were told, "Fake it till you make it." We felt this pressure to always have joy, have the victory. At the end of thirty-five years, I concluded that nearly everyone there was faking it to one degree or another. They didn't know how to be real, and neither did I. So we wore our acceptable Christian masks; we smiled and said nice things. I struggled because I didn't like being fake. But I couldn't risk being shamed and possibly rejected because I wasn't living up to the ideal of a disciple.

It wasn't that I didn't share my faith, but I didn't like outreaches. It felt like they were using high-pressure sales techniques. The best disciples, it seemed, actually enjoyed getting on a bullhorn and screaming at people that they were sinners, headed for a devil's hell if they didn't repent and turn to Jesus. This felt hurtful to me, and I'd been hurt enough in life to know I didn't want to be the one hurting others. So I did my best to conjure up reasons not to go. But I felt like I had to hide more and more. It seemed like we had to be perfect.

Similar to my upbringing, I was starting to feel unseen and invisible. Unless you did something outstanding, you were kind of overlooked. I felt ashamed, like I was not enough. I didn't know it at the time, but I was actually ashamed of not living up to people's expectations. The truth is, I was guilty of not being who God wanted me to be. They didn't spend much time helping people learn who God wanted them to be. They simply believed that they knew best what God wanted for us—just conform.

Individuality didn't seem to have any place in the church at all. They wanted us to all be the same and do the same things: outreach, service, become a pastor or pastor's wife, etc. Anything related to self was bad. We were exhorted to love others as we love ourselves, but, "Oh, we don't need to love ourselves. We're sinners. We're already selfish." They commonly used Scriptures like "Die to yourself. Deny yourself," and "Your heart is deceitful and desperately wicked. Who can know it?" They tried to convince us there was nothing good inside us and that we couldn't trust ourselves. Perhaps they had forgotten that we had a new heart and a new spirit in us?

Over many years, this reinforced my sense of worthlessness. When I came into the church, I was already a doormat. I was confused. What more did they want? Did Jesus want me to be a doormat? I really didn't feel like it was bringing him glory. Does having no boundaries, not being able to say no to people, bring him glory? It sounded more like sanctified co-dependence and people pleasing to me.

But the people we were pleasing were our leaders, just as they were pleasing their leaders and headship. To speak out would lead to being labeled a rebel or at least unfaithful, and we couldn't afford that. We had to fit in to be accepted. Well-known researcher Brene' Brown famously said, "Belonging is being accepted for you. Fitting in is being accepted for being like everyone else."[1]

The only community outreach was street preaching. We were taught not to involve ourselves in social issues. We just needed to get people saved, and God would take care of all the rest. How anyone ever came to Jesus through those outreaches, I'll never know. They invested little in actually growing people in favor of the discipleship ladder. Instead of being actual light-bearers to their communities, they chose to plant churches in far-off places.

The church-planting model Christian Fellowship Ministries employs has a lot of problems. First, at the very beginning of The Fellowship, Pastor Mitchell had declared that we didn't need Bible colleges or seminaries, the very institutions that provide training and safeguards, help people stay true to the gospel, and teach leaders how to care for souls. Instead, Mitchell proudly declared, we would follow Jesus's model of discipling men. I suppose, in a sense, we did do that. Jesus discipled men after himself. Mitchell and those who followed him discipled men after themselves as well.

Second, like myself, the largest percentage of people that came into the church came from backgrounds of poverty, abuse, and addictions. They rarely had healthy relational skills. Disciples were trained in how to start a church and run an outreach, but not how to relate to people in healthy ways. The care of souls, which used to be the domain of the church, was taken up by the counseling and psychology professions, which were anathema to the church. This has had a devastating impact on the organization as a whole. If "it is all about relationship," as they said, we had miserably failed.

Meanwhile, the church environment continued to change. We stopped inviting men from outside The Fellowship to come in and minister. Disciples soon learned to read only from the pastors' list, which came down from Mitchell himself. I once talked excitedly about a new Christian book, only to be asked by a young disciple, "Is it on the pastor's list?"

I'm not sure if I replied or only thought, "Are we a cult?" I had no idea at the time how close to the truth I was. Pastors who disagreed with any of the church directives or policies were no longer permitted to preach at conferences. It became clear there was no place for differing views or dissent. Eventually, all we heard were our own voices echoed back to us.

Rules began to multiply and became more rigid. Some churches were making people sign contracts not to own a TV or go to movies if they wanted to be in ministry. We were also told we didn't need to go to college. The reason they gave was that Jesus could come back at any moment, and we shouldn't waste our time on worldly pursuits. They were teaching doctrine, the commandments of men, one man in particular. Everything came down from Mitchell. Interestingly, the church criticized other churches, which people saw as legalistic. We were as legalistic as any. How could we not see this?

The patriarchal views of men and women are among the most destructive doctrines held by Christian Fellowship Ministries. We were taught to submit to headship, to our husbands, and to our parents, unwittingly, in that order. A woman couldn't hold any position other than teaching a women's Bible study (rarely granted unless she was a pastor's wife) or teaching children's Sunday school. They could work in the nursery or clean toilets. They couldn't even be an usher. It boggles my mind to think what they expected might happen. A woman was never allowed on the church counsel; they would have split their sides laughing at that one!

This explains why women's issues were never addressed. Either they thought women had no issues, or if they did, they needed to just deal with them. We were second-class citizens, and no matter how many times they said this was not so, the proof was in the pudding.

Women were discouraged from going to school. Why did they need an education? God's will for them was to marry and have children. Oh, and to support their husbands in their goals and callings. I still cringe inside when I hear someone say, "It was so wonderful that she released her husband to—whatever." Women did not actually have this power; men did what they wanted for the most part. This was mostly to discourage women for complaining that they had no choice. Strangely, I have never once heard that phrase used the other way around. Some men supported their wives in their own callings, but they were few and far between and often secretly looked upon as weak. But some of those men were actually the strongest, most honorable, and authentic men I knew.

Patriarchy calls men to adventure and conquest: Be strong and deci-sive. Take control, take action, dream big! It honors the self-sufficient, the powerful, and the connected. It is no different from the culture around us; rather, it is an example of culture infiltrating the church. In the church, patriarchy calls women to submit to men, to be meek (more easily controlled). We were discouraged from having dreams or goals of our own. Women who didn't submit were called Jezebels, uncov-ered and rebellious women. Even the world gives more honor and dignity to women than this.

Leaders (men, of course) reassured us of our value and the beauty of our sacrifice, but the truth is, we live out what we actually believe, not what we claim to believe. Women do not have a voice and are regu-larly dismissed unless they agree with a man. They are emotional, and emotions were viewed as untrustworthy; therefore, women were viewed as untrustworthy. Women are the weaker vessel, which is why they need men. They can't possibly be expected to manage their own lives, let alone a position of responsibility and leadership. Women have been effectively silenced, their only impact relegated to raising chil-dren. Unless they change, this will be their downfall. Women in our culture, or in most of the world, for that matter, won't come to a church and give up their freedom for servitude.

Much of this boils down to narcissism, which much of evangelical Christianity today is suffering from. More extreme churches, like Christian Fellowship Ministries, are leading the ranks. Narcissistic leaders are confident, charming, and charismatic. They know how to take control and get things done. This is why they are chosen. It is also why many of these churches become breeding grounds for narcissism. The dark side of narcissists is that they cannot be questioned or criti-cized. Their charisma is often mistaken for anointing. They know how to manipulate others to reach their goals, and they need to be seen as successful. This is not to say all pastors in Christian Fellowship Ministries are narcissistic. Many are good pastors who are humble and genuinely care for their people; I know many of them. Unfortunately, it is very hard to when you are surrounded by this culture to stand out. And standing out is all important.

Our greatest struggles stemmed from marrying in this church. Early in The Fellowship, people dated and then married within three or four months. Perhaps it was because of the preaching that was aimed at avoiding sin. We were told, "God wants young people to get married." We had very strict rules for dating, like always being with a group. Emotions were all but vilified, certainly not to be trusted. Infatuation would surely lead you into sin. Marriage was reduced to a good decision and a commitment. Oh, and about women submitting to men. And that God needed men and those men needed wives. And a woman needed a man.

Early in their church-planting endeavor, leadership had quickly learned not to send out a single man. This obviously added pressure to those who wanted to date and who felt called to pioneer a church. This pressure led to relationships and marriage as a means to an end, the end being church planting. We also learned that we were *all* called. And there was only one primary calling, to pioneer a church.

After several years, my closest friends had gotten married, and I was feeling alone. Based on the preaching, I took that as a sign that God wanted me to marry. I started dating my husband because he seemed kind and responsible and was serving in ministry. I was making a good decision as we'd been taught. I wasn't infatuated with him; I didn't fall in love. I had actually learned as an unbeliever not to trust in those feelings; I'd been taken advantage of too many times. Still, I wondered if I was really in love, but how could I know?

We were taught that God's love is *agape*.[2] It isn't a feeling but an action. The Old Testament informed us that marriages were pre-arraigned by families, and that feeling of love wasn't even a consideration. So I thought I must be on track. What was I thinking? Oh, I was thinking exactly what I was taught to think. My life had long been too broken for me to have illusions about marriage, yet I was not prepared for what was to come.

My husband was a good provider and stable, which my chaotic heart longed for. But he was not emotional; he had two emotions: good and stressed. Unemotional meant he was a good solid man. The church applauded this. I didn't realize that his own childhood home had left him with an emotional void. His father was a career military man, and my husband later entered the service himself. He had learned to perform, achieve, and succeed in life. The church loved their military men, the disciplined ones. Less work for them, I suppose; he could follow the rules and fit right in.

I spent the next thirty years of marriage with very little connection. In the midst of our marriage struggles, I told my pastor that we had no emotional connection. He answered, "What do you mean, 'emotional connection'?" I was floored! Did he honestly not know what I was talking about?

Within a couple of years, my husband was distant and unreachable. When I tried talking with him to connect emotionally, I always left the conversation feeling beat up and confused. I didn't know what gaslighting was at the time, and he was unaware he was doing it. It was a part of his upbringing and also happened frequently in church. I endured it for decades, but the truth is, my heart gave up very quickly. I had well-learned that we were supposed to die to ourselves. I believed and said these types of statements: "More of Jesus and less of me." "It's not about me." For him, gaslighting was a way to distance himself from emotions and real intimacy. Of course, I was a good wife; after all, I had Proverbs 31 to live up to. So I lowered my expectations. I prayed, read the Bible, and did everything I could to be a good wife, mother, and Christian.

I gave birth to my first and then my second son within five years. I loved them with all my heart and still do. Motherhood almost seemed to rescue me from marriage. I couldn't connect with my husband, but I definitely could with my children. The next fifteen to twenty years were some of my best years. I loved them in ways that I had never felt growing up. My parenting lacked a lot. I only had my own dysfunctional childhood to look back on, yet I understood the kind of parent I did not want to be.

The primary teaching of the church on how to discipline children was not to spare the rod and to expect first-time obedience. It was like a military bootcamp. There was no place for foolishness or immaturity, no place for just being a child. It was an interesting church dynamic, this push for maturity, rather than letting natural processes take place. God created us to grow; our physical body teaches us this. Healthy maturity takes time. And just as it was with our children, believers were forced into a controlled and forced maturity that was unnatural and largely unsuccessful. Apparently, they didn't trust God to do the work, so they had to take it upon themselves to control people. What passed for maturity was really nothing more than rigid control and discipline (will power). Discipleship at its best!

Life began to change when my children left home. My heart changed. Marriage had never brought a sense of fulfillment and purpose. It was more like something I endured. Even though I'd done everything I could to be the best Christian and wife, I felt used and resentful. I didn't realize the church had set me up for this with their erroneous teachings. "God created the woman for the man. If a man found a wife, he found a good thing. I was designed to meet all his needs." Yes, these came from Scripture, but the way they were taught under the banner of patriarchy corrupted them.

Even the marriage vows proclaimed this. To the wife they said, "And do you know that God has created you to be a helpmeet and, that in so doing, you will find the dignity and fulfillment that God has promised to you as a woman?" This sent the message that my primary purpose was as a helpmeet and then maybe as an image bearer of God. Women were treated as a commodity.

When my husband was diagnosed with prostate cancer, my first response was indifference, tinged with resentment. I felt like I'd been used for so long, I didn't care. It wasn't my husband's intention; he had been subjected to the same teaching I had. It's just that these teachings benefitted men, not women. He benefitted. Yet God touched my heart; I couldn't imagine what it would be like to go through this cancer and have his wife leave at the same time. So I stayed. I was by no means a saint; I'd just been co-dependent for so many years, I didn't know how to be any other way. The church, however, reinforced this co-dependency in every way they could.

Within a year or so, life was relatively unchanged, only with additional challenges. A Christian author and counselor had asked, "Why are women leaving their marriages after twenty, thirty, or forty years after all they've invested?" I finally realized after thirty years of sowing into my marriage, the ground was barren. After giving everything, I woke up one day and didn't know the man I was sleeping with. When I started having anxiety and panic attacks about physical intimacy, I couldn't do it anymore. I wanted out. My husband was genuinely shocked. He had thought the marriage was fine. The patriarchal teaching left us with a huge imbalance in our marriage; men were entitled, and women were obligated.

After thirty-five years, our marriage had no substance. It imploded. We were pillars of the church, model Christians, in multiple ministries, but our marriage was dead. It looked great on the outside, but it was empty on the inside. We had both desired to be the best husband and wife we could be and filled our God-given roles as the church taught us. The marriage still failed because roles don't make a marriage; it takes relational skills we were never taught. The church was responsible for this. When every effort is given to outward appearance and performance, to planting churches rather than building people, the lack of substance should be no surprise. As the church went, so went our marriage. So went my soul. All that was left standing were whitewashed sepulchers.

Once I realized our marriage was in trouble, I went to headship for help. The pastor said I needed to keep doing what I was doing: keep being faithful, submit, don't complain. "The definition of insanity is doing the same thing over and over and expecting a different result."[3] While this is not in the Bible, it's true nonetheless. I asked if he could recommend a counselor to us. He replied, "Uh, no, not really. The following Sunday, he preached a whole sermon on why we don't need counselors or therapists. "We have God, the Bible and the Holy Spirit." And a pastor who had nothing to offer. So my concerns were dismissed.

Unable to accept his answer, I began my search for a counselor and found an amazing one. She was a strong Christian but had a much more healthy faith. She was kind and compassionate, and she listened. It occurred to me I rarely experienced this in church. Wasn't this more like the example of Jesus? Two weeks later, my husband joined me for couple's counseling and brought up his involvement with pornography.

God broke him; he broke us both, but it was the beginning of change. Statistics say that 68 percent of church-going men and 50 percent of pastors regularly view pornography.[4] The evangelical church in general has failed to address this.

The same week, we met with the pastor to talk about our struggles. He preferred to believe our problem was my husband's travel schedule for work. When the issue of pornography was brought up, he remained silent for a moment and then switched to another topic. As we were leaving his office, he told me, "Oh, and you need to recognize your part in this." I was speechless! Short of being perfect, I'd followed every rule. This pastor, who I had looked up to for decades as a spiritual father and leader, had thrown me under the bus! One thing I knew for sure, I was certainly not responsible for my husband's porn use. Maybe it goes back to the same patriarchal thinking: Blame the woman. I felt like the wind had been sucked out of me.

During the last decade or so that I attended the church, I witnessed more and more marriages ending in divorce. More often than not, the woman was leaving. The husband was then hailed as the righteous one, pitied, and admired for his faithfulness in the midst of hardship. The underlying message to women was to be silent, be a servant, never withhold yourself from your husband, *never* expose your husband's sin, and don't nag or complain. Be sweet, submissive, and have no desires or dreams of your own. You belong to him. All of this was, of course, supported by Scripture, at least according to The Fellowship. But it was really a setup for abuse.

Leaving the church in 2016 was the hardest thing I've ever done. I have never regretted it, but I had no idea what it would cost me. I lost everything: a church family of thirty-five years, a twenty-year ministry I had started from scratch, and friends that I had raised my children with.

The shunning is real. Although my experience was probably less severe than many, the impact on me was devastating. I only have contact with four or five people from there. To be fair, I did not wish to ever see many of them again. When truth and reality hit you at point-blank range, you can't unsee what you've seen.

In belonging to this church, I had lost my identity, my autonomy, and my voice. Even my body had not been my own; it was only mine to give away, to sacrifice for others. My thoughts and opinions, my needs, didn't matter because I didn't matter. I was only meant to be used by those around me for their goals and purposes. What I had learned at home implicitly, the church taught me explicitly.

Over the next months, I suppose the fact that I left was the talk of the church. Apparently, I'd left because my feelings were hurt. I had been in the church for nearly thirty-five years. Did they think my feelings had not been hurt a multitude of times? No, I left because I was betrayed by my pastor and my church. I left because we'd sought help for our marriage and gotten nothing. I left because my eyes were finally opened to the many inequalities, the narcissism of leadership, the manipulation and abuse of power, and the dismissal of those who were wounded or in need by the system they propagated.

Over thirty-five years, there had been many changes at The Door Christian Fellowship. The earlier years hold many great memories. Even in the later years, there were friendships I valued, memories I cherished. God taught me invaluable lessons, both because of and in spite of the church. I left behind many wonderful people, which has been painful on both sides. I don't blame them; I only seek to expose a system that uses and manipulates others to supposedly win the world for Christ. While it seeks to fulfill this mission, it leaves in its wake thousands of wounded people, many, sadly, who have lost their faith entirely. Many more are still in the church, having their genuine spiritual needs sacrificed on the altar of the ego and success of others. This self-propagating system creates unhealthy leadership, leading to unhealthy churches and malnourished and/or wounded congregants. Jesus said, "But if thine eye be evil, thy whole body shall be full of darkness. If therefore the light that is in thee be darkness, how great is that darkness!" (Matthew 6:23).

For several months, I had driven past a church that was set back from the road and up a hill. I finally googled the name and checked out their website. The elders and staff all shared a brief statement about what relationships meant to them. A church that actually valued relationships? Could it be so? It was close to home, so I visited the next Sunday. I've never put much stock in signs, but that day, I was blown away. One of the songs they sang, "Just as I Am," was a childhood favorite I'd learned when I first gave my heart to Jesus.

The pastor had brought a visiting speaker for the congregation to meet. He would be leading the church for the summer while the pastor went on a three-month sabbatical. I was stunned. What, the pastor is going on a sabbatical?! I thought about when my old pastor had scoffed when I'd said I believed God wanted me to take a sabbatical, even though I was exhausted from all the ways I was trying to serve. Everything in this message seemed to speak to me! It was so unlike The Door in so many ways, so many good and wonderful ways.

The church was part of the Evangelical Covenant of Churches, a congregational-style church. That meant key decisions and positions had to be voted on by the congregation. They also had an elder board that included women. It was their job to care for the church above all else, even before the pastor. This was in sharp contrast to what I'd seen in The Fellowship, church councils made up of yes-men. I'm sure they would disagree; somehow, they just all happened to agree with everything the pastor put out there. Women (and men) here were ushers and in other ministries and positions that they were never allowed in at The Fellowship. And it was the healthiest spiritual environment I have ever found myself in.

I was still very wounded, but I loved this new church instantly. I wanted nothing more than to slip in unnoticed and worship God to my heart's content. But God surrounded me with so many wonderful, loving women and truly genuine people. It was still difficult going to church. I regularly experienced anxiety just thinking about it or actually showing up. I was afraid of being abandoned and rejected again or of being used and taken advantage of. It has taken me years to get past that.

I also struggled with hearing certain Scriptures. I began to question everything. I questioned God. I questioned doctrine and tradition. They had been so twisted; I no longer knew how to evaluate the Word of God. I couldn't trust Scripture or people, and I had lost the ability to trust myself. My world continued to crumble, and I couldn't stop it. At times, it would have been easier to give up my faith entirely.

I am forever indebted to the people of Grace Community Church in Oro Valley, Arizona. My brokenness was evident to all, and they overwhelmingly loved me. My longing heart could not get enough, perhaps because of the relational void I'd experienced for the past twenty-to-thirty years. It has been six years now since I left, and my anger is all but gone, replaced by peace, but my heart still breaks. So many loyal, dedicated people are suffering because it is all they know. I pray their eyes will be opened, yet I know what a bind it will put them in; freedom will probably mean the loss of friends and family.

My husband had gotten a job promotion, so we moved out of town. We were fortunate to find an amazing church, a sister church to the one I had attended in Oro Valley. I like to say I went from Grace (Grace Community) where there was so much grace poured out in my life, to Hope, where I have been challenged to continue believing in the God of all hope!

I also left a long-term career and everything familiar. Everything that had previously defined my life—a career, a church family, a ministry, my home—was now behind me. I have never felt so lost. I knew no one here and had no idea what to do with myself. COVID, along with depression, descended within a few months of our arrival to this new city. The struggles with anxiety and the fear of rejection turned to panic attacks and PTSD that continued for another two years, especially when I went to church. Depression told me I was too broken; there were not enough years left in my life for all that needed to be repaired.

I couldn't hide the mess I was in. This wonderful community saw the worst of me but never turned their face away. I saw myself at my worst with levels of shame and wounding that stretched back to my childhood. It was a difficult time, but with the support of my husband, the church family, and my counselor, I made progress and began healing. It wasn't a linear journey but messy.

Every great revolution that needed to happen began with anger, so not surprisingly, my own personal revolution began with anger as well. Therapy was a lifesaver, and as I began to learn the importance of anger, I began to heal. Anger is the guardian of our hearts that protects us from abuse. We had been taught, "Be angry and sin not," but what they really meant was don't get angry. (See Ephesians 4:26.) We were exhorted to forgive. Yet ownership by those responsible was almost nonexistent, especially from leaders.

I cannot overstate the value of a good therapist. Through hours in her office, she was present. She listened, helping me process years of trauma and piece together a fractured marriage. She sat with me when I cried and, at times, cried with me. She helped me see hope when I felt hopeless, and she brought the love of Jesus to me through her own words. I learned what healthy relationships and healthy churches look like.

For several years now, I have been deconstructing and reconstructing my faith, sometimes with fierce anger, just as often with tears. It wasn't a choice; it was that or abandon it forever and I came very close to doing the latter so many times. I struggled as I tried to untangle who God is from the twisted, angry, disappointed caricature that was presented to me. Some Scripture translations that had once been my foundation now triggered me. I soon discovered *The Passion Translation*, which has been a godsend. To be able to read the Bible with fresh eyes has made such a difference.

As of the writing of this (2023), we have been here three years now, and I am making friends and building relationships on healthy and biblical principles. I overcame struggles and fears related to being in ministry: the fear of being overwhelmed, of having more required of me than I had to give, and of not being able to step back when I was exhausted or just felt God redirecting me. These were all rooted in spiritual manipulation. I am now free to serve and worship God from my heart without all the rules telling me how I should give of myself.

I actually love this church and love to invite people to it because I'm experiencing the healing, love, and purpose that church should provide. I'm can minister and serve in the surrounding community without holding the need to bring people to a decision over their heads or mine. Jesus calls us to love people. That's it! It is his job to both draw and to save them. The best part is that simply in loving Jesus and loving people, He shines so much more clearly and powerfully through me.

Our marriage continues to be renewed and redeemed. We still have struggles because of the faulty foundation we built upon. In the process, we are growing in our own lives, and God is opening doors for ministry to couples. Light is shining through the darkness. I have hope and know that God is redeeming everything. He has always been with me and will never leave me.

We have found a community that values love, compassion, empathy, and authentic relationships. I no longer feel that something is inherently wrong with me. I have never been made to feel that I am too much or not enough. I am exactly who he made me to be. My faith is my own, not one that was handed down to me or forced upon me. Jesus says it is more precious than gold and worth fighting for. I am worth fighting for! We are worth fighting for! And his truth is worth fighting for!

---

1. Brené Brown, *Braving the Wilderness*, (New York: Random House, 2019), 159.
2. "Lexicon :: Strong's G26 – *agape*," Blue Letter Bible, accessed March 3, 2024, https://www.blueletterbible.org/lexicon/g26/kjv/tr/0-1/.
3. The quote is of uncertain origin but was probably first stated at a 12-step meeting where the anonymity of participants is carefully guarded. "Insanity Is Doing the Same Thing," Quote Investigator, March 23, 2017, https://quoteinvestigator.com/2017/03/23/same/.
4. "15 Mind-Blowing Statistics About Pornography And The Church," Mission Frontiers, November/December, 2020, https://www.missionfrontiers.org/issue/article/

15-mind-blowing-statistics-about-pornography-and-the-church.

CHAPTER 9

DEMONS CAST OUT ON MY WEDDING DAY

BETTY

*"Beware of false prophets, which come to you in sheep's clothing, but
inwardly they are ravening wolves."*
—Matthew 7:15

I ran a shaking hand down the front of my white dress; the other clutched my bouquet was a sweaty palm as I waited impatiently. Was everyone this nervous before they got married? I was standing in a room ready to walk the short path that led me down the aisle to becoming a wife, my family surrounding me, waiting in anticipation. Time seemed to go so slowly. Excitement and nervousness mixed, causing a flurry of butterflies in my stomach. Soon, I would be a wife.

I felt like I had waited forever for this day, and it was finally here. I looked around the room at all the people who were closest to me, all there to share in the love of that day. I smiled, so happy. The pastor came in, and the minute he entered the room, tension filled the air. There had already been so much negativity. I did not want anymore, not today. I closed my eyes and prayed for a day filled with joy, peace, and happiness. I wanted my day to be perfect. I wanted everyone to get along for once, and I wanted happiness, not anger. I opened my eyes. The pastor approached me. What would he say?

He laid his hands on me and declared, "Get the devil out!" On my wedding day, he was casting out demons from my body. I could only stand there in shock, anger bubbling in my stomach, but I pushed it down. Of course, he would do that just before I walked down the aisle. We were in a room full of people; my family and my father all stood in shock at what he had just done. My father's fists were white at the knuckles, his anger boiling as he held himself back, knowing that an outburst would only upset me more. Why did he feel a need to do this? Why did he feel like I had demons? I was not one to cause a scene, so I kept my mouth zipped tight as the pastor walked through the doors into the church. I could only stare coldly at his back. I refused to let this bother me today.

I took a deep breath and stepped out into the aisle, a smile spreading across my face as I raised my eyes, preparing to meet my husband. Beautiful, understated blue and white flowers decorated the room for my classic, modest dream wedding, but the church was almost empty. Where were all my guests? How odd, the attendance was so much less than I anticipated. When a wedding occurred at the Lighthouse church, every member was encouraged to come and support the newlywed couple. Yet when I stepped through the doors, there wasn't one member of the congregation there who wasn't an immediate part of it. This was not normal.

They had been told not to attend because even my friends who attended the church weren't there to support me. I had personally invited them, my close friends, and expected them to be there, but not one of them was. This was not a coincidence.

I was walking down the aisle with a heart filled with disappointment that this man, the pastor, had so much control over everyone that he could control who came to my wedding. He could make my close friends not want to show their faces for fear of the backlash they could face. Why weren't these people allowed to celebrate our union like they celebrated everyone else's? I couldn't let this ruin my wedding, but I was hurt that we were being treated this way. I didn't understand why we were so ostracized.

I met my husband in college in California, a true meet-cute moment. I was new to campus and excited to meet people, a young girl full of hope and ambition, trying to further my education. Life felt full of exciting opportunities ready to be grabbed. The day I met him, I attended a study group and was on my way across campus when I ran into him. I was just a stranger who caught his eye; he wasn't letting me pass by. At this time, I felt like I was done with dating, convinced I would never meet anyone in this uncertain California dating scene that I was dabbling in. Yet when this handsome man ran into me on campus, my body and my heart seemed to know that this man was special.

We began to chat, and sparks flew; talking seemed so easy with him. This man would be important to me. I now laugh at the memories. What were the chances that we ran into each other that day? How we met was truly fate, which has a funny way of dropping by. Our story is like something you'd read in a romance novel, but to us, it was real life. We fell so madly in love and now have two beautiful children. We were meant to meet that day, and I thank God every day that we did.

Our relationship became serious quickly, and I soon began to visit my partner at his home. He lived in an apartment complex that the church members ran; the apartments and the complex were filled with all the people who attended the church, just a stone's throw away. He lived with his cousin who was also involved in the church. There were married couples, friends living together, and families. The apartments had lots of rules that had to be strictly followed. The all-male rooms did not allow women in the apartment; we did not know this until I came over one evening. One of the neighbors hung out his window screaming at us, "No women are allowed in the male quarters!"

This seemed extreme. Why wasn't I allowed to visit my partner in his apartment? Many unspoken rules were attached to living in this complex, and everyone followed them closely. Different rules seemed to apply to different people, depending on their position within the church. This was odd, it didn't make sense that one rule would apply to my husband, yet other family members didn't have that same rule. I was not allowed to visit my partner in his all-male apartment because we weren't married. Yet although they weren't married, my partner's friend lived with his partner in their parent's apartment. They were pushed to marry, but it wasn't forced upon them.

My partner's cousin was not allowed to have a TV. Extreme rules were attached to his role within the church, yet my partner's other cousin could own a TV. Again, it seemed to depend on the person's status in the church. Your status determined the rules you had to live by. This and other issues started to seem a little off to me, but I was in love, and the church did not seem like a big deal at the time. My partner wasn't heavily involved in the church, but his family was. So although the church rules affected us, their impact at the time was limited.

When we got serious, I was properly introduced to the Lighthouse Church. As our relationship flourished, we started to attend Sunday service with his family. We didn't attend all the time, but I loved being a part of his family, and going with them seemed so natural and lovely. When I first visited, it felt right. I grew up as a Christian, but I hadn't attended a church for a while, so I enjoyed being back in one. It was cool to be with the family, to pray, and to be in a community again. I didn't have an overwhelming feeling of belonging. It just felt nice. People weren't overly welcoming, but I did feel welcome.

My husband's cousin Tyler found this church while walking along the promenade one day; he met a church member who was evangelizing, trying to recruit new members. Tyler heard an argument; intrigued, he went to investigate. There, he met the man who would introduce him, my partner's family, and, in turn, me to the Lighthouse Church. Tyler was heavily involved in alcohol and drugs, and finding the Lighthouse Church was like a beam of light. Seeing the positive change in Tyler influenced the rest of his family to join the church, first, my sister-in-law and husband's other cousin and, with them, my husband and the rest of his family.

My husband didn't like a lot of the rules that came with joining the church; although Tyler was heavily involved, my husband held back.

When he lived with Tyler, he could see everything they had to do to abide by the rules. They weren't allowed to watch TV, they were only allowed to listen to certain preachers, and any preachers outside the church were strictly forbidden.

They could not consume alcohol, and anyone caught drinking would be severely reprimanded. The environment felt very controlling. My husband sometimes turned on the TV while living in Tyler's home, and Tyler snapped at him, making the whole situation a very big deal. We once saw his other cousin with a beer in his hand, and he freaked out, worrying that he would be caught and the church would find out. This sense of complete control over people's lives just seemed so odd. Why would a church need this much control over its congregation? Surely their private lives were their own.

My sisters-in-law and their husbands attended the church regularly. My husband's other relatives lived in the apartment complex too. They attended the church a few days a week, but Tyler was much more heavily involved, sometimes attending six days a week. The church used him as a pawn, bringing him up to the pulpit, using him as a positive example to motivate the congregation. "If you follow God, you will get a car like Tyler," or "If you commit to God like Tyler, you could have lots of money."

This did not seem right to me at all. If you follow God, you don't just get material blessings from nowhere; it doesn't work like that. But the church massively targeted his family. With their history of drug addiction, they were an attractive pawn in the church's games. The Lighthouse Church looked for vulnerable people: ex-drug addicts, people who served in the military, alcoholics, and the homeless. The church sucked them in and used them as great examples of how the church can turn people's lives around. In many ways, this was positive; they wanted to help and support the vulnerable. But they were only interested in these people if they appeared to turn their lives around. If they resorted back to their old ways, the church didn't want anything to do with them.

When my husband and I first began dating, we faced an extremely strong negative attitude from his older cousin who was dating the pastor's daughter. He had a huge issue with us dating, which was strange. He didn't know me, so why was he so against our relationship? I now realize that this was because I was a Christian from another church (not the Lighthouse). I was an outsider, and looking back, I was always treated as such. The pastor had a large family, and every single one of them was extremely cold toward me. Even after I saw them at many events, baby showers, and family occasions, they always stuck with their clique, singling me out. I never felt welcomed or wanted within their circle.

They didn't treat me this way when I first met them. They were welcoming, but when they learned that I had come from a different Christian background, they began to shut me out. This exclusion wasn't sudden but rather a slow change in how cold they were as they learned more about me. This came to a head on our wedding day.

My husband's older cousin began dating the pastor's daughter around the same time that my husband and I were getting serious. When my husband's cousin wanted to marry the pastor's daughter, there was a huge fiasco over it. When he asked her to marry him, she said no. But with the pastor's influence and his guiding hand, it suddenly became an arranged marriage. It didn't matter that she didn't want to marry him or that she had said no. She had no choice now. She was extremely unhappy with the situation.

The wedding came. From the body language radiating off the two of them, they both felt forced to be there. The wedding pictures looked awkward; there was no love between the two of them, no happiness or eternal joy. Two people came together to fulfill somebody else's will, and everyone could see this. I was dating my now-husband at the time, and during their wedding, others made me feel extremely unwelcome. I was standing with the group, preparing for the photographer to capture the moment. My partner's cousin turned to me and asked why I was in the picture because I wasn't welcomed. I felt hurt and shunned.

But despite all that, I always tried to stay kind. I was excited to be joining a family and build relationships with them. I have always dreamed of bonding with my husband's family, so I wanted badly to make an effort with everyone, form a connection, and become a family. I wanted to welcome my husband's cousin's wife and show her kindness, but she never returned my affection. There was always a coldness about her. She always kept me at a distance as if she had secrets to hide, and she always acted as if she was in competition with me. Bad energy radiated off her as our conversations were just focused on knocking me down. I should have seen this as a red flag, but I never did. I was always kind to her but never received it in return. She seemed set on having a bad relationship with me, and nothing would deter her from this.

My husband's cousin and the pastor's daughter lived together in an apartment complex, but they soon started to have marital problems. This was no surprise since they didn't want to get married in the first place. The pastor began giving them martial counseling and eventually took control of their marriage, keeping them very close under his watchful eye. This was a way for him to control both of them. My husband's cousin was committed to the pastor; the pastor had a hand on him 24-7.

Five years later, it was my turn to get married. I wanted to include the pastor's daughter in my wedding, so I made an effort to make sure she was involved as much as possible. I had a wedding coordinator who was supposed to plan and organize everything, yet the pastor's daughter wouldn't allow this. She wanted to be involved in every detail herself and messed things up on purpose. She told my husband's sister lies about me, trying to pit her against me. She canceled scheduled meetings and had her hand in every decision made about my wedding. She told me that she could always have full control over me and that she was better than me. I got angry. I had always tried to show kindness toward her, and this was how she was treating me.

Before the wedding, the cliques I had mentioned earlier were out in full force. No one was welcoming to my family; they kept to themselves and seemed paranoid of anyone who wasn't a part of their church. We could feel the negativity around us, keeping us at arm's length. It was so obvious, yet my husband's family seemed unaware of what was transpiring. I am not one to cause a scene or raise an issue, so I didn't want to say anything.

But when I look back, this time was an extremely hard time. I didn't fully know what was going on, and I didn't understand why we were so disliked. All I knew was that things weren't right, and I was being pitted against others. Days earlier, my husband's sister screamed at me only days over some sort of issue with the church music, which I had no idea about. I soon learned that the pastor's daughter had gone to her, spreading lies. Now they were all mistreating my family, and I wanted to speak out so badly. But I did not feel like I could do that; I preferred to stay in my lane and keep the peace. But this made me miserable.

This should have been the happiest day of my life, but it felt like everything was being controlled and manipulated around me. They controlled the music we played; of course, it had to be Christian. I chose a classical piece to walk down the aisle to, and they told me I couldn't use it. I had to pick music and flowers that they had agreed to. I wanted a simple bouquet of dark-blue flowers, and they said I had to use light-blue flowers. I would schedule meetings to discuss wedding matters with my coordinator, and they purposely went against everything that I organized. Their total control caused internal arguments between people who shouldn't have even been involved. The people who were most important to me were being shunned. I was so stressed and upset and couldn't do anything about it.

At the wedding reception, my father spoke a Scripture about the husband. "Therefore shall a man leave his father and his mother, and shall cleave unto his wife: and they shall be one flesh." (Genesis 2:24).

The pastor and his wife mocked him. "Oh, you think you know the Scriptures?"

He also mocked me and my husband. He did it in such a way that people thought he was funny and friendly, but he was purposefully mocking us. A lot of people were not happy about our wedding, including the pastor's daughter. You could feel the negative energy throughout the entire day, and in the wedding pictures, you can see their sour, pinched faces. Our union did not please the people of Lighthouse Church.

I didn't know why they couldn't take to me or my family, but on reflection, I was a threat to them. I was already a Christian, so they could not manipulate me because I had grown up knowing the Bible and knowing about Christianity. They couldn't tell me their lies. Maybe they were worried that I would find them out or annoyed that I couldn't be molded into their perfect church member. I will never know for sure, but I did know that they didn't like or accept me.

We lived in Arizona and were traveling to California to get married so that my husband's family could be involved. This made sense to us. We already had a church there where we could be married, and we were close to the pastor. Before we got married, we had to meet with the pastor, and he gave us the book Healing: Commission, Confrontation, and Compelling Witness written by Wayman Mitchell. During this meeting, he began discussing other couples within the church and how he had a file on them all. Why was he discussing other couples with us? He then began to mock my Christian background; it was as if he was joking about my faith. He acted as if I wasn't a Christian prior because I didn't go to church often. There was no reason to bring this up.

The wedding itself was so overly controlled by the church. They wanted to be involved in every single aspect to the point where I didn't feel like I had a say in any of it. It didn't matter to them that we had a wedding coordinator. If we went against anything they said, they made a big deal about it. They said that we needed to go by the handbook.

One big thing that stands out to me about the wedding was a gift that we received. I was staring at the table of gifts from our guests when a statue caught my eye, a large brown totem-like statue, just sitting on my wedding table. It had no name or gift card on it. What did it mean?

My sister-in-law's friend gave it to us; she was heavily involved in the dispute about our music. It reminded me of witchcraft and gave off bad energy. I wanted nothing to do with it. I didn't understand why she gave it to us, and I felt incredibly uneasy. It felt like a threat, so I decided that I did not want it in the journey of our new life, so I left it at the reception. It felt like an angry dig at us, and I didn't like the message it gave me. The whole wedding, although utterly amazing, felt off and strange. It didn't feel like my day. I felt as if I were the main character in someone else's story, and I was hurt that our guests were encouraged to not come.

When we returned from our honeymoon and were back in Arizona, I decided to look through the book that we had been gifted. I then started to uncover all the lies and deceit in it. I started to connect the dots and didn't like what I was seeing.

One thing that I heard about all the time was the concept of arranged marriages. The pastor asked the men who they were interested in, and when the man chose, they arranged their marriage, even if the woman was against it. These women were often really young, just teens or slightly older. This happened in our own family. The pastor's daughter said no to marrying my husband's cousin, yet they still insisted on it. This is crazy to me. The book claims that you can get certain ailments, depending on what sins you have committed. If a woman doesn't obey her husband, she will get ovarian cancer. If you step out of line, then you will get an ailment. This is crazy and doesn't make any sense. The more I thought about everything going on within that church, the more I wanted to stay away. This new distance helped me put my thoughts into perspective, and I made the decision that we would no longer be a part of that world.

We never truly left the church; in a lot of ways, I was never really involved. I was only involved through my husband and him through his family. Although we attended services, we were never heavily influenced by the church, not compared to a lot of his family. So when we moved away, we naturally stopped attending. My husband attended when he visited, but for the most part, we stepped away. So many of my husband's friends no longer associate with us. They don't talk to us anymore or make any effort. It's sad, but that is what happens. None of the church members acknowledge our existence.

When we visit for family occasions, we can feel the awkwardness, the rejection, the quiet hatred that comes our way. We are ignored and isolated; they don't want anything to do with us, which makes these incidents hard to bear. It hurts to be shunned just because you no longer attend a church.

But one of the hardest things that we deal with is the relationship with my husband's cousin and his wife, the pastor's daughter. They have cut us off completely. This is due to her. She always seemed so paranoid around me, like she was keeping secrets. But it hurt my husband that he was no longer close with his cousin who was so important in his life.

I have recently decided that I will no longer travel back to California to be around that church and those people. I am fearful. I have two children; they have family who are still heavily influenced by that church. I am so protective of them. I don't want them to be a part of that life. I don't want them to be subject to an arranged marriage or doing things they don't agree with. But what choice do I have? What control do I have? So I need to cut them off.

As it stands, that life and people have been cut off, but they are still my husband's and my children's family. I don't know how the future will unfold, which terrifies me for my children. I thank God for the distance between us; it gives me some control over my choices, but my husband's family are so heavily involved with the church that I don't know how long it will last.

I often wake up from nightmares, the trauma haunting my dreams. I mainly hold a lot of trauma from my wedding day. I can never get that day back, and I am annoyed and hurt that they controlled so much of it. The more aware I am of everything that is going on, the more anxious I become. My husband's cousin is currently being groomed to become a pastor along with their children who will be groomed into this life, which makes me angry. I want to protect them, but I have no power to do that. I want to protect my own children and I'm scared that I will lose my power. I worry that my husband's family will always be this way.

We have tried to tell my husband's family; we have tried to make them see the truth, but we are told that our words are from the devil. They are taught to say that to anyone who speaks out against the church. At times, the church has taken matters too far with my husband's family so that they question what is happening. My husband's younger sister, my sister-in-law, was removed from her job at the church because she was told it was not God's work. At least the church gave her a home. They grab people and trap them by using financial benefits to draw in their congregation to keep them on their side, to continue to control them, and to build trust. Surely any church that makes sure its followers are housed is a great church.

My husband struggles daily, and some part of him is still attached to that church although he does see the truth more clearly now. He has lost a lot of friends, people he has known since childhood. He has separated from his family. He is still on the fence about everything. When I voice my opinions, he sees the sense in what I am saying, but he struggles: struggles with his family so heavily involved, struggles that he is not close to them, struggles with the rejection from the people he grew up with, struggles with his family's anger. He struggles to accept the truth because that means his life and childhood were a lie. His family still lives a lie. I understand his worries, but this terrifies me. What if he can never fully step away? What if he gets dragged back in and brings my children with him?

Sadly, my husband's other cousin, Tyler, passed away. He relapsed into drugs. One member of the church truly believed that the high control the church had over him played a role in his death. I truly believe that too. When my husband returned to the church in his cousin's memory, the pastor didn't even acknowledge him. This was the man who married us, and he didn't even acknowledge a mourning man in his church.

Tyler was always kind to me. In a family that was often cruel, he was a light and warmth, and it breaks my heart that he was driven down the path that led to his death. Tyler was a huge part of the church and heavily involved in everything they did. He went down to the promenade and preached and sang to draw people to church. He lived in the apartment complex and ran groups. The church used him as a shining example of a great member until he relapsed. Tyler's grandfather needed medication, and soon, Tyler began to take his prescriptions, quickly getting hooked and relapsing. You would think that the church would assist him, help him out of his addiction, pray over him, and support him, but they didn't.

They kicked him out of the apartment complex, leaving him homeless and vulnerable. They abandoned him, which angered us. Why didn't they help him? They used him so heavily in every part of their services and in running the church, yet when he needed them most, they kicked him to the curb. His family tried to help in many ways but were heavily influenced and guided not to do so; they were guilt-tripped and lied to by the church to stop them from helping. They were told not to be too heavily involved with him because the church had severed ties.

The pastor claimed that Tyler didn't want any help, but that was not the case. He died on the street not too far from the apartment that he was kicked out of. I think of him often, and it makes me angry that church damaged him. No wonder. Anyone who lived under the rules of that church would eventually snap from all the pressures they made you live under: not watching TV, not drinking alcohol, living up to such high standards, and being terrified that if they broke any rules, they would be chastised. That would mess with anyone's mental health. Yet when they do snap, the church acts as if they never existed. Even now, after his death, no one ever talks about him. He was used as such a positive influence among the community but has been all but forgotten.

He was homeless because of the church after they kicked him out of his apartment. They used him for years and then kicked him to the curb. They took away his home, forcing him to stay on the street just down the road from where he once influenced a whole congregation.

Surely, he felt utterly rejected by the people he called family. He felt abandoned by his church and by God. I can only imagine his mental state. And then he overdosed and died.

Would that have happened if he had the support of the one place you would most expect it from, his place of safety, his church?

CHAPTER 10
CURIOSITY KEPT ME ALIVE
MARIA

*"That we henceforth be no more children, tossed to and fro, and carried about
with every wind of doctrine, by the sleight of men, and cunning craftiness,
whereby they lie in wait to deceive; But speaking the truth in love, may grow
up into him in all things, which is the head, even Christ."*
—Ephesians 4:14–15

She was standing on the corner, her long blonde hair scraped into a tight ponytail, her blue eyes shining, a kind crinkle appearing in their corners as she tried to get the attention of passers-by, offering them a flyer. She looked like a soldier on a duty call, her face set in determination. Some people just walked past, ignoring her, and others took one without a second glance in her direction, yet her compassion and serious determination never faltered at the ignorance of other people. When someone refused her flyer or threw it away, she simply approached the next person. She continued to hand people flyers and offered a safe space to talk about the church. There was something intriguing about her.

It was just an ordinary Thursday morning; I had just finished a physio appointment and was walking home through the streets of Arnhem in the Netherlands. But this day, seeing this blonde-haired girl on the street corner handing out flyers, changed my life. I only caught sight of her out of the corner of my eye, and before I could even acknowledge her presence, she approached me, a serious look in her honest deep-blue eyes as she handed me a flyer for a Bible meeting. "Have you ever thought about Jesus Christ?"

I thought for a minute. "Yes, yes, I have." I wanted her to know that I had thought about him, and I did know about him.

"Are you sure that you will go to heaven when you die?"

Again, I thought deeply. "No, I can't be sure."

"Have you made a choice for Jesus?" she then asked me.

I wasn't sure what she meant by making a choice for Jesus. I wasn't familiar with this way of speaking. It made me think, have I? I had read the Bible. I knew about Jesus—I understood his teachings and even tried to follow them but not with much success. Still, I tried. I prayed when I really needed help. But had I made a choice for Jesus? How did one do that? I replied to her, I did not know.

"You would know for certain if you had made a choice for Jesus." I scrunched up my face. She continued, "You would know for sure. It is not something you are unsure about. You either have made a choice or you have not."

She must have been right. Whatever this making-a-choice-for-Jesus thing was, I had not done that. I knew about Christianity, but I had been viewing it all from the outskirts without ever truly taking any decisive step or leap of faith. I had just been thinking about it. The girl looked at me with concern. "To go to heaven, you must make a choice for Jesus. You have to let him into your heart once and for all, and when you really have done that, you will know it for certain. You will also know for sure you are on your way to heaven. So you have never made such a choice?"

"I guess I have not, then," I told her. I must not have, or I would know.

"Would you like to?" she asked.

At this moment, a thought came to me. Usually when people address you on the street you tend to walk by. If strangers ask you to do something, you tend to automatically say no. I thought, *What will happen if I say yes? Where would this take me if I took a chance on a kind stranger's words?* So I made up my mind and I said, "Yes, okay. I will make a choice for Jesus."

"Shall we pray together?" she then asked. Pray? Well, I suppose so. When you make a choice for Jesus, that must involve prayer. It seems only reasonable. "Yes, all right."

And so, we said a simple prayer together, allowing Jesus into my heart, for my sins to be forgiven and to change my life. When we were finished, the girl looked at me with a hopeful gleam in her eyes. "Do you feel the peace?"

Feel the peace? This was another new concept to me, and it was not even noon yet! I figured she was expecting me to feel some sort of magic afterward, an epiphany or a feeling of peace wash over me, and truth be told, I did not feel that much. I didn't want to disappoint her, though, so I gave a confirming answer that seemed to satisfy her. She called to a red-haired guy who was passing out fliers on the other side of the street. He came to congratulate me, and while he wrote a few encouraging Bible verses for me on a piece of paper, the girl asked for my address, which I gave her. We chatted further for a little while, and then my new friends continued to pass out fliers.

On my way home, I was reflecting on my life and this choice I had made. I knew I had done the right thing. I had not lived a life that God would be happy about; I hadn't been good and worthy. Even my attempts to be a Christian had not been much of a success. I needed Jesus in my life, and this blue-eyed girl really was on God's business. This choice I made for Jesus was important, something I did not want to lose, even though I did not feel peace. Back at home, I dutifully looked up the Bible verses I had been given and found them helpful. Wanting to know more about my new faith, I headed to the library and borrowed a pile of Christian books.

After a while, the blue-eyed girl and the red-haired guy visited me. He appeared to be the pastor of a tiny new church. They invited me to a coffeehouse meeting to watch a movie, one of those apocalyptical movies. It was called *The Years of the Beast* about the rapture and the end times and how a small group of people who stayed behind became Christians and had a hard time, but God helped them. I liked the movie; it touched me. I might face hard times too, and without God's help, I would not make it. That evening, I called to God and asked for his strength and power, and he answered me. He has been with me ever since.

I didn't have a Christian upbringing; my parents weren't believers. If anything, they were against anything to do with religion. I, on the other hand, was always very curious. I knew quite a lot about the Bible and Christianity and had even read the Bible for myself. I had many friends who were believers and who encouraged me to follow Jesus, so it wasn't totally new to me. From time to time, I had even tried to be a believer myself, but it wasn't until I started to attend this church, encouraged by the blue-eyed girl, that my faith walk became more than a series of trial and error.

It was a tiny church, the first baby church in Holland. It did not look like a church as it was held in a scout center, so it appeared more like a community center than a church. It was a simple place. The church did not own the building. There was a big church in Zwolle, and our tiny church was the first baby church that had been sent out. Church planting, that's what they called it. A bunch of young enthusiastic people attended this church. They wanted to be my friends, and they really did their best to make me feel welcome.

I started to attend the meetings, which I found both helpful and pleasant. I especially enjoyed the coffeehouses and got to know the people of the church a lot better. To this day, I am not sorry I met this blue-eyed girl, and I am not sorry I attended the church. However, I wasn't the model new convert they thought that I would be. A lot was going on in my mind that I wanted to know more about, but I did not feel free to ask the church people. I was not sure how they would react.

I went to the library instead, and I became a regular client at the local Christian bookstore. Not all the books I read were good books. The church people would not have approved of many, but I wanted to explore the information, good and bad. I was curious and open and wanted to learn all that I could. I am also sure they would not have approved of some of the things I did if they had known. Some of my adventures I do not even approve of myself now, while I have absolutely no regrets about other things, such as visiting other churches.

The first months were nice. We had revival meetings with visitors from all over the world: America and other countries. Someone prayed over me, which really helped me grow further. It was all about the basics, becoming a Christian, trusting God, praying, building up your relationship with him, coming to meetings, and sharing your faith with others. At the time, I did not know anything about The Fellowship. All I knew was this little church and all these nice and honest people.

I had never heard about Pastor Mitchell or even knew what the Foursquare denomination was. I later understood The Fellowship in Prescott was still a part of the Foursquare Gospel denomination. It was just before they left in 1983, right before Mitchell took his disciples and newly planted churches out of the Foursquare. I was not aware of any of these developments, though. The denomination was different from today. It was still kind of hippyish, and even though obedience to God was highly valued, they did not have that many rules about clothing or other outward matters. At the first coffeehouse meeting with a rock band, the guitar player had long hair. That would never happen today, which is kind of a pity. He was very nice; he came over to me and asked if I liked his band. I said, "No!"

He laughed and thought it was the funniest joke that someone didn't like his band. I was impressed because I thought he would be offended, yet he just thought it was funny. Maybe I would have been angry if someone had said the same thing to me, but it was totally okay for him that someone didn't like his music.

The girls in the church were also very devoted and helpful. They gave their best efforts to be good friends to me; I have no negative feelings toward them. However, it was hard to be open and honest with them. They knew everything so well. When something bothered me and I asked questions and shared my thoughts, I always felt like I was asking the wrong questions or sharing thoughts I was not supposed to have. I was either snapped at or given an answer that was straight from a book. I once asked something controversial about people who did not know the gospel. What would happen to them when they died?

The girl I asked first took a minute and thought about it. She then took out a little booklet, like an index for complicated questions. She browsed through the book and gave me the answer right as it was printed. At that moment, I thought, *I will never ask you a question ever again*. And I didn't. The booklet was okay, and I even bought one for myself later. But I did not appreciate, however, an answer from a catalogue to my serious question. I wasn't unhappy, but I felt unheard. I distanced myself from them and was even more determined to sort things out between me and God.

I also had some questions about their loud praising and clapping hands during the worship services. I had no problem with it myself, and in fact, I liked it. But some visitors snuck out during the worship service, and others looked uncomfortable. I mustered the courage once and asked one of the girls whether we were doing it right because people were leaving. Were we not supposed to get more people into our church and reach our city for Jesus? The girl turned around and corrected me sharply. "We are not doing this for the people. We are doing this for God!"

I should not have said anything. When she snapped at me, I understand these girls were not the kinds of friends that I could talk to freely and exchange ideas with. They knew everything already. It was their idea or none, and that was the end of any discussions. Yes, we did remain on friendly terms, and I still appreciated the girls, but I no longer confided in them. We got along better if I kept them at arm's length.

So I decided to chat with the Bible Guy who attended my school. We were kind of friends. We sometimes drank coffee together, or I visited him at his home and ate macaroni while he showed me his Bible collection. We talked about Christianity and sometimes even argued a little. He sent me home with a pile of edifying books and magazines about faith. He was a Christian but attended a different church that he was equally devoted to. I was advised by people from my school to stay away from him because he was a fanatic. This just made me curious. If someone says to me, "Don't have anything to do with him," then I become more intrigued.

I wanted to find out more about him, so I did, and I liked him. We were friends and no more. By the time I met the blue-eyed girl, we were not even on the best of terms, for something he had said had upset me, and I had not spoken with him in a couple of months. I still wished to talk honestly about what kept me busy and not just with anyone but with someone who was a Christian too. I decided it was time to lay aside our differences and talk to the Bible Guy again. At least he would not snap at me.

I met him on the way to class and told him what had happened. I had become a Christian and been baptized. I invited him to my place and cooked a vegetarian stew of some kind. He was surprised that his stories, books, and magazines about the Bible had worked out and that I had become a Christian. I felt comfortable around him. I spoke with him about my questions and how I had approached the church with them. We talked about it all, discussing my questions. "What would God do if this happened? What would God think about this? How do you know?"

Some of his answers were like those of the girls', but the difference was that he was thinking about them himself and listening to me. He talked with me like an equal. He also had many questions for me, for he was interested and even fascinated with The Door church. He liked the way they evangelized; he was intrigued by them and wanted to know them better. We started to visit each other's churches now and then. I especially enjoyed the prayer meeting group, hosted by the kindest family I had ever met. The Bible Guy liked everything and everybody at The

Door. Whether they appreciated him as much, I'm not so sure. We finally became great friends, and after a while, we liked each other. We wanted to be together always, and so we decided to get married. The Door people thought that this was not a good idea because he was not a part of our church. My pastor told me bluntly, "This is not God's will."

The only way we could work this out so that the pastor would give his blessing was if my future husband joined The Door Church. So then the question arose whether he would join The Door Church or whether I would go to his church. If I chose to leave and go to his church, the pastor believed that this was completely wrong and that my future husband was stealing me away. At the time, I could not find the right words, yet when I had a chance to process what the pastor had said, all I could think was, "No one owns me. How could someone steal me if no one owns me? You do not own me. I am not your property. If I go to another church that also believes in Jesus, then why is that wrong? I would still be serving Jesus and still belong to him."

We had made our choice, and I was to follow my future husband to his church. He was very happy and active there and had many responsibilities that he didn't want to drop. I was fine with joining them. I thought they were nice and that the church was pleasant. They were just as devoted as The Door, and it was all about God after all, wasn't it?

After a while, we got married in this new church. No church is perfect, and they soon began having problems. Many people left due to some sort of dispute. As a result, we decided that this church was no longer the right fit for us. We could not do what we wanted for God here, so we left. My husband told the pastor we had decided to leave and although he was disappointed, he was not upset. He said, "May God bless you."

All the congregation came up and shook our hands and said, "God bless you in your new church. We hope you will be very happy."

They let us leave with a blessing. The Door Church would never have done that. They had no ill will toward us. We could meet them for coffee any time, no problem. They were a lot calmer than the congregation at The Door Church. We were used to loud praising, clapping, and rock music while this church sang much quieter songs. The whole experience was a lot more soothing. We were used to more enthusiasm, and at the time, I did miss it. Yet on reflection, back at The Door, I began to miss the simple goodness and obedience to God that this church possessed, the love and forgiveness, the openness to leave and come back.

The pastor of The Door Church had been visiting us for a while and asked us, "I have had it in my heart to ask you to come back to our church." We thought that if he wanted us back, maybe there was a good reason for it. Maybe God was behind it.

So we went back, but it was different from the church that I had left. The church had been changing. When we were away, The Fellowship that we now know was born, and that was what we entered. We heard new teachings that we had never heard of; for example, you now had to have a vision, and everyone was calling the pastor, "Pastor" whereas they previously called him by his Christian name. Many new people were attending, which was great to see. The word *discipleship* was introduced to us. The pastor was speaking about the new phase of discipleship; young men becoming disciples. This was appealing to my husband; he liked the idea of learning from the pastor and growing.

But all this made me very uncomfortable. I was more reserved and was paying attention to what was happening, my curious nature still very much in the forefront of my being. The pastor had small children, and they were always yelling at their toddler and slapping her on her fingers. Why weren't they nice to their children? Why were they so angry? I saw more and more behavior like this.

The children were dragged to all the meetings—at least three church services per week and the coffeehouse evening—and their parents never seemed satisfied with how they behaved. The children were always yelled at. I was concerned by this treatment. Would they expect us to treat our children the same?

In the beginning, when there were only the pastor's children, there was no nursery. We met in a Scout club building. The toddler was sleeping on the floor, under a chair. The baby was put in a camping bed in the kitchen behind the meeting room. She was supposed to be sleeping too. And if she was not, she was yelled at or punished.

Sundays must have been heavy and hard days for the little girls. They had to spend all day at church: first, the morning meeting; then, a follow-up meeting to discuss the progress of the new converts; and finally, the evening service. Their mom, the pastor's wife, was supposed to participate in all these meetings. The poor little girls were dragged along, and if they were not quiet enough or they made too much noise or asked for too much attention, well, they were yelled at or punished. I have never seen such awful dads as The Fellowship pastors in Holland.

At times, they allowed their baby to cry until the scheduled time to pick him up and feed him. I was not prepared to treat my children this way; if they were hungry, then I would feed them. I worried that they expected us to treat our children the same way. I was not happy about this. We were then told that we were not strict enough with our children. The natural instinct to love and care for your baby and feed them when they were hungry was used against us. When I asked about it, I was snapped at and told it wasn't my business.

I regretted coming back but told myself that perhaps I need to be patient. After all, Christians should be patient. Maybe it would get better, but it did not get better. It was an extremely hard time. Seeing all these changes made me sad, but I did not see them right away; it took time. Like a slow burn, I was noticing more and more that disappointed me about The Door Church and how they were behaving. Maybe if it had happened quickly, I would not have stayed so long, but it slowly ate away at me, gradually getting worse. This just made me sad.

We were told that if we were good enough, we might be sent out one day to plant a church as part of the discipleship training. My husband felt like he had been called by God; he wanted this so much. But although he didn't say it, I could sense that the pastor did not like my husband through his behavior. His body language was off, and he spoke disrespectfully to my husband. He made snide remarks and often yelled at him. I don't think my husband fully realized that he was not favored, but my husband irritated him. They didn't get along well, and if you don't get along well with your pastor in The Door, you're stuck and won't go anywhere.

My husband wanted to be a good disciple; he wanted to be approved and accepted, and he worked really hard to achieve this. But he was never good enough. Once, he created a drama piece that was good. But he had misunderstood some details that were written in the screenplay and did not do it correctly. The pastor began to shout at him, telling him how wrong he was. My husband just took it. When the pastor screams at you in this way, it's called a correction, and as a good disciple, you must take the correction and the yelling.

And that is exactly what my husband did. "Thank you for correcting me." He bowed his head, genuinely thankful for being shouted at publicly. I found this really hard to watch.

The pastor also didn't like it that my husband had stolen me away from the church. This was a black mark against his name, a disadvantage. My husband came from another church, which was suspicious. He had studied Latin and Greek at school, so he was probably proud too. If you knew anything that the pastor did not, it was bound to blow up your ego and pride. The pastor soon dropped him as a disciple; he became just another church member and received no more training. He did not belong to the inner circle; other men were put first, and my husband grieved over that.

I was secretly relieved, for being a disciple is hard on the relationship as you try to jump through all the hoops to be approved by the pastor, and his approval did not come cheap. During the discipleship meetings or counseling, my husband was often told that our children were not obedient enough and they should be disciplined more. Consequently, when he came home, he was determined to make the children more obedient. So, when he was no longer a disciple, all of us were relieved, the children included. Our relationship improved, and little by little, we became almost as happy together as we had been first.

After we went back to The Door, we stayed for three years. We were extremely committed to going to all services, outreaches, and coffeehouses. We liked these social meetings, preaching, and teachings, so we went as often as we could. I still have fond memories of these positive things and of some helpful pastors who came to visit and preach. But then, there were many negative things that bothered me, such as the attitude of The Door people against any other Christians from any other church groups. They made statements like the following: "Well, they are Christians too but not as devoted as us, and they don't do things like we do."

But it got worse. They made jokes about other Christians and churches, how they were doing everything wrong: worship, church services, and evangelism. It was never good enough. Nearly every sermon included a snarky remark against other Christians or other churches. I found it hurtful. I knew many other Christians from other churches and had good friends who belonged to these churches. I knew it was wrong. I had read the Bible many times. We were supposed to love anyone who believed in Jesus and treat them as our brothers and sisters, not make nasty remarks about them.

The attitude of arrogance bothered me a lot. God cannot bless arrogance and pride. When you think you are the best, that is pride. God has ways of humbling us, and I was concerned when I heard them speak this way about others. They said they were cutting edge and the best while everyone else was lukewarm. If they kept speaking like this, God would discipline them. I was worried because, despite the negatives, I loved my church and the people. I did not want to see them disciplined or humbled. I would rather see them blessed by God.

For three years, my husband never got along well with the pastor. They didn't fight, but the relationship was not good. We knew they would never send us to plant a church, even though that was all my husband wanted. They didn't trust us to do this. My husband had seen the positives of the church and wanted to try them for himself; he wanted to pastor his own church.

My husband got a job in another country in the career he was trained in. It was an amazing opportunity, so we decided to move there. He wanted to start a church alongside his new job, but the pastor was not happy about it. He was angry and didn't want my husband to do this. He wouldn't give his blessing. "I can't stop you from doing this. If that's what you are going to do, then that's what you are going to do. I will not give you my blessing. Goodbye."

So we decided to go without his blessing. I don't know if it was a good idea, but I'm happy we moved. We still live in the same place. But we couldn't try to keep the relationship with The Door, with people who did not appreciate us. We couldn't wait for them to accept us and give us their blessing. But that was what we did. We began hosting meetings as soon as we could. But we had no mentorship or support: physical, emotional, spiritual, financial, nothing. We had to pay our own way and figure everything out on our own.

We asked if we still could come to the conference, and the pastor of the big Zwolle church said, "Yes, that is fine. You are welcome." After a year or two, he even began to invite us along with other pastors. This surprised us because I thought they disliked us and hated the idea of what we were. The first few times we went, others didn't consider us pastors or a proper pioneering couple. They looked at us funny when we walked in. We tried to talk to people, network, and make relationships, but it never worked well. At the third conference, the pastor of the Zwolle church approached us. "You really need to settle matters with your own pastor. Otherwise, I can't help you. You must admit that you committed some kind of violation for moving and creating your own church. Maybe if you do this, then I can help you."

So my husband and our pastor had a conversation. I was not involved; I was never asked. Women are never asked to be involved in anything, although we do stay around to assist. Whatever my husband did seemed to work. They managed somehow to settle their dispute, and from that day on, we were sent back to Finland and accepted as a pioneering church.

To start with, I was ecstatic, yet the very night that it was announced, Greg Mitchell, the main conference speaker and Wayman's son, gave a very weird sermon. He was preaching about spiritual warfare and deliverance from demon bondage, which was all fine and well. Suddenly, however, he made a very strange remark: He claimed that we should release the spirit of peace if there are quarrels and disputes. I almost fell off my chair. This was New Age teaching and not from the Bible. It's true, we do have authority over evil spirits, and we can rebuke demons and tell them to go away in the name of Jesus. But we should not try to do the same with "spirits of peace and love," for such spirits do not exist. Good spirits, which are the angels, receive their orders from God, not from us. It is foolish to release imaginary good spirits, for we have not received authority or instructions to do such a thing. It is dangerous.

I was really upset, and I thought, *Is it never going to be good? First, my husband has had a dispute with our pastor for years and years, and now that is settled. But we hear New Age teaching in our Bible conference. What is this place?* They asked the couples that were to be sent out to come forward for prayer. I did not want to go. My husband almost had to drag me. "Come, honey, I know this was not right, but anyone can make a mistake. We will pray about it, and God will take care of it," he whispered. So he managed to get me to the prayer line.

What this pastor was saying was so clearly not biblical, and it created so much suspicion within me that I started paying closer attention to the sermons and everything else that was said and done. The more attention I paid, the more I noticed that the teachings were not right and not according to the Bible. They were not from God, and they were not healthy. They were, however, dangerously mixed with some truth. It is like eating a piece of meat sprinkled with speckles of glass. You don't notice the harm at first until it cuts your throat. I had to be careful and keep my eyes open. Little by little, I realized that we were not involved in a healthy movement of God after all. Too many man-made and alien ingredients had been smuggled in.

Our new position in Finland, planting our church, and increasing our numbers was nice. We were happy, and our work felt meaningful. We were meeting new people and were a positive influence in our small town. But back in The Fellowship, we dealt with all sorts of quarrels and splits. Many friends left the church because their pastor had split from The Fellowship. We were told that we could no longer have any contact with them. These things were happening more and more often, and although we weren't directly involved, we were expected to take sides. We had to make a choice for our church. They thought the right choice was to choose The Fellowship. So we had to cut ties with people we wouldn't have chosen to cut ties with. We still regret that to this day, annoyed that we complied with everything they told us to do.

The people who came to our church were young, but they were not stupid. Even if we did not discuss the problems in The Fellowship with them, they sensed that something was not right, which put them off. Little by little, they began to leave until we were left with an extremely small number of people. This was difficult for us, and we did everything we could to stop the leak. My husband gave up his job so that he could be a full-time pastor, which he thought was the right thing to do. He thought God would bless that decision, but that was not the case. During this time, we went through a huge financial struggle. The attempt to save our little church from going down had the opposite effect. Nothing was going our way.

We decided to host a revival and invited a pastor from Holland to come and preach a series of meetings. He was our good friend, and he had heard that we were struggling. He knew people were leaving, so he thought that he should preach something radical. A lot of our members struggled to follow Fellowship principles, such as calling their pastor "pastor" and breaking contact with people who had left the church or failing to be over-enthusiastic about the way wedding ceremonies were conducted.

So he decided to preach a sermon on rebellion. It was about obeying your pastor, no matter what, and if you didn't, you would be struck down. You should call your pastor "pastor," and if you don't, you are a rebel. God is only waiting for the right moment to cut your throat (this was illustrated by a lively pantomime). If your pastor does something wrong or sins, you are not supposed to do or say anything about it. He is still your pastor, and if you even lift your little finger against him, God will strike you with leprosy, just like he struck Miriam who criticized Moses.

This mixture of death threats and Bible verses pulled out of context did not deserve to be called a sermon, and the whole experience was just horrible. It was the most terrible sermon I ever heard in my life, and as a result, more people left. I cannot blame them. We shrank and shrank and shrank until, eventually, we were told that we should come home. We should leave our church here and return to the church we came from in Holland. We didn't want to do this; we felt there was no home for us in Holland. We had been here for so long, and this was our home. We did not see any future for us in the Arnhem church, for the relationship with our pastor had remained complicated. I told my husband, "If it is allowed, I might consider going back to Zwolle church. But I will *never* go back to the Arnhem church, and I will never go back to that pastor."

They would not allow us to go to the Zwolle church. So that was the end for us. On reflection, I am not sure what would have happened if we were allowed back at Zwolle. At the time, the pastor who had been at that church for many years and helped us in many ways had been sent to South Africa. Another pastor had taken over the Zwolle church, and while we considered him a sensible person at first, later, we learned that he was doing some very strange things. I am glad we didn't see or experience that.

In the beginning, when we were part of The Door, back in the eighties, there was no dress code. One sermon was about a Bible text that described how horrible it was if a man wore women's clothes and if a woman wore men's clothes. But the pastor preached that this was not about clothes but about the roles of men and women. He said that men should do certain things and women have their role as well. He said that it didn't matter what you wore. Back when Jesus was alive, everyone wore dresses.

As the years went on, however, what you wore became one of the most important topics. Your clothes mattered. If you were part of the disciple process, men had to wear a shirt and tie. At first, it didn't matter what a woman wore, but this has now changed. Now, it is frowned upon if a woman does not wear a dress. These rules about clothing and other outward matters have become more important as the years have gone by. Even now, when you speak to people from The Door, they are creating more and more rules. Each year, a new rule is created, and a new way of living is added to the pallet. It was not this bad when I first joined but just got worse.

During the conferences, they introduced a new guideline and rule that we needed to spread to the church members. In the beginning, there was no such thing as a member of the church. You either came to church or you did not. One day, they told us that now you could become a member of the church; then a year later, they said that if you want to be a member, there were a list of conditions.

A few years before we left, they introduced signing contracts. If you wanted to be an important part of the church, such as run a coffeehouse or lead a group, then you had to sign a contract promising that you didn't do any of the following: own a TV or a VCR, drink alcohol or smoke, and go to movies or the theater. I found this weird. They never asked us these questions because when these rules came out, we were already pastoring. We did not want to impose these new rules on our church, so we just ignored them. We also saw no point in making nonsmokers promise never to smoke or teetotalers never to drink alcohol or anybody promise not to do things they did not do anyway. I saw all the papers. My husband wanted me to know what was going on, even though women were not supposed to know what was discussed in the pastors' business meetings.

One particular point—about becoming an evangelist—was extremely weird. Reading it, all I could think was that these people didn't have a life. This contract instructed people where they should be. During the month, you were supposed to spend three weeks in the field and one week at home, but when you were at home, you had a schedule as well. Everything was regulated: You had to be at prayer meetings at given times, and you were never to miss a church service. These people seemed to be on constant surveillance. An evangelist was not even supposed to take his wife with him if he was preaching in a nearby city. I was not the wife of an evangelist, but I thought, *That is weird. I would never agree to that. If that was my husband and he wanted me to come with him, then why would I not be allowed to go? I am his* wife. *I am not some piece of furniture in the home church.* This bothered me a lot."

Little by little, things were getting worse. The straw that broke the camel's back was the issue with a beard. It was never announced out loud that if a man wanted to be a man of God, then he should not have a beard, but if you had a beard, then you were subject to snide remarks. I don't know where this came from; it was an unwritten rule. My husband grew a beard, and they held this against him when they told us to leave our small church and come home. They ridiculed him because he had facial hair. "You have a beard. You don't shave it off."

We had read the Bible many times; the Bible didn't support the notion that a man of God should not have a beard. After this, we finally realized that we had had enough. This was ridiculous. We don't want to be a part of a church with these types of inane rules. It was nonsense. When we told people outside of The Door about these rules, they laughed out loud, exclaiming how absurd that was. They said it was the most bizarre thing that they had ever heard. So we made the decision not to go back to Holland but to stay here. If we didn't have our small church, then we would find another, but we would never go back to The Door.

Eventually, we did have to dissolve our little church. We encouraged the congregation to go to another evangelical or Baptist church. "There are some great churches in the city. We can no longer keep you secluded here in this little group. We encourage you to go out and serve God, and we will do the same."

I am very happy to say that most of the people from our church that have left The Fellowship are still Christians, and they are still serving God. Thankfully, there are no hard feelings between us. We found a little old-fashioned, traditional Pentecostal church in a small country town. We sing from an old black hymn book; there is no loud clapping or hands raised in praise. Even though we sometimes miss the loud worship services like we had at The Door, this church suits us.

Sometimes I wonder what our friends from The Door church would say if they could see us now. Would they still call us Christians? Maybe, but they would probably call us religious too, and they would call our worship style lukewarm and claim we have lost the vision. They probably would not be impressed by how we serve Jesus or by the people of our church. I really could not care less. If I must choose, I'd rather sing from the old hymn book with them. They are Christians, they believe in God, they tell others about him, they love each other, and they do good works, particularly good children's work. They believe that it is so much better to be at a church and to serve God in any way possible than to not serve him at all. There are no weird rules, no disciple training, no contracts, no dress code, no yelling at us if we do something wrong, no snapping if you asked a question. They are just normal people.

I was always curious and wanted to know why certain things were done. I wanted to understand God and faith on a deep level, and I still do. My curious nature kept my eyes opened and kept me alive. It allowed me to see what was going on in the background, yet even I didn't realize until we left the ridiculousness of what The Door was asking of its members. I do not regret my time there; I loved the members, and they had good hearts. But the church was spreading dangerous teachings in their sermons, and I am happy that I got out. I am happy where I am now, in this small church. I often think of that blue-eyed girl on the corner of the street with her flyers. I am happy I met her and that I stopped to speak to her. I will never regret that meeting.

But I am happy my eyes have now been opened.

ADDENDUM

DENNIS CROSBY

I've spent the last seven years reassessing just about everything. I have a very long memory and have been busy turning over events in my mind. I've discovered an unbelievable amount of material about The Fellowship online, including documentaries going back to the eighties, and have also contacted many people who left through the years. Former members have been complaining about the same things I've witnessed all along, but we've been warned many times not to read negative material about The Fellowship online. I knew better because I also did web development sometimes, but what little criticism I ran into, I dismissed outright. The use of the internet was discouraged, and my efforts to put The Fellowship online were initially met with skepticism and hesitation.

After I left, I started searching for information to try to understand what had gone wrong. At one point, I was starting a Facebook group about The Fellowship, but I found an existing one and joined it instead. It was better than what I was attempting, so I deleted what I was working on and joined Escaping the Potter's House. I've met people there who were members before me, and others have left since. The US, Europe, and Australia are heavily represented, but people join from everywhere. I've met people who knew the same people I knew and people who knew parts of the story I didn't. The familiarity is uncanny. People have had their lives upended time and again through the manipulation of narcissistic, sometimes sadistic, so-called pastors. Same stories, different accents. It's been documented for a long time. A couple of old documentaries about The Fellowship, along with a lot of newer information, are on YouTube. Since the pandemic, ironically, there are a lot of Fellowship videos as well.

Not every Fellowship pastor is guilty, and some are still sincere. But they are all part of a corrupt system, and any Fellowship pastor who knows about the abuses and doesn't expose them is guilty of covering them up. They can call it "covering sin with the cloak of love" to excuse it, but that refers to confessing (exposing) and repenting, not ignoring, denying, and hiding. The Fellowship has been involved in a series of lawsuits, often involving church property. Few people in The Fellowship have heard those stories. Google "Fiji lawsuit Potter's House." Wayman had a truly vindictive streak.

The hierarchical structure of The Fellowship becomes a financial pyramid scheme. It's a business, managed like a business, with contracts like a business. The corruption at the top makes it a corrupt business. Now they're building the same kinds of big buildings they always criticized other organizations for building when The Fellowship first began, and they have new arguments as to why that's okay now. Pastors have been instructed to begin with and emphasize the acquisition of property, which contractually belongs to The Fellowship. The pastor who has to sign the document and fill out monthly reports to the mother church does not own the property. So it's no surprise that leaders who've been around a while have accumulated reserves as a buffer against falling into disfavor, and those who haven't are desperate brown-nosers who can't even hide the fact, because it's career-ending to be in disagreement with someone too high in the hierarchy.

The pastor does, however, control the spigot of the money flow in the local church, although they usually go through someone with the title of treasurer. It's rough on beginning pastors because there's not much in the spigot, but with time and experience, they can comfortably manage an increasing amount of cash. Nobody wants to go back to the old days. It's generally accepted that twice the average wage of the members of the congregation is proper for the pastor's salary, although some pastors require even more than that. Don't be too crazy. Poverty is no longer for successful clergy. How much cash sticks to the pastor varies and would always be a temptation, but few pastors are willing to risk a lifetime career and choose "tact" and "unity" instead and call this "wisdom".

So they defend The Fellowship and blame the victims whenever they can't make problems go away quietly. After all, the whole world conspires against The Fellowship; it's not surprising the internet would be filled with so much slander. That's their standard comeback, anyway. Slander is exactly what Wayman did when he accused the victims of lying. I think Greg Mitchell is even glibber. Anyone who leaves The Fellowship is against God's will and therefore a rebel.

By Any Other Name

Corrupt men corrupting Scripture, devising doctrines to manipulate— this is incredibly malevolent and satanic. It happened in a few short decades, all because of ego. Pride was the downfall of the King of Tyre as well, who is commonly interpreted as referring to Satan himself. (See Ezekiel 28:17.) It's been unpleasant reevaluating everything because I've seen, in addition to the corruption in The Fellowship, that I became corrupted myself. Not in the same way, but in my own way. If it isn't Christlike, it's darkness. When you are surrounded by undiscerning people, it's easy to hide from yourself. I've only begun to realize how cynical I've become. Being in the army also helped foster a cynical view of life, but being in The Fellowship probably made it worse. Still, it's a character flaw that troubles me and does no one any good, other than to get a few laughs due to my abundant sarcasm. (Like a Scott Lamb sermon. There are examples on YouTube.)

Part of being cynical stems from deceiving myself into thinking I was better than most people. I've had that tendency most of my life, but although those lessons also began at an early age, time has taught me that I'm not. My own efforts subtly made me feel better disciplined, more diligent and more critical toward people who didn't seem to be either. I kept the rules better than the pastors, even though I refused to sign anything saying I would follow the rules. The heart is indeed deceitful. But that's more of a symptom. The problem is, I'd become so wrapped up in doctrine, apologetics, and Fellowship nonsense, I was moving away from Jesus by trying harder to work for the organization. I was becoming more like a Pharisee among Pharisees.

Humanity is obviously in darkness. A rational mind can only come to correct conclusions based on detailed, accurate information, but humans have limited senses, and infinity requires a longer time to analyze than our life spans. We don't have long enough to adequately investigate.

This is the real reason people believe that life is relative; if you can't know absolutes, they don't exist. This is further complicated by the fact that numerous groups and countless individuals actively try to deceive to their advantage. Even our own personalities are full of justifications so that we can live with ourselves in public anonymity. Relativism lets everyone get away with what they can. That's how you end up with a world like the one we're in. The Fellowship devised a way to stay busy and feel better without being troubled by study. (Who has time to study anyway?)

Rather than by knowledge and logic, God chose to call his own through three means: his story, history, and the Holy Spirit. I've been running on the wrong track, shooting in the wrong war, arguing for the wrong cause. After thirty-seven years in The Fellowship, there's a lot to unravel. How someone can be so colossally blind to what is glaringly obvious? I've asked that many times. Spending over half your life in a cult because you continued to trust in people who had long since ceased being trustworthy is a special kind of stupid, isn't it? Well, that was me.

I didn't look at what I didn't want to see and stayed too busy to let it bother me for too long. I suppose I might have caught on more quickly if I hadn't moved so much or been sick for so long. But I can't deny that wanting things to be true that weren't had a lot to do with not seeing what *was* true, like the fact that The Fellowship had turned into a cult. Rather than raising my kids in an ongoing revival as I'd hoped, they instead witnessed a cult go over the edge.

The Fellowship covers up for themselves and each other while they blame and slander their victims as well as anyone who stands up to them. They sit in judgment over their congregations and try to regulate everyone's lives. People have been kicked out for going to the pastor with proof Wayman was corrupt. They are guilty of far more than I ever suspected and don't care how disruptive their actions are or how many people's lives they ruin. A string of victims and many others have told their stories online. You can confirm this yourself. They are unrepentant although they can fake a formal apology. They're especially good at blaming the victim. "I'm sorry if you feel like I wasn't fair." What they mean, though, is I'm sorry you feel that way, but you're wrong. God's grace heals all, but presumption and vile pride just won't submit. You can't fix that.

A common denominator in The Fellowship's list of sins is that people cling to power that wasn't given to them. It's how The Fellowship split off from the Foursquare with all who followed Wayman's schism, and it's how The Fellowship has subsequently tightened its grip on those who stayed because of those who left. The claim that they have authority over people's lives is false. They do not. They try to claim God gave authority over you to your pastor and that you must do what your pastor says. They falsely claim that God honors obedience even when the leader (and command) is wrong.

Mislabeling anything that casts a negative light on the organizational leadership as criticism is brainwashing. This has been reported to include intimidation on the part of zealous supporters of leadership. Righteousness isn't even a consideration in how they behave. The degree to which leaders are defended closely resembles taqiyya, which is a Muslim practice of self-protection due to the fear of leaders.[1] The leaders can't ever be wrong, and The Fellowship has to be protected.

Manipulation is justified to keep people on the right path as they have assessed that path to be. As God's appointed covering, they think they are responsible for doing what is necessary. This is a convoluted doctrine that encourages pastors to attempt to assert authority over someone else for their own good. This cuts both ways because pastors actually feel responsible if someone shipwrecks, but that triggers the "look for someone else to blame" reaction. Vicious circles abound where people are labeled witches. The Fellowship has long characterized opposition as satanic (*satan* means "adversary"), and dissension is already characterized as rebellion which dovetails nicely with the following verse to assert witchcraft is being used against them.[2] "For rebellion is as the sin of witchcraft, and stubbornness is as iniquity and idolatry. Because thou hast rejected the word of the Lord, he hath also rejected thee from being king." (1 Samuel 15:23).

Multiple embellishments are possible, depending on the unrest in the church. Truth doesn't really matter to them if a statement produces the desired effect. A visible sign of behavioral change is the only assurance they have of control over you. Effectively, they preach Fellowship propaganda—not the Bible, not the gospel, not Jesus. Mitchell wrested control of a group of churches and taught their leaders that control of their churches depended on "keeping people too busy to get drunk." They invented doctrines and adopted those invented by others to get people to accept that degree of control. They were anti-tv, anti-internet, anti-outside influence forever until the pandemic threatened their grip, and then they began live-streaming. Now you can even donate online. Suddenly they're posting online, and many churches are even on Facebook. However, Scott Lamb has preached very harshly against Facebook. I guess they didn't watch that video. My wife found a flyer after the last conference with Fellowship T-Shirts available to order. Someone left it in the hotel where the pastors had been staying. They're contradicting themselves everywhere.

It took this for me to see, in spite of my wishes, in spite of what I believed, that The Fellowship leadership, organization, and structure is irredeemable. Seeing their indifference to truth, being in the hospital, my last conversation with a dying friend, and too many good people leaving the church all brought me to this conclusion. Everybody in The Fellowship needs to find a new church. Many already have. I left because I couldn't stand what they'd made of it. It's taking a bit longer to see what I had become in that environment.

Of course, some people—not everyone—don't want the responsibility and are glad to have someone decide everything for them. Certainly not nearly as many as The Fellowship expects.

Children growing up in The Fellowship are encouraged to seek counseling, and talking to a leadership figure like the pastor makes them feel important, so they quickly look for advice about everything. This turns out wrong in too many ways. People don't realize that some pastors (not necessarily the majority) in The Fellowship keep notes on counseling. Valk's notebook from Amersfoort became a hard drive directory in Zwolle. He left his second daughter in charge of it, although I doubt she knew what was on it.

Mitchell started out with a vision. Whether it was literal as I once thought or merely metaphorical as it now seems, the vision was the goal, and Wayman departed from it. He became a control freak after 1990 but had already been maneuvering behind the scenes, absorbing the original Fellowship into his collection of churches and using it as a framework to build the structure of his new empire. He didn't talk openly about that, but I think that's what caused churches to split off, usurping power.

Even the wording of The Fellowship bylaws prior to and after Wayman seized control show how fundamental this shift had become. It went from a "fellowship of like-minded churches cooperating in world evangelism" to reducing the pastors to "stewards of local churches" that belonged, with their property and members, to The Fellowship.

I had wondered when the name Christian Fellowship Ministries (CFM) first started popping up in the eighties, "What's wrong with The Fellowship?" The Fellowship described perfectly what the churches were, and suddenly, it changed to this bland-sounding Christian Fellowship Ministries, logo, and even talk of church membership. Now I know it was the result of a business merger.

As I mentioned in the introduction, Wayman was over Foursquare churches in Arizona. He later left Foursquare, and The Fellowship became Christian Fellowship Ministries. The tax exemption had been signed over to Wayman. I was never told any of this and only learned about it online after I left, although I'd talked to Silver Gaddis (from the original Christian Fellowship Churches) when he visited Zwolle while we were still at the *Blekerswegje* address. I didn't know how he fit in at the time.

Wayman became obsessed with keeping what he obviously felt was his, in spite of what he preached about "God's work" and "God's church." He appointed men who would be loyal and, increasingly, men who were dependent on him, propping them up after their own failures, for which they would remain grateful or lose everything. He recycled people most organizations would've expelled. Frequently (more frequently than you'd expect), pastors were caught in "moral failure" and reassigned (redirected is the Potter's House term) to another church. They tried to recycle Evert Valk too, but he had become too great a liability after too much publicity and that he even lied (and was caught) to Nomdo Schuitema. These were the kinds of people who become fierce defenders of Wayman, who could make them do whatever he wanted.

And of the people he couldn't manipulate, Wayman became increasingly suspicious. Wayman also instituted the pastor's contract, which placed every single thing in a church building, including the members, into Wayman's hands. Any pastor in conflict with Wayman could see his career end with a phone call. In so many words, Wayman said that God placed you in this Fellowship and if you leave The Fellowship, you leave the will of God.

If you were deemed a troublemaker who asked too many questions, you were to be expelled from the church, because in that case, you weren't placed in The Fellowship by God but planted there by the devil. One pastor called Valk, who called Wayman, who said about a certain woman, "Kick her out." Mitchell based his on only one thing: the kinds of questions they said she was asking. It turned out she was only reading a book by Andrew Womack and asked her pastor what he thought about it. And she wasn't alone—other people were kicked out after asking questions their pastor couldn't deal with. That's how much authority they wielded and how little they cared about people who were in the church before the pastor and his pastor, even as that woman was. And how many had been kicked out? After I left, I contacted many people I'd wondered about to find out why they left.

"You have to pay tithes to The Fellowship, otherwise you are robbing God, and he may kill you for it." I always thought this was hyperbole, but I have a video of Wayman Mitchell and another of Scott Lamb preaching just that. Fundraising had to keep up with expenditures. This also gave them justification to define generosity as more than 10 percent.

Oddly enough, Wayman Mitchell's own sermon about "the old prophet and the young prophet" clearly contradicts the teaching of obedience to your pastor, no matter what, but he did preach that sermon in spite of also preaching you must obey your pastor. Ironically, Wayman himself is the only person I ever heard preach that you should listen to God and ignore what the old prophet says, based on 1 Kings 13:11–32. In this passage, the young prophet listened to the old prophet and died as a result.

One of the vilest practices that has crept into The Fellowship is playing family members off one another. If someone leaves the church, everyone else in the family is encouraged to remain and, if necessary, sever ties with the rebel. My own son was counseled to find someone else in the church to look to as an example because I was a rebel.

But my wife, oldest daughter, and her husband left around six months after me, and my son left the following year. My son had actually asked me and my oldest daughter for a list of reasons as to why The Door was wrong and went to Nomdo Schuitema for answers so he could refute us. In his blundering arrogance, Nomdo's response led to my son leaving instead.

I still have one daughter in the church, and her husband threatens to leave during visits if we talk about De Deur. You can't listen to criticism. It is self-imposed mind-control of whatever makes you doubt leadership. It's too hard to reconcile the criticism with the narrative, so you avoid criticism. Ignore what doesn't fit, and what doesn't fit in The Fellowship has accumulated exponentially.

Paul Stevens' son preached a sermon after his father kicked him out of The Fellowship and tried to give his church to Paul's grandson. He correctly pointed out a particular word for this in Greek in the New Testament that describes this trait as one that will grow as men become more corrupt. This is the definition of the Greek word ἄστοργος (astorgos): "a presumed derivative of στέργω (stergō) (to cherish affectionately); hard hearted towards kindred: - without natural affection."[3]

Wayman refused to go to his own daughter's funeral after she and her husband left The Fellowship and expected no less from anyone else in The Fellowship. Paul Stevens has recently demonstrated that he's living up to this with the way he's treated his own son in a sermon you can find on YouTube.

These leaders in The Fellowship are demonstrating a character trait that the Bible presents as a diagnostic as to the extent of corruption that humans can descend to. And they encourage others to do this as well. In many posts online, people complain about this, and it's actually one of the most common complaints—the wedge pastors actively try to drive between family members. They are not only "without natural affection"; they actively try to extinguish it.

One of the last sermons I attended at *De Deur* was a farewell sermon by one of the young people in the church who was about to be launched out for the first time to pioneer in another city. I had taken baptism photos of his parents and had known his family for a long time. He preached about the warnings to the churches in Revelation. Wrapping up, he actually said that Zwolle didn't suffer from any of those shortcomings, implying that the church was perfect. At that, I immediately thought of Ephesus. Actually, the word *Ephesus* seemed to scream inside my head from the passage in Revelation. "Nevertheless I have somewhat against thee, because thou hast left thy first love. Remember therefore from whence thou art fallen, and repent, and do the first works; or else I will come unto thee quickly, and will remove thy candlestick out of his place, except thou repent." (Revelation 2:4–5).

Observations, Conclusions, and Other Considerations for Current Members

The Fellowship reads into the text what they want it to say. Unfortunately, this is how they approach the Bible. They only use the Bible to convince people they should do what The Fellowship teaches. Expository preaching is rare, and eisegesis is really their whole point. They use whatever translation best supports what they want people to believe. Citing alternative views is only done as a contrast to clarify "what we believe," and "what we believe" is always God-inspired.

Pastors become afraid to deviate from what Prescott teaches and care more about what others are preaching than what the Bible actually says. With very rare exceptions, none of them have gone to Bible school and for many, being sent out was their best career option. Over the years, many have ended up with no other job options, and Christian Fellowship Ministries owns them now. They are the blind misleading the blind, too often with malice, but they think God gave them the right to do what they believe.

Some people, usually people still in The Fellowship, don't understand what the problem is. They say, "We still get people saved, healed, and delivered." That's what they call it, but is that what happens? They hold a rally and get someone to answer the altar call and repeat the sinner's prayer—but is their life changed? Honestly, in The Fellowship view, there isn't much hope for someone who doesn't lock in because to them, the change that counts is the adaptation of the habits and mannerisms of The Fellowship. Christ didn't die for that.

I actually got to the point that I didn't want to evangelize for fear that someone would get saved and I'd end up taking them to a Fellowship church. I honestly didn't want that on my conscience.

Healed? For his last twenty years, Wayman always asked, "Is anyone here sick in their body who has been saved six months or less and you need prayer? Come to the front." Six months or less? Does faith fade quickly in The Door? Observing corruption erodes confidence, so maybe it does.

Delivered? People are delivered into a system of doing what the pastor says because that's God's will for you. He knows it because God talks to him. God doesn't talk to you. You're not anointed. The Fellowship doesn't deliver people except into indentured servitude.

The Fellowship isn't God's will; it isn't the church spoken of in the Bible although they use *the church* to mean The Fellowship, which Greg says is God's plan. They teach constructed doctrines because they tinker with Scripture. These doctrines seem to be derived from Bible passages, but they conflict with what the Bible teaches. They don't do what the Bible teaches but distract people from Bible teachings with all kinds of other activities: rallies, revivals, conferences, coffeehouses, services, and outreaches. Keep busy, don't think. Volunteer to paint the church, and let's arrange a pot-luck to celebrate how long our current pastor has been here. We have a franchise to run.

Wayman loved to preach about the common sense of the business world. He imposed the suit and tie standard early on and openly opposed beards, usually successfully. He credited his education to the Columbia Book club subscription he always canceled after getting his free books.

I always intended to learn Greek, and kept returning to it through the years, progressing slowly. After my cancer operation, I quit all the opiates, and my mind cleared up. I started focusing on Greek to the point that I stopped reading other translations. I started following the sermons using the Greek texts, and I saw that the Greek wasn't supporting the arguments being made on the basis of certain translations.

In fact, Fellowship doctrine started to seem as though it were based on a very slippery slope. The translation of a given passage may seem okay according to what The Fellowship taught, but that meaning seems unlikely, given what is actually written in Greek. And no one seemed to care.

Since leaving The Fellowship, I've gone to a whole new level of studying the Bible. I decided to read it for what it says. So far, I've copied all but five books of the New Testament by hand in Greek, like a scribe. I recommend it as a method of careful study. It makes you appreciate what's involved, what mistakes can be easily made, and somehow, when you're paying attention to spelling, you pay more attention to what is being said.

I am now aware of a completely different understanding than what The Fellowship teaches, an understanding of passages, not just verses. The interplay of words shifted my perspectives because translations just can't capture everything that's there. A consideration of longer passages also makes you follow the reasoning and the train of thought of the argument being presented—Paul isn't the only one who builds his arguments over larger portions of his writing.

I also realized that it wasn't just The Fellowship that was wrong, but I'd taken the Bible out of context myself. This was highly confrontational because I saw that while I thought I had been doing well, I hadn't been doing well at all. Fellowship teaching had distracted me from what the Bible teaches.

The Bible is inspired by the Holy Spirit, and the Holy Spirit still reverberates with what it says as long as you don't try to make the text say what you want. Each detail of biblical knowledge sharpens the resolution of the whole image because everything is interconnected. In that sense, it is holographic yet dynamic, which is what you'd expect of a Being which is Spirit, Light, and Life, unrestricted by time and space. The truth is a lot different than the game being played in Fellowship churches. The most amazing thing is, I knew this, but I'd forgotten. I had gotten distracted, busy, and lost my focus from what I had known in the beginning, which in the end was still true.

I can no longer focus on the doctrines and methods or activities of an organization.

The Fellowship hides the truth; it makes them look bad. They don't follow the Holy Spirit but instead have become manipulative and even malicious toward people in the congregation, not generally in the open but often during counseling. They don't follow the Bible but quote selected passages at length to argue that they are right. God's Spirit is not present in the counseling sessions with the pastor when he is trying to manipulate and demean someone. They didn't consult God or the Bible. What have they got to say worth listening to?

Aside from covering up their own misdeeds, the worst thing might be what they do with families. They drive wedges between family members to keep everyone in line but also encourage marriages between couples in the church to send out and start a new franchise. They tried turning my family against me when I left. The leadership has condemned themselves beyond what I could add.

But that brings me to the worst part. The Fellowship teaches a certain unbiblical standard that masquerades as sound doctrine (with a few idiosyncrasies that are explained as superior). This is called Fellowship standards or Fellowship Principles. The Dutch name sometimes used is Fellowship *voorwaarden*, which means "conditions." It's all a decoy, a distraction, and puts a barrier between you and God. If you follow their rules, you'll end up feeling like you've done better than someone who doesn't, even though the rules are arbitrary, superficial, and meaningless.

Paul minces no words telling the Galatians how foolish that path is, and thinking you're better than someone else is biblically ridiculous. If you're lucky, one day you'll wake up and realize you are a Pharisee, one among many. If not, you'll continue on that path without realizing it. The Fellowship plays the same game the Pharisees did. If you want to go through the motions and be religious without being transformed by God's Spirit, Christian Fellowship Ministries is the place to be. It's an atmosphere of assumed superiority, disdain for the untidy and uninitiated, and a mockery of other organizations and cynicism about humanity. That rubs off on you over time.

I'm not saying being in The Fellowship will make you cynical, but you certainly won't stop being cynical either. You can rise up in ministry and still be a jerk if you shave, smile, and wear a tie. Throw in some actual people skills, and you've got a bright career without changing your character at all as long as you kowtow to the right people. It's a waste of time! And in my case, decades. The Fellowship is set up in a way that harbors unregenerate ideologues but doesn't value discernment or understanding because they preach the authority of the pastor. They didn't in the beginning, but they were structured differently then too.

If The Fellowship wasn't full of the wrong spirit, why is there so much gossip? Why do good people leave? Why are people who've left always called rebellious (or "unable to maintain the level of commitment The Fellowship expects" as they like to word it. They also ignore the valid reasons people have left through no fault of their own). They have always made fun of people who say The Fellowship doesn't have enough love. Why is that?

"But the fruit of the Spirit is love, joy, peace, longsuffering, gentleness, goodness, faith, Meekness, temperance: against such there is no law." (Galatians 5:22–23). That doesn't sound much like The Fellowship, does it? If these stories aren't true, why do people from all over the world have the same kinds of stories?

---

1. Matt Stefon, "taqiyyah," Britannica, accessed March 3, 2024, https://www.britannica.com/topic/taqiyyah.
2. "Lexicon :: Strong's H7854 - *śāṭān*," Blue Letter Bible, accessed March 3, 2024, https://www.blueletterbible.org/lexicon/h7854/kjv/wlc/0-1/.
3. "Lexicon :: Strong's G794 – *astorgos*," Blue Letter Bible, accessed March 2, 2024, https://www.blueletterbible.org/lexicon/g794/kjv/tr/0-1/.

TERMINOLOGY

Accountability

The teaching that the pastor has a right to meddle in your life.

Amen

Normally a statement of affirmation, it is a reflex expression of agreement with the speaker.

Altar call

A phase usually at the end of a service where the speaker addresses the audience and tries narrowing the set of addressees to people he can persuade to come to the front of the room and pray. Responding is seen as submission to the challenge of the address, which was presumably related to the preceding sermon.

Authority

The right or obligation to do something or instruct others to do something. The Fellowship falsely claims authority in all kinds of areas and use it as a basis for controlling members' lives.

Backslider

Someone who used to be involved in the church, but no longer is to the degree they previously were, if at all.

Baby church

Any church founded and supported by an older church (the mother church).

Bible conference

Semi-annual gatherings at the Conference Church, depending on which church is in charge. These last a week and consist of seventeen sermons, repeated shake-downs for more money, a film, some people singing and two evenings when couples are called on stage where it is announced what city (or country) they will start a new church in.

Biblical standards

What The Fellowship traditionally calls their made-up rules, especially related to dress and behavior.

Bitter

One of the residual effects of encounters with The Fellowship. Ironically, current members have been taught it is a symptom that confirms that the person is wrong for leaving when the assorted post-traumatic effects resulting from the experience in the cult should be seen as a warning to stay away.

Blessings

Perks of godly living as described and endorsed by leadership.

Born again

In Fellowship usage, your passage to heaven has been confirmed. Properly, it refers to the passage in John 3 in the New Testament where Jesus, in a discussion with Nicodemus, declares that you "must be born again" to enter the kingdom of heaven. Literally, it says "born from above," but the King James Version has influenced the terminology. This has been commonly equated with saying the Sinner's Prayer in evangelical circles.

Calling

Biblically, God inviting an individual to do something for which they are suited, often uniquely so. This is different than the common secular idea of being spectacularly good at something or hopelessly compulsive about something. It is also different from The Fellowship pressure to join the franchise.

Called to (fill in ministry)

Selection by Fellowship leadership to perform some task.

Carnal

Deviating from Fellowship standards, especially when your own needs and interests are given a higher priority than church activities.

Church planting

The cult is metastasizing. The term is based on the idea of sending a couple to pioneer a Fellowship church in an area where one does not currently exist, which is ideally subsequently supported financially and with impact (evangelism) teams that are intended to bring local potential converts into contact with the new pastor. This is usually also accompanied by an advertising blitz.

Covenant

A really strange made-up doctrine that you are bound to The Fellowship. This applies especially to pastors. It seemed to pop-up out of nowhere with Wayman's imprimatur when it first came into prevalence around 2007.

Discernment

The ability to distinguish between evil and good intentions.

Discipleship

Wayman's on-the-job pastor training methods utilized by all franchises to train potential new management. A disciple is the term used for pastor's gopher.

Demonic

Involving demons and demonic activity, e.g., contradicting a Fellowship pastor

Dynamic

In Fellowship usage, usually, not boring.

Evangelism

Demanding attention of a preferably captive audience to loudly recite or present a printed copy of your creed. When done in public, exotic, or notorious places, this enhances the person's status.

Follow up

Refers to new converts. Methods to confirm and strengthen the level of indoctrination in recently new contactees of a Fellowship cult member.

Gathering dirt

Collecting, categorizing, and verifying evidence of past or present crimes and cover-up attempts.

God's economy

Wayman's obsession with the business world reflected in his choice of illustration about the Kingdom of God, symbolized as a large prosperous household. *Economy* refers to *oikos* + *nomos* "*house* + *law*" (but the Greek compound *oikosnomos* means *steward*).

Grandbaby church

A church founded by a church founded by a church.

Heavy shepherding

A heresy adopted by The Fellowship from the wider church world. It involves micromanaging the lives of members of the congregation and all the abuse that flows from that.

Headship

The idea that someone is in charge of the people who are in charge of you.

Locked in

Locked in refers to a person reaching the point that they enthusiastically support the goals of The Fellowship and participate in church activity. It usually follows becoming convinced that the teaching of The Fellowship is more valid than the competition.

Jesus-people wedding

A Jesus-people tradition where the weddings are simple and the occasion has been adapted to recruit potential new members, especially family members.

Jezebel spirit

Biblically, a dominating evil woman. Fellowship-wise, a woman or women whose influence threatens the hegemony of Fellowship assertions.

Matriarchal spirit

While the meaning isn't clear, it appears to be a good insult in Wayman's mind.

Ministry

The activity of the elite or the tasks the elites assign to you.

Manifest

Apparently supportive.

Moral failure

Anything a pastor (or his wife) is found guilty of, or suspected of, that the Bible condemns, that is considered grounds to replace them. An adulterer's homecoming.

Miracle

God's endorsement. There aren't that many anymore, so close counts.

Mother church

A church that founds another church.

Outreach

Going somewhere else with the official rap.

Pastor

The Fellowship use of the word *pastor* is an amalgam of every New Testament Ministry, with the exceptions of apostle and evangelist. Apostleship has been attributed to Wayman, but it was a really good batch of Kool-aid. Evangelists, ironically, are nearly always failed pastors these days, with some exceptions. The Fellowship also regards passages referring to bishops (overseers) and elders (presbyters) in the New Testament as also referring to pastors, who are considered authoritative leaders in every church. Anyone disagreeing with the pastor is a rebel, and the proof of this is drawn from Old Testament passages about kings and prophets. Fellowship pastors sit on thrones and preach about sacrifice. All ministry not from the pastor must be sanctioned by the pastor. Women can't do anything unless they're married to the pastor, in which case they sometimes run everything, but only behind the scenes.

Pioneer

The act of moving to another city or country and attempting to establish a Fellowship franchise where one does not currently exist. Also, someone who has done so at least once, or is currently in the process.

Powerful

An emphatic similar to "very" or "way more". A superlative reinforcer.

Praise

To speak highly of, especially to speak highly of God. Also, a phenomenon of enthusiastic, joyful expression of the greatness of God. In Fellowship usage, an interval, usually less than two minutes unless following an offering (money collection) or an altar call (soul collection), in which tongues-a-la-Prescott and standard rote phrases continue until it ends.

Rebel (noun)

Someone who doesn't agree with leadership, especially an ex-member. The Fellowship definition is replete with references to Old Testament events where people who opposed prophets and kings were severely judged. Since The Fellowship defines the authority of the pastor using Old Testament passages referring to kings, they inherently assume the behavior of kings and banish dissenters.

Rebel (verb)

To contradict, ignore, or disobey the pastor.

Reprobate

The Fellowship uses this word to indicate unsalvageable resistance to Fellowship teaching. Actually, they have no idea what the word means. It means *reject*, more or less, and has its roots in the results of assaying precious metals.

Resistance

Hesitance to whole-hearted acceptance of whatever teaching the pastor is spewing from the pulpit.

Step up

To fill in empty ministry spots, assume responsibility to fulfill a role no one wants without regard to the aversion you feel.

Sinner's prayer

A specific prayer with these words: "Jesus, I admit I'm a sinner. Thank you for dying on the cross for me. Forgive me and save me from my sins. Amen." A lot of churches believe saying this is enough to go to heaven. Some believe you have to mean it and live by it as well. Others see it as an attitude that has to be maintained, and many wonder where it came from. It's not in the Bible anywhere but is considered mandatory in The Fellowship. Saying it confers the status of being "born again," whether or not a change takes place in someone's spirit.

Slain in the Spirit

When, as a result of being prayed over, or more often touched, a person falls over. This phenomenon is attributed to the Holy Spirit. The Fellowship has distanced itself from the practice, although it enjoyed some popularity in the late 1980s.

Spirit of X (rejection, illegitimacy, etc.)

A diagnosis according to Wayman's crackpot pray-for-what-you-can-name method of praying for the sick. Spirits are behind all difficulties and usually sins of the suffering gave the spirits access to the individual. Wayman's solution was to get the individual to confess whatever they could be persuaded to confess and then repeatedly assert that the spirits' access had been canceled. Very similar to what occurred in Australia when an accident killed four police officers.

Standards

Law part 2, according to the council of Prescott.

Submission or submit

Acquiescence, especially to Wayman's (or his representative's) supplemental guidance.

Supernatural

Events, beings or phenomena that exist or operate outside the laws of science but nevertheless appear to affect the physical world.

Tithe

The belief that 10 percent of your income should be given to the local Fellowship church you attend. Always seen as mandatory in The Fellowship, it became a diagnostic fairly early, determining your sincerity along with attendance at all events. Outside the Fellowship, some churches believe it, some don't, but few preach that you'll "go to hell" or "that's how you keep God from killing you and your family." However, The Fellowship does teach this.

Vexing spirit

Anything that troubles you, especially if it persists. It is intentional and the fault of a spirit that wants you miserable. While such things may exist, they are probably not responsible for the abundance of misery ascribed to them by Prescott papacy.

Witchcraft

This is the most common translation of the Greek word *pharmakeia*, which has at its core the idea of manipulation and deception and is the source of the English word *pharmacy*. For this reason, many people conclude that it means drugs. In context, however, manipulative deception is a broad definition that seems to fit the instances when the word is used. It is also at the core of what The Fellowship leadership does. They manipulate church members in a variety of ways for their own purposes, employing false doctrines. Witchcraft is a common Fellowship method, especially in the face of resistance.

A word

When a leader (a pastor or more often an evangelist) calls out someone in the congregation, usually publicly, and says what God has told them to say. It usually mentions a problem or area of struggle area for the person being singled out and ends with something encouraging and often a promise. Sometimes time spans are given for when it will be solved and, in some cases, conditions, i.e., "If you'll get a hold of God and read your Bible and pray," or "If you'll believe God and start paying your tithes."

World evangelism

Opening franchises in foreign countries to repeat all the things that are wrong with The Fellowship.

APPENDIX I

1. The Christian Fellowship Church is a loosely affiliated group of churches tied together by a common bond of vision and relationship. There is no legal structure holding any congregation to the others. These congregations are not sub-ordinate units but are totally autonomous and responsible for their own affairs and financial obligations. Any oversight is purely relational and functional, not legal.

2. All pastors licensed by the Christian Fellowship Church are given this privilege because of a common bond of vision and ministry based on his qualification and training in a Fellowship Church, recommended by his pastor. Other ministries previously trained and qualified by other like minded ministries may be licensed from time to time.

3. According to The United States Constitution and Internal Revenue Publication #557 (Rev Jan. 1982), any church organized according to chapter 3, page 8 and page 13, Section 501 (c) (3), are automatically recognized as a tax exempt organization and all contributions are automatically exempt from tax by the donors. These are recognized as churches and are not obligated to file Form 1023 to obtain this status. In other words, any church duly organized and fulfilling the 5 basic requirements that constitute a church has the right to operate without any of the formal religious corporation structure that is generally belived to be necessary to gain recognition with the I.R.S. and give tax exempt reciepts.

4. Here are the 5 requirements which need to be stated in a minimum constitution for your church.

    1. Exclusively for religious purposes, church will be governed by officers including a secretary and treasurer, an annual business meeting to he held and accurate records kept.
    2. No part of the proceeds to inure to the benifit of any private individual. All property to be held in name of church.
    3. No substantial part of activities are which is carrying on propaganda or otherwise attempting to influence legislation.
    4. The income to the church to be from free will offerings and gifts.
    5. Upon dissolution all assets will be given to a tax exempt religious or charitable institution or religious organization or church.

5. You are not required to file the yearly form 990 if you are operating as a church. In some states there are varying requirements for reports to the state if you are incorporated in that state on a yearly basis, by the state itself.

6. All churches entering into a real estate purchase and some leasing agreements for vehicles or buildings will be required to have a State Corporation before they can contract financialiy. It is advisable that churches of some size should incorporate for these purposes.

7. All churches are required to have an employer I.D. number. This can be obtained by application #554 obtained at any IRS office. After application you will recieve Form 5372, notice of new Employer Identification number assigned. It will show the church's EIN # in the upper right hand portion. This number should be given to the bank for each account with which you open an account. Do not open a church account with your social security number.

97 MIMOSA CRESCENT
SINGAPORE 2880
TEL: 481-8001

THE POTTER'S HOUSE
Christian Centre

To Pastor Mitchell and the Elders
October 1990

For almost a year now, I have agonized in my spirit over the divisions in the fellowship. Being in an overseas setting I have tried to stay out of it and submit no matter how I felt. I must now speak up.

I have not found sufficient Biblical backing to satisfy me concerning the actions to dis-communicate certain leaders (Jack Harris, Ron Jones, Peter Edwards, Ron Simpkins and any who associate with them) who have chosen for various reasons to break-a-way.

There has been time for me to retrospect and view this in light of:

1. My Personal Christian and ministerial ethic.
2. Scriptural reasons for total dis-association from fellowship.
3. Moral justification.

I can not agree with the way these men have been:

1. Disassociated from all relationship with fellowship ministers.
2. Their Character attacked.
3. Families and friends separated and fighting.

I understand loyalty and commitment. I'm aware some who broke-away have been moved by <u>wrong</u> and <u>divisive</u> spirits. But, we are not dealing with young converts in a local church, rather with Men of God who have years of proven and fruitful ministries. There must be a difference in handling them than just simply saying "he's a rebel." My Christian spirit and beliefs cannot allow me to treat fellow ministers of the gospel that way. I cannot just cut these men off as though I never had any relationship with them.

Jack Harris: Has spent years helping every man in this fellowship. He has been an encouragement and a partner in ministry to me. I know of no Biblical, doctrinal, or moral reason

Mitchell & Elders CFM

why I should not associate with him.

Ron Jones: Has been called a rebel, immoral, power hungry, church splitter, liar, and much more. I cannot accept that. I see no Biblical stand to disassociate myself or ministry from him.

Ron Simpkins: Is a personal friend of mine. I have no Biblical reason to break relationship with him or not allow him in my pulpit.

Peter Edwards: I believe Peter to be a man of integrity. One of the main accusations against him was that he choose not to abide by a rule which required him to break relationship with a relative and friend many years.

I can't imagine what would happen if "The Fellowship" would draw me into a conflict with my own brother, my father or my son. As I have seen happen this past year with some families.

Structure is not divine. It is human and flawed at best. It must always be flexible to adjust with growth, maturity and circumstances. It must become large and flexible to allow for mature men to exercise their personal visions. It must allow for complete release at some point in a man's maturity and fruitfulness.

What drew me to the Arizona Fellowship 13 years ago was the vision to invest in men and see them fulfill their destiny. Planting churches was the means to release them. Now planting churches has become the process whereby men are used to build "The Fellowship." The worker becomes expendable. The work becomes more important than the worker. The investment is in equipment, cars and buildings. The "Indigenous Church" has become the "Fellowship Church."

I am no longer the 27 year old young man who sat across from Pastor Mitchell when he offered to help me establish a church. I am 40 years old and have a much larger vision and a driving desire to see that come about in the next 10-20 years. With the actions that have been taken against men in the past year or so I begin to wonder if the structure is not becoming a threat more than a help and assistance. If a man's vision is to step into new areas of ministry, enlargement, or if he does not fully agree and submit to every "letter of the law" he might find himself cut off and black-balled from all he helped build for years. That is very difficult to live with, commit to and continue to sacrifice for.

Larry Reed is an example of this. For 20 years he helped build this fellowship, labored and had a positive impact. I had Larry and his family in my church for 2 years and I know of nothing morally or Biblically wrong with him any more than many men of "feet of clay." Here is a man over 60 years old, out. In all of my Christian life I have never seen a church or organization cut men off like that. Out of respect for the leadership of our fellowship I have abided by the decision toward Larry. That kind of submission and discipline I now bring into question.

I understand the need for disciplinary action in moral issues. Even in relational ethic violations. But, all discipline should be for reconciliation. I believe there should be a healing sought. That process must start with Headship and the Elders. I am not saying there can or will be reconciliation. We can not go back to where we were. But there can be healing in relationships. Ungrounded actuations can be checked. A way can be paved for Christian families and friends to once again share Christian love and relationship.

My personal vision has always been "World Evangelism." I was involved in Miracle Crusades and Conferences in nations of the world before I came to Prescott. This vision is why I have given years of my life to missions. Now, after 8 years in missions with the fellowship I have come to the conclusion that I cannot fulfill my missionary vision within the structure of the fellowship.

1 Corinthians 9:9 "For it is written in the law of Moses, Thou shalt not muzzle the mouth of the ox that treadeth out the corn..." The way we are structured, no matter how fruitful a missionary is, how large his church is, or how long he has been on the field he will have generally the same amount of resources as a pioneer. I have had basically the same amount of support for 8 years in Asia. I have promoted crusades for most every pastor who comes to Asia yet I have never been able to preach one crusade which required more than a few hundred dollars investment, because I have no resources. The heartbreaking thing is that I foresee no means in the context of The Fellowship which will allow us to make impact upon Asia or have resources to do any more.

A number of times I have brought this up to Pastor Mitchell and some of the leadership. I have been told that the only way I can ever have resources beyond basic support is to return to the States or another developed country and build a base like other men have done. Because of my burden for Asia, I have not done that but stayed here functioning under our structure. I always believed that by helping build The Fellowship I was also building a base which would release me, but that has not proven to be true.

APPENDIX II

Recently God reaffirmed a promise given to me years ago, that I can see powerful miracle crusades and make impact in Asia. I am now going to believe God to raise up a missionary ministry that will service this purpose. This means I am going to step out by faith for the finances needed to respond to the opportunities in Asia. This will require that I move beyond the boundaries and limitations set by The Fellowship and open the door for other churches, ministries and individuals to partner with us in ministry.

I am releasing Pastor Mitchell and the Prescott church from their commitment to support me in missionary work. I will not send a budget to the Prescott church after October 1990. I am also resigning from the position of elder in the Christian Fellowship Ministries.

Yours in Christ,

Larry Neville
Singapore

APPENDIX III

Pastor Contract

Dated this_____day of_____,200_

I_____hereby subscribe to the by-laws of the Christian
Fellowship Church Inc.,an Arizona Corporation;
DBA The Potter's House
Christian Fellowship. I submit myself to the
Leadership and
Board of Elders put in place to minister order
and discipline in
oversight of this Fellowship. I submit my
ministry to Pastor Wayman
Mitchell or his successors. I make a solemn
commitment before God and
this church in _____State
of_____

I will abide by the standards, doctrines and
vision to make disciples,
plant churches and work in unity with
the Fellowship as a pastor and
steward of this church. If at any time in the
future I decide I can no
longer work in good faith with this church or
Leadership, I will
resign from my position, leave the church in
good order and not cause
any further disruption in that church or any
other Fellowship church.

I further state; I am in subjection to Pastor
Mitchell and the Board
of Elders of the
Christian Fellowship Ministries. Should they
see fit
to remove me for moral indiscretion, financial
insolvency, doctrinal
error, or a disruptive spirit causing harm to
the church or
Fellowship; I will submit to their direction
and surrender all church
bank accounts, buildings, equipment and assets
and go quietly on to
redirection, discipline and relocation.

Signed_____ Dated____
_____

Notary
public_____ Dated____
_____

Pretoria, 5 March 2003

To all the Pastors in the fellowship.

Hereby I am sending you a copy of the Pastors contract
that Pastor Mitchell wanted me to
sign, and if I would have refused to sign it, he would
have stopped the support of our church. I
not only had to sign it, but also I had to go to the
notary public and let them sign it to. So the
worlds court <u>system</u> and money domination is being
used as a threat to keep Pastors in line.
This form sooner or later every Pastor will have to sign.
This is the direction Pastor Mitchell is
taking the fellowship. It is not a fellowship anymore-it
is an organisation.something we never
wanted to become. A business organisation.

It is very very crucial for all of you to remember how
we started. We started as a fellowship of
friends. Support was a gift of love. The vision of
our fellowship is that all over the world
indigenous autonomous and self-supporting fellowships
would arise with their own conference.
Anyone that would plant 25 churches could start their
own conference agreed upon in the
<u>Phoenix leadership</u>. Some conferences started out of
need of location. The vision of
multiplication is that all over the world men were going
to function as a powerful copy of Pastor
Mitchell's leadership. The vision is to train men and to
train them so well that they fully can and
will function totally separate from you, and a
new fellowship is formed. And over that new
fellowship the first Pastor has totally NO AUTHORITY,
otherwise multiplication is impossible.

Through that multiplication of disciples and churches
and leaders totally released in the world,
the world is going to be reached with the Gospel of
Jesus Christ. That is the risk Jesus Christ
took, that is the risk we will have to take. If we do not
want to take that risk, than we need to
start looking for another job. 2 Tim. 2:2 // on this text
our fellowship is based.

APPENDIX IV

Pastor Mitchell appointed an eldership over the
entire fellowship, which is a violation of our
vision. Elders are Pastors. So to appoint 7 Pastors over
our whole fellowship creates a
headquarters in Prescott-something we all, including
Pastor Mitchell, never wanted. If you want
to appoint an eldership (actually not necessary) you will
have to use your own men as leaders
over your own fellowship. That's why the new eldership
appointment of the 7 according to our
vision should have been Pastor Mitchell's own disciples
over his own fellowship. And in
Harold's fellowship Harold's men. And in Joe
Campbell's fellowship Joe Campbell's men. And
in Mike Mastins, Hank Houghtons, Bill Coolidge, Tommy
Alvarez, Dale Reece, Greg Johnson'
fellowships, their own men. And in Rudy van
Diermen fellowship Rudy van Diermen's men etc.
etc.

Pastor Mitchell is violating our vision of discipleship and
multiplication. In an old sermon of
Pastor Mitchell I found the following quote: "A
movement will start with a man, that man is
given a message, that movement starts developing
methods, than that movement starts to
develop into an organisation. Than unavoidably it
degenerates into a grave tomb or
mausoleum or museum. This is the course of history in
which it always goes..."

Read the contract for yourself.

Pastor Rudy van Diermen
Pretoria.

APPENDIX V

LEADERSHIP COVENANT – JANUARY 2004

I, the undersigned, being a leader in good standing in the fellowship of believers known as the Christian Fellowship Churches, acknowledge that I am acting as a pastor and a leader in this fellowship at the behest of the fellowship and not as a proprietor or as an independent agent. I have read the letter from Pastor Mitchell to the fellowship at large, dated July 10, 2000, regarding a basic structure for dealing with conflict resolution and the discipline of errant pastors, and I am in agreement with the principals put forth in that letter. I further submit that any changes in the members of the Board of Elders from those set forth in the letter will not affect my acceptance of the aforementioned principals. Therefore, I herein bind myself to that structure and if, in the future, I choose to no longer abide by that structure, I will resign my position of leadership and my pastoral post without rancor or disruption and allow the fellowship to arrange for my replacement as they see fit. Furthermore, as much as is within my power, all human and financial resources at my disposal at that time will remain in the fellowship and I will relinquish all claims to them.

I understand that in our ongoing effort to avoid a rigid legal denominational structure it is necessary that we bind ourselves together in good faith by solemn covenant. I therefore willingly sign this covenant before my God and Savior Jesus Christ, and the witness of my brethren at this leadership table.

Signed _____   Dated _____

Witnessed _____   Dated _____

APPENDIX VI

Pastor/ Missionary Contract

Dated this _____ day of _____

I _____ hereby subscribe to the Constitution of The Potters House Christian Fellowship of Australia Inc. I submit my ministry to Pastor Payne or his successor. I make a solemn commitment before God and the church that I am pioneering or am being entrusted with _____ in the Nation of _____.

I recognize that this church and any equipment or other resources acquired are not my property, but that I am only stewarding them for the Fellowship. It is a great privilege and opportunity to have someone invest in my ministry and not an entitlement. I am not an Employee of The Potters House, but a self-employed minister of the Gospel. I understand that I am responsible to provide for my own medical expenses and insurance and clearly state that the Potters House is not liable for any of these. I understand that all financial support, settlement monies and redirection expenses are simply an offering given to me at the discretion of the Potters House and are not a salary paid or an entitlement.

I will abide by the standards, doctrines and vision to evangelize, make disciples, plant churches and work in unity with the Fellowship as a pastor and steward of this church. If at any time in the future I decide I can no longer work in good faith with this church or Leadership, I will resign from my position, leave the church in good order and not cause any further disruption in that church or any other Fellowship church.

I further state, I am in subjection to Pastor Mitchell or his successor, Pastor Payne or his successor, and the Board of Elders of the Christian Fellowship Ministries. Should they see fit to remove me for moral indiscretion, financial insolvency, doctrinal error, or a disruptive spirit causing harm to the church or Fellowship; I will submit to their direction and surrender all church bank accounts, buildings, equipment and assets and go quietly on to re-direction, discipline, and relocation.

Signed _____ Dated _____

Witness _____ Dated _____

Membership Covenant

"Having repented of my sin and received forgiveness; been baptized in water; submitted myself to the Lordship of Jesus Christ; and being in agreement with the Potter's House Christian Fellowship's vision, Credal Statements, and Membership Covenant, I count it a privilege to apply for Membership. I understand that in applying for Membership I submit myself to the Leadership of the church and to other members. I also commit myself to a godly lifestyle by adhering to the very best of my abilities to the following..."

1. I WILL SHARE THE RESPONSIBILITY OF MY CHURCH...by praying diligently for its growth; by consistently inviting sinners to attend and to be converted; by warmly welcoming and serving those who visit.

"To the church...we always thank God for you and pray for you constantly." (1Thess 1:2) "Go out into the highways, the byways and the hedges...and urge anyone you find to come in, so that My House will be full." (Luke 14:22) "So, warmly welcome each other into the church, just as Christ has warmly welcomed you; then God will be glorified." (Rom 15:7)

2. I WILL PROTECT THE UNITY OF MY CHURCH...by being Kingdom minded and always acting in love towards other members; by refusing to gossip or slander or discourage; by submitting to the leaders God has over me for my benefit.

"So let us concentrate on the things which make for harmony, and on the growth of our fellowship together." (Rom 15:19) "Do not let any unwholesome talk come out of your mouths, but only what is helpful for building others up according to their needs..." (Ephes 4:29) "Obey your leaders and submit to their authority. They keep watch over you as men who must give an account. Obey them so that their work will be a joy, not a burden, for that would be no advantage to you." (Heb 13:17)

3. I WILL SUPPORT THE TESTIMONY OF MY CHURCH...by attending faithfully; by living a godly, biblical life; by tithing regularly.

"Let us not give up the habit of meeting together as the habit of some is...but let us encourage one another." (Heb 10:25) "But whatever happens, make sure that your everyday lifeis worthy of the gospel of Christ." (Phil 1:27) "A tenth of the produce of the land, whether grain or fruit, belongs to the LORD and must be set apart to him as holy." (Lev 27:30) "Bring the whole tithe into the storehouse, so that there may be food in My house, and test Me now in this," says the LORD of hosts, "if I will not open for you the windows of heaven and pour out for you a blessing until it overflows." (Mal 3:10) "Each one of you, on the first day of the week, should set aside a specific sum of money in proportion to what you have earned and use it for the offering." (1Cor16:2)

Name: _____ *Date:* _____

Church Vision and Credal Statements

Vision Statement: *"Our vision is to build a Christ-centred, contagious, contemporary, disciple-making Christian community – every person is a soul winner."*

Mission Statement: The Potter's House Christian Fellowship of Parramatta exists as a local congregation to witness to the world of God's love as revealed in His Son Jesus Christ, our crucified, risen, exalted and soon returning King. We seek to teach the Word of God and spread the gospel of Jesus Christ in the power of the Holy Spirit.

Our goal is the shaping and equipping of our church family so that disciples will be nourished and empowered to fulfil their God ordained purpose and ministry. As members of the church our desire is to bring glory to God through our public and private lives.

We do this by rejoicing in Christ Jesus; increasing in knowledge of God through the study and application of the scriptures; by growing in godly character; by practicing Biblical fellowship; be serving one another with our spiritual gifts, our time and our money; by proclaiming the Gospel in Parramatta, Sydney, and to the ends of the earth.

Core Values: Our mission is accomplished by keeping focused on our core values.

- God's Word as the final authority for life: We seek to grow through the consistent application of scripture to our lives, our attitudes and our relationships. (1Peter 2:2)

- Spirit Filled Witness to our world: We seek to proclaim the Gospel of Jesus Christ through personal witness, evangelistic, endeavours as a church and through church planting both at home and abroad. (Matt 28:18-20)

- Worship as a priority: We live to worship God joyfully and gratefully for who He is and for all He has done. (John 4:23,24)

- Fellowship: As an interdependent people, we understand the value of meeting together as a corporate body and in smaller groups in homes to encourage each other and to bear one another's burdens. (Heb 10:24,25)

- Giving and Stewardship: We recognize that all our material possessions are a gift from God given to further His work and glory in the world. It is God who gives us power to gain wealth. We value giving money to further the ministries of the church through tithes and offerings. (2 Cor 8:7)

- Commitment to service: The Holy Spirit gives each of us abilities to serve one another, the church at large, and the community in which we love. Discovering, developing and deploying those gifts to serve others is our constant aim. (Gal 5:13,14)

APPENDIX VIII

CONDITION	SPIRITUAL ISSUES
Arthritis Osteoporosis, painful joints	Hatred, unforgiveness, bitterness and rebellion
Asthma Sinusitis, sinus infections, restricted breathing	Fear, fear of rejection, rejection
Blindness Poor vision, cataracts	Idolatry, false religion, Spirit of Blindness
Back pain Herniated discs, injury	Hatred, bitterness. rebellion
Breast cancer Tumors, cysts	Gossip, evil speaking, unforgiveness, hate of husbands
Bone spurs	Hatred of husbands
Cervical cancer Bladder infections	Curse of Promiscuity, hatred of husbands
Ceserean pain Loss of feeling	Hatred of husbands, Spirit of Death, unforgiveness
Colon cancer	Inherited curse, Spirit of Death, cast out fear command cancer to leave
Deafness	Fear of death, deaf spirit
Deafness One ear, in children	Curse of Illegitimacy
Diabetes	Self-hate, self-pity, rejection
Digestive disorders Ulcers, hiatal hernia, intestinal	Anxiety, fear, anger, temper tantrums, hate, worry
Ear infections Recurring in children	Inherited curse, involvement in pregnancy classes e.g. Lamaze and touch therapy
Eczema Psoriasis, skin problems	Witchcraft, inherited curses, masonry, secret societies
Female dysfunction Cysts, tubal infection, tumors	Fear, stress, hate and unforgiveness of husbands
Gall bladder	Hate and bitterness
Heart High blood pressure	Resentment, cast out Death, unforgiveness, anger and temper fits
Injury Trauma, accident, sports, surgery, wounds, industrial	Unforgiveness, cast out death and Spirit of Infirmity, speak resurrection life
Kidney failure or infection	Anger, unforgiveness, temper and hate
Nerve damage Loss of feeling or function	Cast out death, unforgiveness, command nerves to live, speak resurrection life
Scoliosis	In most cases for women a connection with molestation, cast out hate, unforgiveness, bitterness
Stroke Paralysis, loss of feeling	Hate. self-pity, cast out Death

Magical healers	Chiropractors, Touch Therapy. Witchdoctors, Curandero(a), Reflexologist, Iridology
Objects	Talismans. medals, crystals, crucifix, scapular medals, copper, brass and silver healing bands and bracelets, prosperity spires
Witchcraft and Occult	Ouija boards, tarot cards, palm readers, friends (lovers) involved in witchcraft, horoscopes, Dungeons and Dragons
False Religion	Cults, secret societies like Freemasons, Eastern Star, books on the occult or cult 'bibles'

While this list is not complete, and does not exhaust all the areas that are relevant; many cases
have validated that these spiritual issues can be 'roots' of the conditions mentioned.

** Feel free to pull out this page **

ABOUT THE AUTHOR

Joel E. Crosby is an e-commerce manager at an automotive aftermarket company, leading a small team of interns. He was born into The Door and attended until halfway through June 2019. Before he left, he met his wife, Nellen, there in 2017 at her sister's birthday party. He fell in love with her right away, and she thought of him as only a nice friend but later fell in love with him too. Joel especially enjoys collecting coins and banknotes and has an extensive collection.

In his spare time, Joel manages a Facebook group called 'Escaping the Potter's House,' where former members of The Fellowship discuss and process their experiences.

You can connect with Joel on Facebook at facebook.com/JoelECrosby or on Instagram @JoelECrosby. You can also visit his website, JoelCrosby.com, to sign up for emails about new releases.